Praise for *The Universi*

'As Higher Education Minister early in ... ... enlightened leadership of Charles Clarke), I was constantly being told by members of the public that we needed plumbers not graduates. It was never their kids that were going to be the plumbers incidentally. To me this phrase summarised Britain's uncomfortable relationship with its world-class university sector. In this book my old boss has (with Ed Byrne) used his passion for education and his great gift of foresight in order to provide a blueprint for how universities and governments can help to resolve the problems of our age and, in doing so, addresses the kind of nihilism that led to Michael Gove's famous contention that people had heard enough from "experts".'

The Right Honourable Alan Johnson, UK Minister for Universities 2003–04, Secretary of State for Education and Skills 2006–07

'Finally we are seeing some light and heat around the frozen notion of universities as static creatures, not responsible for the outcomes of our society or our planet, through the work of Professor Ed Byrne and Minister Charles Clarke and their new book, *The University Challenge*. Byrne, who is one of the world's leading university presidents, and Clarke, a firebrand Home Secretary from the UK, outline for all of us how to begin the mental process of freeing emerging and future universities from the ice ages. Frozen in time, universities have not adapted well, nor are they prepared for what lies ahead as a result of technological change, political and social complexity, and global changes, both climatic and geopolitical. Byrne and Clarke outline in a hard-nosed way how modern universities should evolve and how they should take on these challenges by freeing themselves from the bureaucratic structures of the past, and why and how they must begin to focus their energy on the positive outcome of society. This is a must-read for anyone thinking about universities and their responsibilities for the future.'

Michael M. Crow, President, Arizona State University

'This is a call to arms. Ed Byrne and Charles Clarke demand universities understand themselves and their potential influence for good. In difficult times, higher education can help society manage change, grasp alternatives, develop skills and promote knowledge. Should they fail … '

Professor Glyn Davis AC, Chief Executive Officer,
Distinguished Professor of Political Science,
Crawford School of Public Policy, ANU

'This is a timely book which addresses the role and challenges faced by universities across the globe. Byrne and Clarke are well qualified to comment on universities. It is an important read for many within and well beyond higher education.'

Professor Dame Nancy Rothwell, FRS, FRSB, FMedSci,
President and Vice-Chancellor, The University of Manchester

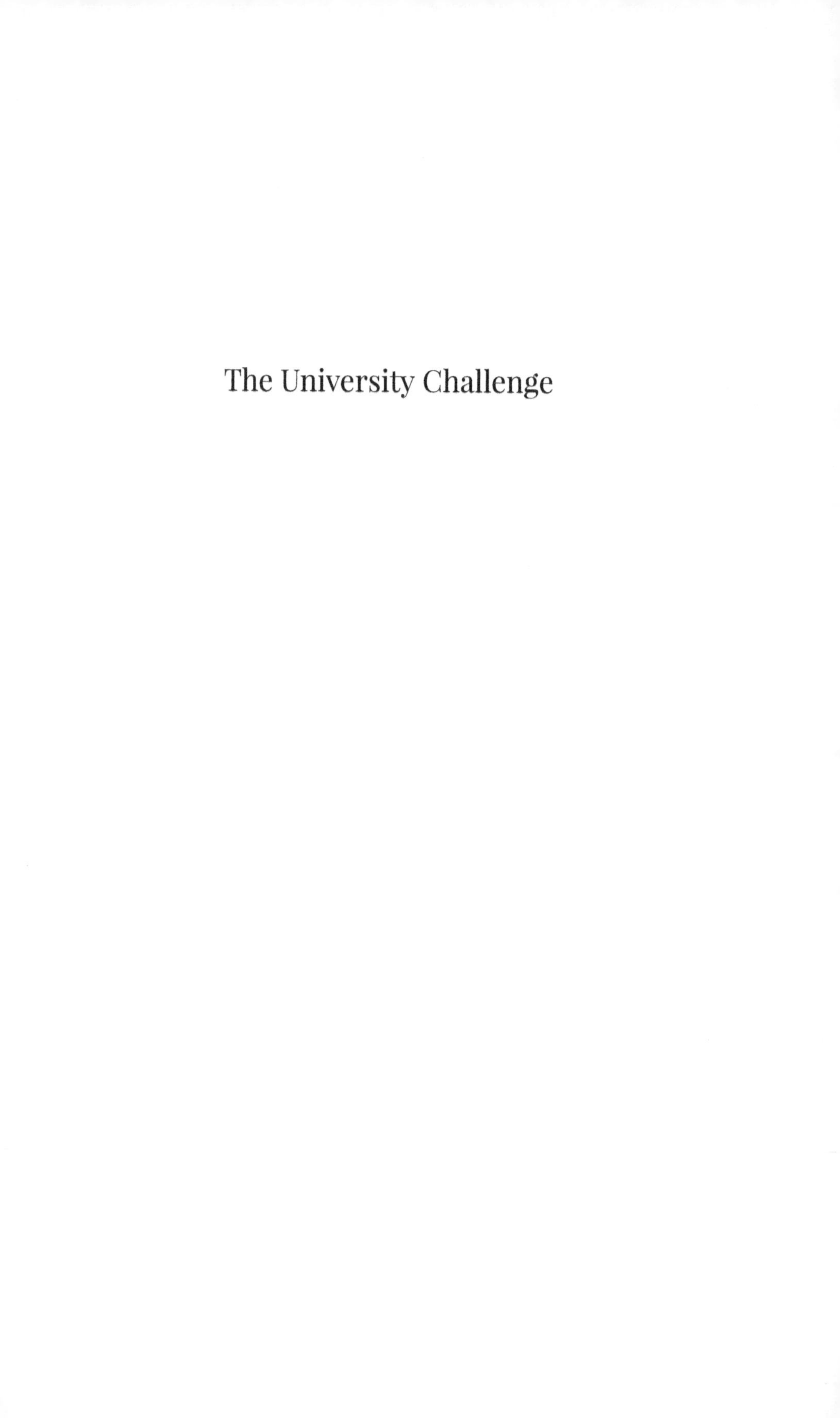

The University Challenge

The University Challenge

Changing universities in a changing world

Ed Byrne and Charles Clarke

Harlow, England • London • New York • Boston • San Francisco • Toronto • Sydney
Dubai • Singapore • Hong Kong • Tokyo • Seoul • Taipei • New Delhi
Cape Town • São Paulo • Mexico City • Madrid • Amsterdam • Munich • Paris • Milan

PEARSON EDUCATION LIMITED
KAO Two
KAO Park
Harlow CM17 9SR
United Kingdom
Tel: +44 (0)1279 623623
Web: www.pearson.com/uk

First edition published 2020 (print and electronic)

ISBN: 978-1-292-27651-9 (print)
978-1-292-27652-6 (PDF)
978-1-292-27653-3 (ePub)

British Library Cataloguing-in-Publication Data
A catalogue record for the print edition is available from the British Library

Library of Congress Cataloging-in-Publication Data
A catalog record for the print edition is available from the Library of Congress

10 9 8 7 6 5 4 3 2 1
24 23 22 21 20

Cover design by Madras
Cover image © ikryannikovgmailcom/iStock/Getty Images

Print edition typeset in 11/14pt Electra LT Std by SPi Global
Printed by Ashford Colour Press Ltd, Gosport

NOTE THAT ANY PAGE CROSS REFERENCES REFER TO THE PRINT EDITION

Contents

Publisher's acknowledgements

xv Neil Kinnock: Joe Biden plagiarised Neil Kinnock's speech in the British General Election, August 1987; **3, 5 MIT Press:** Joseph E. Aoun 'Robot-Proof: Higher Education in the Age of Artificial Intelligence', MIT Press, 26 Sep 2017 https://www.amazon.co.uk/Robot-Proof-Higher-Education-Artificial-Intelligence/dp/0262037289; **13 Queen Elizabeth:** Quoted by Queen Elizabeth; **19 The National Archives:** Higher Education Funding Council for England – HEFCE; **31 Adam Smith:** Adam Smith, 'The Wealth of Nations', who lectured in Edinburgh and was professor at Glasgow University from 1751–1764; **32 Oxford University Press:** David Willetts, A University Education retrieved from https://www.amazon.co.uk/University-Education-David-Willetts/dp/0198767269; **48 World Economic Forum:** 'The Fourth Industrial Revolution: what it means, how to respond', https://www.weforum.org/agenda/2016/01/the-fourth-industrial-revolution-what-it-means-and-how-to-respond/; **52–53 Henry Holt and Company:** The Times Good University Guide 2020, John O'Leary, Times Books retrieved from https://www.amazon.co.uk/Times-Good-University-Guide-2020/dp/0008325480/ref=dp_ob_title_bk; **62 Times higher education:** Best universities for graduate jobs: Global University Employability Ranking 2018, November 14 retrieved from https://www.timeshighereducation.com/student/best-universities/best-universities-graduate-jobs-global-university-employability-ranking; **74 United Kingdom Research and Innovation:** Mission Statement of UK Research and Innovation. Used by permission. Retrieved from https://www.ukri.org/about-us/; **77 Carnegie Classification of Institutions of Higher Education:** Created by the Carnegie Commission on Higher Education in 1970 and most recently published in 2018; **91 House of Commons:** The Office for Students' response to the Education Committee report on value for money in higher education,

House of Commons; **92 The Economist Newspaper Limited:** Tsinghua University may soon top the world league in science research, Nov 17th 2018; **92 Hans Peter Hertig:** Quote by Hans Peter Hertig; **95 Higher Education Funding Council for England (HEFCE):** King's College London and Digital Science (2015). The nature, scale and beneficiaries of research impact: An initial analysis of Research Excellence Framework (REF) 2014 impact case studies. Bristol, United Kingdom: HEFCE; **104 Hachette UK:** Agtmael, A. W., & Bakker, F. (2016). The smartest places on earth: Why rustbelts are the emerging hotspots of global innovation; **153 The Brookings Institution:** Tale of two Rust Belts: Higher education is driving Rust Belt revival but risks abound John C. Austin Wednesday, December 20, 2017; **106 Penguin Random House:** James Fallows, Deborah Fallows 'Our Towns: A 100,000-Mile Journey into the Heart of America'; **165 United Kingdom Research and Innovation:** United Kingdom Research and Innovation annual report retrieved from http://www.rcuk.ac.uk/about/aboutrcs/research-funding-across-the-uk/; **119, 121 Neil Kinnock:** Joe Biden plagiarised Neil Kinnock's speech in the British General Election, August 1987; **139 Department for Education:** Free speech in the liberal university, A speech by Jo Johnson at the Limmud Conference, Birmingham, 26 December 2017; **140 House of Commons:** House of Commons, Official Report, Parliamentary Debates Hansard, 17 May 2018; **140 House of Commons:** Serious barriers limit free speech in universities retrieved from https://publications.parliament.uk/pa/jt201719/jtselect/jtrights/589/58902.htm; **140 BBC:** 'Intolerance' threat to university free speech by Sean Coughlan, BBC News; **140 BBC:** Universities: Is free speech under threat?, by Rachel Schraer & Ben Butcher, BBC; **141 The National Archives:** Counter-Terrorism and Security Act 2015; **165 Aneurin Bevan:** Quote by Aneurin Bevan **169 Office for Students:** Quality and standards, Office for Students (OfS) **175 Institute for Fiscal Studies:** Institute for Fiscal Studies, retrieved from https://www.ifs.org.uk/publications/9965; **176 Universities UK:** Higher education in numbers, retrieved from https://www.universitiesuk.ac.uk/facts-and-stats/Pages/higher-education-data.aspx **177 Higher Education Statistics Agency:** Destinations of Leavers from Higher Education 2016/17, 19 July 2018. https://www.hesa.ac.uk/news/19-07-2018/DLHE-publication-201617; **179 Her Majesty's Stationery Office:** Independent panel report to the Review of Post-18 Education and Funding May 2019. https://assets.publishing.service.gov.uk/government/uploads/system/uploads/attachment_data/file/805127/Review_of_post_18_education_and_funding.pdf, Chapter 7; **198 Lord Acton:** Lord Acton, the historian and moralist, expressed this opinion in a letter in 1887; **238 The National Archives:** Counter-Terrorism and Security Act 2015.

About the authors

Ed Byrne is an Academic Neurologist who has worked in Australia and the UK. His research contributions are in the fields of mitochondrial disease and neuromuscular disorders. He was Professor of Neurology and Director of the Centre for Neuroscience at the University of Melbourne, and then had a number of leadership positions in health and in the university world including Dean of Medicine, Nursing and Health Sciences at Monash University, Vice-Provost for Health at UCL and Vice-Chancellor of Monash University. He is now the President and Principal at King's College London and is currently the Chairman of the Association of Commonwealth Universities. He has long-standing interests in working to improve the contribution that the university sector can make to society at large.

Charles Clarke studied at King's College, Cambridge. He was President of the National Union of Students from 1975 to 1977, and then advised Neil Kinnock, Education spokesman and then Leader of the Labour Opposition.

He was MP for Norwich South from 1997 to 2010 and served in the Cabinet as Secretary of State for Education and Skills. He introduced and implemented the major university reforms of the 2004 Higher Education Act. He also served as Labour Party Chair and Home Secretary.

He works on international education reform for parts of Cambridge University and has held Visiting Professorships at the Universities of East Anglia, Lancaster and King's College London. See www.charlesclarke.org.

Introduction

When we were talking about writing this book, and the challenges that universities face today, we asked each other why we became so interested in universities. We discovered some surprising similarities in our family backgrounds and these were our answers:

From Ed Byrne

My parents left school in the mid-teenage years. My paternal grandfather was a coal miner who was illiterate. My father graduated from Durham University as a medical doctor because of opportunities that opened up for him as a returned serviceman after the Second World War. It was axiomatic in my family that education has a transformative value both in personal growth and in opportunity in life.

When I in turn became a medical doctor and a consultant neurologist, I understood that our knowledge of the causes of human illness was at best patchy and that the research to address this was undertaken largely in universities. These two factors – hereditary respect for education and a growing passion for research – drew me like a magnet to the university world.

As, a little unexpectedly, I became more senior, more involved in large collaborative multidisciplinary projects and more exposed to the rich and deep talent of a multi-faculty university, I came to appreciate the contribution universities make as an essential and irreplaceable element of civilised society.

Now that the winds of change are blowing as never before with information and technology revolutions re-shaping both the workplace and society at large, I have become increasingly interested in how that respect for knowledge that is at the heart of the university mission can not only be preserved but developed into something evermore powerful that is fit for purpose in these challenging times.

The opportunity to work with Charles is a special one for me. My experience as a researcher, teacher, dean and university president in both hemispheres complements his as a government minister engaged in making change happen. It is a difficult line between the devil of complacency and the deep blue sea of unbridled futurism and in this short book we set out some ideas that should stimulate discussion and debate. Some of them are likely to be right!

From Charles Clarke

My maternal grandfather was also a miner, in County Durham. Her parents were both teachers in Weardale, where she was born and brought up, and from where she was allegedly the first child to go to university, Bedford College London (now the private Regents University). My father was born in Derbyshire. His parents were also both teachers, and he went as a scholarship boy to Christ's Hospital and then to Cambridge to read Maths, where I followed him in the late 1960s on the conventional middle-class school-to-university escalator.

I got involved in student politics and campaigns to open Cambridge more widely, get student representation in the university and promote ethical university behaviour, for example by not investing in then apartheid South Africa. In the mid-1970s, I ended up as President of the National Union of Students. Its many campaigns at the time included trying to end the binary division between universities and polytechnics, ensuring that student teachers could get jobs when they graduated and stopping student grants being means tested on parental income.

I started working in politics for Neil Kinnock when Jim Callaghan appointed him Labour's Education spokesman. We tried to set out clear policies for the future of universities and 16–19 education.

After Neil finished as Labour leader in 1992, I worked on a project for the Standing Conference of Principals, now GuildHE,[1] a group of about 50 higher education institutions, to make the case for them to have university status on the basis of the strong quality of their undergraduate education.

So when, after becoming an MP, it fell to me to take through the major reforms of universities in 2003/4 it was on the basis of a conviction in the power of universities to benefit society, but also of the need for them to change to do that effectively.

And working again with universities in recent years, I am reminded of the constant battle in the university world against the strength of forces of conservatism who refuse to accept that change is needed. As I discovered, Ed is one of those most committed to the need for change, from his experience at both Monash and King's College London. I have enjoyed working with him to make that case as strongly as we can.

Of course, we share histories of this type with millions of people. The story of university education is one of empowerment and liberation that resonates across continents. That's why, in August 1987, Neil Kinnock's speech in the British General Election earlier that year – 'Why am I the first Kinnock in a thousand generations to be able to get to university?' – was plagiarised by Joe Biden during his presidential campaign. It's a powerful and motivational message, perhaps greater than any other, and it applies everywhere. It's an appeal for change for a purpose.

In this book, we outline the steps that universities can take to bring themselves into the front line of the changes that are so necessary for the whole of society in order to meet the challenges we all face.

Chapter 1

Changing universities in changing times

Introduction

Many people have lost confidence in universities at a time when we believe that they are more important than ever. The planet, and all of us on it, face huge challenges in the decades ahead. By the mid-21st century we will need not only to feed 10 billion people but also to ensure fair access to often costly heath care and a reasonable quality of living around the globe. All of the creative and innovative capacities of humanity need to be aligned and applied as never before in human history.

The central contention of this book is that high quality universities are a key contributor to addressing and overcoming those challenges. Universities prepare outstanding young people to become confident citizens and changemakers, and they make their own contributions across a wide variety of sectors, fields and social arenas. Universities drive much of the world's most promising and innovative research and are seen as the jewels in the crown for advanced knowledge-based economies. Universities typically bring great people together from many disciplines and are ideally suited for multidisciplinary approaches. All of the grand societal challenges require an approach of this type. It follows that if universities are to perform this role well they must not only continue to excel in more traditional ways but must reform and adapt to become truly fit for purpose for the challenges we face. They must find a higher gear and not only do things differently, but do different things, if they are to continue to play a major role in making the world a better place.

Some say that the present reputational issues facing universities in the West in particular are a product of poor communication of what universities do. But we contend that it is about much more than this – and there is a need for real change and humility.

We argue that the leadership to enable universities to perform their roles effectively must come from universities themselves, and should not be driven by governments. The role of governments generally should be to encourage and enable transformation to happen, though not necessarily to drive the direction and processes of change themselves, though that might be necessary in some situations. Indeed, we warn that over-detailed government regulation threatens the ability of universities to make the contribution that they need to make. Creating excellence through high degrees of regulatory control is not only impossible but dangerous.

For example, in the UK, there is a very real danger that the massively increased powers of the new national regulator, the Office for Students,[1] will constrain energy and creativity in the sector. The way in which the government has established this office could significantly diminish one of the strongest university sectors in the world if the regulatory framework does not respect institutional autonomy over standards, pedagogy and curriculum.

Our analysis begins with the context within which modern universities have become what they are now. We then explore the way in which university research develops understanding of our world and the ways in which change is taking place; we cover the modern relationship between universities and work, particularly as artificial intelligence extends its reach; the need for universities to serve the whole community, and not simply a relatively small subset, mainly of a particular age and class. Oxbridge and Ivy League institutions have made and continue to make superb contributions to humanity but they also, perhaps inevitably, perpetuate an elitist mindset and educate a small number of students. Here we look broadly at what universities can and must do to help to form future generations and equip them to meet the challenges they face; the role that universities need to play in promoting global interrelationships; and how universities should be funded and governed so that they can operate in a truly sustainable way.

On the basis of this analysis and these assessments, we will make recommendations about the ways in which universities should address these challenges and prepare themselves to play the kind of role they need to play. We set these recommendations out in detail in the final chapter.

The change that is all around us

It is commonplace to point out the rapid change in the world around us, to the extent where even recent past generations would have found it difficult to understand the world in which their children and grandchildren now live. This reality extends to every aspect of our lives. For example:

Work

Work, with its associated income, has been at the core of our societies and economies for millennia. But it has changed, and is changing, incredibly rapidly in terms of who is working, where work takes place and how work is done with what types of machines. The current changes in occupation types, work patterns and, in particular, the development of automated systems and artificial intelligence have a revolutionary flavour.

An example of the massive changes in the structure of work since the Second World War is the fact that today's largest and most powerful companies didn't then exist at all and are all in the information world and not manufacturing. Young people think of Google and Apple in the same way our generation thought of IBM and Kodak and our parents thought of GM and Ford.

But there will be much more change in the next couple of decades than in the previous century. Joseph Aoun, the President of North-Eastern University, has set all this out very clearly in his book – *Robot-Proof: Higher Education in the Age of Artificial Intelligence*.[2] As he says:

> **The only real certainty is that the world will be different – and with changes come challenges as well as opportunities. In many cases they are one and the same. Education is what sets them apart.**

Change is accelerating at a time when the university world, often seen as fairly left wing, retains a conservative mentality in respect of its institutional culture and professional practices. It tends to think in terms of small increments, though increasingly rapid major transformation is inevitable. Fairly small changes that would be seen in other sectors of society as modest are seen as exceptionally challenging and become difficult to achieve (though, nevertheless, universities have experienced and successfully implemented major change in the past three decades). But the process of change is not over and so any conservative state of mind needs to change rapidly. It is in part a consequence of flat, non-hierarchical and collegiate structures. Vice-Chancellors that succeed typically do so by influence rather than diktat. This collegiality is a positive quality at the core of all great universities and the key challenge or dilemma is how to accelerate change without diminishing that quality.

Communication and travel

The laptop and the mobile phone, with their supportive technologies, have utterly transformed our ability to communicate with each other across the world, with our friends and families and in the ways in which we live our ordinary lives, for example managing our money and doing our shopping.

We travel around the world for holidays and for work in ways that were unimaginable to our grandparents.

In almost every social context now, if one scans the room, one sees that almost everyone is glued to a mobile device. Put simply, the personal space of individuals has extended enormously from contact with people who are physically nearby to people who can be reached in a second across the world. Steve Jobs has changed the world at least as much as Henry Ford.

Families and social structure

In many countries, it is less than 50 years since homosexuality stopped being illegal. But now, in most countries, it is a generally accepted and welcomed part of modern life. In addition, because of the fact that people live far longer and because of the ways in which modern telecommunications have developed, the essential structure of families and society is changing. Many places of employment manifest exciting new approaches to gender equity across the workforce and there is a wider recognition that a fair society that fulfils its potential needs to ensure that everyone, irrespective of gender, race or sexuality, can fulfil their own potential. There is a long way to go but this is undoubtedly the journey the world is on.

Although most modern societies are more tolerant than their 19th-century forebears, there is still much to do, notably in the areas of cross-cultural and cross-religious understanding, both crucial arenas where university work should be part of the solution.

Better health and living longer

Medical advance is enabling most of us to live longer and better, which of course has big implications for our social welfare systems and the ways in which we organise work and leisure across our lives. This also has implications for the distribution of wealth across society.

The key demographic tendency in all Western countries, and now spreading across the world, is an ageing population as people live longer and birth rates reduce. Parents who are over 50 typically have significant capital wealth, including a family residence that has escalated massively in value, but their children often can't enter the property market at the comparatively young age that their parents did. This leads to generational unfairness and often to understandable resentment.

The cost of care of elderly people is rising, even more so as new technologies, often developed in university, come into day to day use.

Major strategic issues surround the development of optimal systems of health and social care, which bring together both traditional medical sciences and the social sciences, economics and law, among others. Multidisciplinary universities are in a strong position to contribute solutions to this.

Arts, culture and cuisine

Most people are massively expanding their artistic and cultural experiences, including the food they eat and the clothes they wear.

The changes in working patterns, which we mention above, with increasing wealth, are likely to reduce working time and increase leisure time significantly over a lifetime. A high-level education increases the intellectual scope of individuals for a full intellectual embracement of cultural activities across society as a whole.

In this context, the study of arts and humanities, about which some voice doubts and to which many universities in the world do not give priority, will become more important, not less, in all societies and will be seen as crucial to the ongoing human journey as never before. Indeed, as Joseph Aoun points out as he makes the case for humans to strengthen their comparative advantage over machines in the economy:[3]

> **Creativity combined with mental flexibility has made humanity unique... They will continue to be how we distinguish ourselves as individual actors in the economy... The most important work that human beings perform will be its creative work. That is why our education should teach us how to do it well.**

The study of arts and humanities is our means of archiving and reinterpreting the past, transmitting cultures, and giving individuals the ability to live reflective lives in conversation with past as well as present human knowledge and creativity.[4] It initiates them into ongoing streams of culture and allows them to become full participants. This type of study has a very high utility for society, and indeed is increasingly important for the future of work in the changing environment. It is something that should very much be encouraged.

Poverty

Economic development across the world has dramatically reduced the levels of poverty and even famine, though of course enormous challenges remain. Optimistic thinkers, including Stephen Pinker,[5] Bobby Duffy,[6] Hans Rosling[7] and Yuval Harari,[8] among others, have huge confidence in the capacity of the human to succeed and overcome the challenges of the next century.

At the same time, developed economies have become less equal, with tiny numbers of people possessing an enormous proportion of the world's assets and often not using their money and power well. Indeed, not only in the most advanced countries but also in countries that were regarded as part of the third world, the spread of affluence has increased, not decreased, financial equality, with huge wealth held by a few.

Climate change and energy use

Science has increasingly demonstrated that human behaviour is changing the climate of the world, slowly but steadily. This leads to enormous risks, particularly for communities vulnerable to climate change, and requires us to find and then use forms of energy that will reduce those risks.

It is particularly noteworthy that this area, more than any other, has seen what are loosely called 'alternative truths' in Europe, the UK and Australia.

In these countries, there is an increasingly vocal anti-climate-science voice on the right wing of politics which thrives on denigration of scientific opinion (in this and also other fields) and causes real fact confusion for many in the general public. This sentiment is driven, in the main, by a view that fossil fuel will continue to be essential as an energy source. For political or personal reasons, a significant subgroup, including some prominent media individuals, have felt able to ignore scientific evidence and even decry the scientific process as a whole. For example, Michael Gove, a senior UK politician, famously decried reliance on 'experts' in the 2016 Brexit referendum campaign in the UK. His views prevailed in the vote.

Universities have a crucial role to play in combating the view that 'alternative truths' are acceptable. Of course, universities are by their nature apolitical and, quite rightly, must give a forum to all views. But they must also promote proven science and this is sometimes a fine line to draw.

It also makes it important for university researchers to accept that their audience is not only their scientific peers and therefore they need to engage proactively in sometimes robust and dishonest public policy debates and exchanges.

Global politics and conflict

Our politics and public life are now international, far more than ever in the past. Phenomena like migration and extremist political techniques like fake news and terrorism impact upon all of us.

Such changes, fundamental as they are, are relatively easy to describe retrospectively but their impacts are absolutely enormous. They range from causing industrial desolation in parts of Europe and areas like the mid-Western 'rust belt' in the US to stimulating immense mass migrations, provoked by a variety of social, environmental and economic transformations, and universalising violent political conflicts and bringing them directly into our communities.

Governments, and international institutions like the United Nations and the European Union, have tried to address parts of this process of change, and have tried to promote change in beneficial directions. The UN Millennium Development goals and the newer Sustainable Development Goals are both good illustrations, but there are many more.

However, so far, these efforts have been only partially successful and often seem to be well-meaning but ineffective, while at the same time the actual process of change is contentious. Simultaneously, the processes of globalisation, the increasing role of artificial intelligence, the ageing of society and transnational migration are very real and immediate and are often seen as negative in overall impact.

It should therefore be no surprise that, faced with the challenges that arise from these changes, millions of people across the world have used their political power to protest, in particular at the perceived failures of governments and institutions to deal with these challenges. Often the protests are purely symbolic and fairly small scale in numbers, such as the regular protest seen at the annual Davos meetings, the 'Occupy movement' and 'Extinction Rebellion'.

But there have also been substantial political movements, so in the US, we see the Tea Party movement and then the election of Donald Trump; in Southern Europe, the rise of Syriza in Greece and Podemos in Spain; in the UK, the progress of UKIP and then the Brexit referendum; and there are similar examples across the world. In general, the process is characterised by rejection of the political parties and mainstream ideologies that have governed us since the Second World War. And with that comes uncertainty and instability as people are crying out for solutions to the problems that they perceive.

A key tenet of populist movements is the lack of utility of 'globalisation' and the internationalist approach which has dominated global political culture over the past seven decades. Accentuated nationalism, growing calls for enhanced barriers to people movement, rising hostility to free trade and, in Trump's America, even rising trade tariffs are all now everyday features of politics in a way that would have been unthinkable 15 years ago. 'Nativist populism' is an international issue in ways unseen since the Second World War. The confidence of several generations that a global mindset is now hard wired is under real practical threat. This has massive implications for universities which have been and still are absolutely committed to a global mindset and the development of global connectivity. They support and thrive on free movement of scholars, teachers and ideas.

In the round, universities have been marginal to this process of massive social and economic change while the values they represent have been attacked by politicians such as Donald Trump and Michael Gove, without a coherent overall response. Universities are indeed a key source of derision for those who disparage globalism and the concept of a liberal centre consensus in Western politics. Many of their critics argue that mass participation in higher education has harmed economies and devalued the academy.

Universities deal in knowledge. 'Alternative truth' politics is an attack on everything that they represent.

Despite universities' undoubted contribution to many of the positive changes that have taken place, they have offered less in dealing with the dimensions of change that are big and threatening. They have been complacent in a worldview based on a healthy self-esteem. Thus it has been a real shock for university communities to begin to appreciate that they are not as well regarded externally as they regard themselves. The sector has been rife with hubris.

It is essential both for societies and for universities themselves that they work out the ways in which they can use their skills and knowledge to help societies deal with these potentially earth-shattering transformations.

Traditionally, universities are judge and jury of their own performance and could (sometimes unfairly) be characterised as 'ivory towers'. That state of mind must be firmly relegated to the past because, in the future, society at large will increasingly be judge and jury and universities, as part of their mission, will have to perform in a way that seeks to exceed and not just meet or manage rising social expectations. Universities must face up to growing political and public scrutiny, which is both appropriate and inevitable in an era of massive public funding for universities.

For about 60 years after the end of the First World War, there was a boom in public money going into UK universities. This both drove up funding per student and fuelled the expansion of the sector. The unit of resource then declined from about 1980 to about 2000 and, since then, UK universities have once again experienced real growth in funding and the sources of funding have diversified. Though universities have sought to categorise the funding derived from income-contingent student loans as 'private' rather than 'public', the debate about university governance and accountability has been fuelled and has given rise to real tension. This has arisen across administrations with, for example, the Lambert review[9] and the establishment of the Office for Fair Access (OFFA)[10] and then even greater intervention through the new Office for Students established in the Higher Education and Research Act 2017. At the same time, universities have become very large institutions driven by international income for both research and students. Many universities are now institutions *linked to* their city rather than being institutions *of* their city. Big money, globalisation and a lack of community strategy have exposed an attitude of mind and vulnerability in university leadership teams.

The effect of this steady process of change is that the activities and behaviours of universities are four-square part of the public debate. One of the issues we consider in this book is whether the current balance is right.

Many of the issues that need legitimate public debate are complex and mired in political disagreement. The controversies about such issues as genetic modification of food, or the alleged link between vaccination and autism, ought to be capable of scientific evaluation. While issues such as these are complex and require scientific input, the loss of public confidence in scientists by a significant proportion of the general public creates major policy challenges, which are ethical and sociological. The debates on these matters are not only for government and politics; universities and science must play a full and accountable role in the public debate.

Four key contributions to addressing global change

Traditional university thought would suggest that the key role of universities is to educate and to research. We agree with this but see these roles as underpinning processes that are even more fundamental.

Universities have four vital contributions to make in helping the world deal with accelerating change and address the challenges that change creates. They are the pillars of university impact in the modern world:

- *understanding and interpreting the process of change;*
- *offering approaches that would harness the process of change for general benefit;*
- *educating and training to high quality the specialist workers whose skills are necessary to address change properly;*
- *creating a general intellectually engaging climate and culture across societies that promotes the virtues of understanding and science.*

Universities are already very major contributors in each of these areas, but of course not the only ones.

At a time when inputs from many areas of knowledge are crucial to all complex problems, universities have the opportunity to be the most interdisciplinary of institutions. This gives them a rich opportunity to play a special role as highly interdisciplinary institutions in addressing grand challenges which require increasingly interdependent and interrelated approaches.

There are already striking examples of what universities can do, such as Arizona State University in the US, which is pioneering a new model of excellence with inclusivity; Warwick University in England, which is leading the industrial rejuvenation of the Midlands; and Keele University in England, which pioneered new educational paradigms some decades ago.

Currently, universities probably make this contribution best in the field of medicine and health, where they are directly responsible for some of the most far-reaching, profound and positive changes in our society, and so it is worth looking at this illustration of what universities can offer in an important field. We give brief examples here and expand on this in Chapters 4 and 5.

University research, often these days in partnership with charities and private companies, has created major breakthroughs in most areas of medicine in recent years. This includes really major advances in the understanding of cancer and cardiac health problems. These advances have made an important contribution to significant increases in life expectancy across the world.

Through achievements such as the sequencing of the human genome, stem cell research, treating HIV, Zika research, human papillomavirus vaccination, targeting cancer therapies, laparoscopic surgery, bionic limbs, face transplants and spinal cord stimulation, and many others, medical research has transformed the lives of millions of people. And of course breakthroughs in contraception and in public health research, including those that have led to smoke-free laws, have been enormous components of the change that we are all experiencing.

This research, driven by the desire to expand understanding, has led to immensely important outcomes like increased life expectancy, lower child mortality, elimination of debilitating diseases and healthier populations. These of course also contribute to ageing demographics which creates a new set of challenges.

Some of this research is controversial and sometimes contested but it remains an enormous contribution made by universities.

This happens at various different levels of research. Ground-breaking basic science (sometimes called blue sky research), like the discovery of DNA and the genetic codes, cell behaviour, or the mapping of the workings of the brain, is essential to enable health improvements. Universities have always been about such blue sky research as well as applied research. While society today expects more immediate outcomes, it is always important to remember that the blue sky research of today drives the outcomes of applied research tomorrow, more so as the pace of change accelerates.

Research considered esoteric for many decades, such as quantum physics, is now as important as Newtonian physics in technological advancement. The ethical implications of the new biology require innovative work in philosophy, ethics, public policy and law, to complement the scientific advances.

Then university research applies this acquired knowledge to particular health problems and begins to identify solutions. There remain enormous areas of ignorance (for example about the brain and dementia) where research still has to identify possible ways forward. An equally major area is the increasing recognition and importance of mental health problems around the world.

In parallel, research identifies the propensities of particular groups of the population to particular health problems and, through randomised control trials, seeks to find the best means of raising levels of health. Personalised medicine based on the DNA revolution is already with us and the potential for stratified medicine is immense.

In short, the research and understanding into health problems that is carried out by universities (often in partnership with clinical health systems such as the UK NHS service) is indispensable to enabling the wider world to deal effectively with the health challenges that it faces.

It is universities again, often in industrial partnership, for example with pharmaceutical companies, that lead the way in finding approaches, such as new drugs or therapies, which enable changes to health practice that are of general health benefit. These spread across the world and have an enormous impact in raising standards of health and health care.

It is the universities that educate and train health workers, doctors, paramedics, nurses and the whole range of health carers. Again, this happens throughout the world and, as a direct consequence, health standards rise and health problems are reduced.

There are perpetual issues of the standards of health education, its capacity to adopt innovation and improvement against traditional ways of doing things, and the sufficiency and adequacy of what is done. But the contribution of universities to educating and training the specialist staff upon which all health systems depend is undoubted.

And then universities play a major role in creating the intellectual culture regarding health and medicine which is the foundation for the way we do things. Universities can and do spread understanding across society about what we need to do in order to raise the quality of the health of our population.

Recent progress in the NHS illustrates the power of university health system partnerships. A prevalent view some years ago was that the NHS in the UK was relatively rigid and slow to take up essential reforms. A series of reforms underpinned by the work of Sir David Cooksey[11] led to much closer integration of university health research with health systems with resultant improvement in clinical outcomes. The NHS is now well advanced on the journey from a rigid system to a flexible system based on this partnership where staff are empowered to find knowledge-based ways of doing things better.

The example of health and medicine shows clearly how, under each of the four pillars identified above, universities can and do contribute to helping the world deal with the accelerating process of change in that field. It is a strong record of achievement. Even though far more remains to be done, and of course there is certainly room for improvement, for example in contesting obesity in parts of the world and fighting disease in others, the work of universities shows what can be achieved.

Fields like information and communications technology, and engineering are similarly strong across the range and there are others.

But an interesting contrast is the field of the environment and climate change. In this area, university research has identified the reality of climate change and its challenges, and has influenced most leaders of government and public opinion of the need to address the threats, to the extent that the 2015 Paris Agreement committed governments to targets intended to reduce the risks.

As mentioned earlier, there is no room for complacency and several major governments, including in both the US and Australia, are already moving away from the Paris accords in response to lobbying from the fossil fuel industry.

This may be because universities have been far less successful in offering practical approaches through which the threat of climate change can be mitigated, in educating and training specialists to work in this area, and in changing the overall intellectual climate and culture through which these issues are thought about.

There are also areas, such as education, good government, law and order and policing, migration, eliminating poverty and promoting equality, where universities have been much less able to make a decisive contribution in any of the four ways identified to meeting the challenges of change in the modern world.

Great people are working in these areas and excellent work is being done but impact on society is not yet at a sufficient level to meet national and global needs. Just look at the difficulties in dealing with the refugee crisis and how easy it has been to mobilise xenophobic populist sentiment in certain countries.

When Queen Elizabeth, in November 2008, asked economists at the London School of Economics 'Why did nobody notice it [the financial crisis]?', she was speaking with the grain of public sentiment. She got an answer when she visited the Bank of England in December 2012, which some might say is typical of the speed of response in the academic world.

This might be one of the reasons why the word 'academic' is pejorative as meaning something that is not understandable, relevant or accurate.

Clearly, this is not in fact the case but it does highlight the communication problems that universities have. In a highly connected world where social media and on-demand content have changed social expectations, academic research and engagement can seem ponderous.

Lord Mervyn King's recent book, *The End of Alchemy*,[12] which criticises current approaches to financial stability, illustrates the extent to which theoretical economics is currently failing to influence the practice of economics and finance throughout the world.

So we contend that the challenge facing universities is to make themselves essential to addressing the modern challenges of a changing world, in each of the four pillars identified at the beginning of this section. This requires a more focused approach and is not just a matter of communication.

The challenge needs to be addressed systematically, to be stimulated from the universities themselves, and to be achieved by changing the ways in which universities currently work.

Some universities have begun to address this by identifying the challenges that they hope to tackle and emphasising that these need to be thought about in cross-disciplinary ways. Princeton stands out as a global leader and Warwick and UCL are good UK examples. The University of Wollongong in Australia has been running such a programme for six years and there are many other outstanding examples, such as Delft University of Technology. University College London's six 'Grand Challenges' are typical:

Global Health

Sustainable Cities

Human Wellbeing

Cultural Understanding

Transformative Technology

Justice and Equality

Universities have addressed this in different ways but a central part of our argument is that universities have to do far more to identify the ways in which they can contribute to meeting the challenges of change and to do that well they have to change themselves. Their historic task is to inform and guide the world we are moving into and not simply to interpret the world of yesterday.

Change in universities

We contend that universities themselves need to change if they are to play an effective and positive role in enabling our societies to address the changes that they face.

Such change would need to take place against the background of change, which is already happening, notably in the areas of research, teaching and learning, financial investment and reform, national structure and an increasingly challenging international environment.

In each of these areas, the changes vary since different countries face different challenges. But there are some common features that can be identified. We recognise that universities are conservative institutions at their heart and their vitality comes almost entirely through the intellectual endeavours of their staff and students. Change in universities cannot simply be mandated from the top but must engage the whole university community. This can only be done if both the value and the moral imperative that drive change are well understood across the university community.

Research

There are two developing aspects of university research policy that will become increasingly significant as countries consider how policy should evolve, and funding should be distributed. These are the highly variable distribution of the quality of research across different universities and the way in which research impacts upon addressing the overall challenges that are faced by society as a whole.

Even within the UK, let alone across the world, the quality of research is highly variable. Of the UK's approximately 160 universities only about 50 would have a good claim to be producing substantial amounts of world-class research in many departments/areas – that is to say research that provides genuine understanding of the changing world.

Though it is true that there are islands of real excellence in a wider group of universities, the fact is that research excellence is very concentrated and a large number of universities cannot really be truthfully described as research-excellent in cumulative terms.

This skewed distribution is reflected in the various world rankings that are regularly published, in the distribution of research funding from both state and private sources, and in the informal but powerful assessments of academics themselves. It is also seen in the quality and power ranking of the very detailed UK research exercise, the Research Excellence Framework (REF), which in varying forms has been carried out every five years through several cycles and then funds much of UK university research. Australia has a roughly similar assessment exercise, which also reveals striking asymmetries of institutional research strength, that is concentrated in 8 of the 39 universities.

Similar variability is the case in all OECD countries. And, even though there is plenty of room for scepticism about how accurately the world university rankings reflect research capacity and the extent to which research citations reflect quality, the fact that in every country some universities are seen as research-leading and others are not cannot be denied.

In some countries, such as Germany, this truth is reflected in the institutional arrangements for organising and funding research (with the development of an elite research university stream), but in others the overall narrative of university education is not yet ready openly to acknowledge this variability. For example, the situation in France is rapidly changing to follow this pattern. There are, of course, a variety of alternative models including, in some cases, direct funding. Others, such as the UK, have evolved this through carefully calibrated policies on the basis that excellence should be funded wherever it is found, which has driven concentration in a relatively small number of universities.

The debate is typically phrased in terms of the crucial role of research-led teaching, which implies that high quality education and teaching is only feasible in an environment where quality research is also being undertaken. This concept, at the heart of the Western university tradition as we describe in Chapter 2, underpins the view that research and teaching in university must always co-exist and ideally be undertaken by the same person. This view is the philosophical driver for the suggestion that all universities should be research-active in all the areas in which they teach, even though this clearly does not reflect existing reality.

So, in the UK, for example, 'academic drift' towards research has characterised many new universities, former colleges of advanced technology, former polytechnics, and former colleges of art or education as they have acquired university status. Indeed, any suggestion that research should be confined to a limited number of universities has been very strongly resisted as it is maintained that research is essential to good quality university teaching in all universities.

It is also true that, over the past 30 years, traditional universities have responded to the challenges from non-research universities, such as the former polytechnics, by establishing business schools and professional training in fields such as nursing and there has been some mission creep towards applied subjects.

The massive and economically important strength of the UK's research, for example, is concentrated in about a third of our universities. If no research were to take place in the other two thirds, the overall damage would be quite limited.

As this variability continues to become clearer, the narrative of the relationship between research and teaching will have to change and the structure of universities will change. This may involve a recognition that even a wealthy country like the UK can support only a limited number of research-intensive universities.

One bar to this process is that esteem in academic life has been almost totally research-driven. Any rebalancing would require institutions to improve recognition and esteem for the outstanding university educator.

The second evolving change is the growing significance of 'impact' in deciding which research to fund and which not to fund. The existence of 'impact' as a criterion for funding research has been resisted by many in academic life, but is gradually becoming accepted. In a number of countries, including the UK, major government research funding has been focused more on major national and international priorities requiring research at scale than on the traditional research of funding good projects in any area that is shown to be excellent through peer review. This process also drives concentration of expertise at major new centres such as The Francis Crick Institute in London.

The reasons for the resistance to impact are not just conservative opposition to change of any kind. There are worries that such a criterion for state funding might suppress original or challenging thinking ('blue sky' as referred to earlier) or might inhibit 'academic freedom'. In other words, it might impose a crassly utilitarian template on academia.

And it is also true that it is difficult to fix properly the metrics that can measure 'impact'. This is perhaps easier in fields like medicine and engineering than the social sciences or humanities, but any metrics are bound to be controversial, refined though they have been over time.

Nevertheless, the idea of 'impact' is becoming better established and more accepted and will spread more and more widely as a criterion for determining the location of both public and private funding for research.

Universities should organise themselves in the best possible way to help us all understand and interpret the process of change in the world in which we live, and then to offer approaches that would harness the process of change for general benefit. As well as changes unique to particular institutions, this will involve new types of international partnerships.

A great deal of thought will be needed to find the best ways to do that. The variability of research quality and the significance of 'impact' will be at the centre of that consideration.

Success on this journey will go some way towards restoring public confidence in the value of their universities. Universities are not owned only by current communities of staff and students. It is dangerous to neglect the major national investment over many generations that has made these institutions succeed.

Teaching and learning

Despite these questions about the future of research, a far greater concern is the quality and utility of teaching and learning.

Again, the nature of these concerns varies widely across the world, and is very much related to the function of universities in particular countries. But the determination of national political and economic elites to get their children's university education in countries like the US, the UK and Australia is evidence of their doubts about the teaching quality of their own country's universities.

And, in the OECD countries, concern about teaching quality is very high too. This comes from students, who often now have to pay substantial fees and want to be sure of the quality of what they have paid for (potentially using their power as consumers with the legislative strength that gives them); from employers who want to get the highest quality recruits; and from governments who want to ensure the quality of the graduating population, which is getting towards 50% of the age cohort in some countries. Another pressure for governments is convincing young people in or about to enter voting age groups that they have had or will get economic utility – or value for money – from their own educational investment. This concern remains a substantial component of contemporary policy debate about university education.

These pressures cast a light on the indisputable fact that universities and their academic staff have generally been more focused on their research interests (which still dominate university world rankings) and are diverting money that they receive for their teaching to fund their research in considerable amounts.

These tensions have led to development of 'student satisfaction surveys' and are leading to new government approaches, such as the 'Teaching Excellence Framework' in the UK, which are designed to measure teaching quality.

To address these issues in the UK, a new regulator with dramatically enhanced powers, the Office for Students (OfS), has recently been established. With its system of formal regulatory powers it has sought to distinguish itself from its predecessor body, HEFCE, which was viewed as 'of the sector, and for the sector'. The advent of the OfS brings with it the prospect of a significant reduction of university autonomy in England. In contrast, Australia's powerful new accreditation agency, TEQSA,[13] adopts a lighter touch, nearer to the traditional UK model.

As attempts to measure teaching quality at school level have shown, such efforts are fraught with difficulty, particularly if the teaching quality metric becomes a performance indicator that determines future funding and such issues.

The concept of 'value-added', another government obsession in England, is particularly difficult to measure.

Nevertheless, this discussion heralds the change that has already begun, and will keep coming, to raise the standard of teaching in universities.

Anyone who does not recognise this has their head in the sand.

This will have a particularly big impact at Year 1 of university life, where there is increasing pressure to ensure that all university students are well educated across both arts and sciences, and fully equipped, for example in statistics and logic, as advocated by Professor Steven Pinker, to play their full roles in national life. A particular problem for countries like the US and UK is the relatively low level of mathematical literacy where many young people lack even a basic competency.

This takes on particular significance in a country like England where early specialisation in the English school system is a particular problem and the 'A' Level system, driven by university entrance demands, is far narrower than the 'baccalaureate' approaches of most other countries.

But also at Year 4, master's qualifications (typical structure in England, honours year equivalent in Scotland and Australia), which are an important source of income for universities, are decreasingly seen as simply a route to a PhD and academic study and increasingly as an educational development that better develops the student for modern working life. However, both the funding arrangements and the university commitment to master's degrees will need to change if this trend is to develop properly.

The increasing prominence of both early and midlife postgraduate courses and qualifications aimed at career enhancement will be complemented by a further strengthening of e-education programmes.

And, in the world of change in which we live, a qualification at the age of 22 will no longer be sufficient for a career for life. Individuals, and their employers, need continuous professional development and, more widely, citizens live in a world where lifelong learning is essential.

From the outset, universities have offered some of this, but lifelong learning will need to become an increasingly important, even central, component of universities' teaching responsibilities. Often, this will be in partnership with an organisation such as the civil service in the UK or with industry.

Overall, the challenge of teaching quality will not go away nor should it. Teaching provides the greatest source of income for universities and getting this right will remain a big challenge for them. To the public at large, of all the things that universities do, teaching is undoubtedly the most important. The general reader may be surprised that there is a need to say this because, for many years, it has not been the case inside some of the greatest universities.

Financing it all

The finance of universities is changing rapidly across the world.

Difficult and controversial judgments are being made, in the fields of funding both for research and for teaching, as to the best balance between payments by the state, by the student and, to a limited extent, by employers.

There is not a stable funding state where everyone can be confident that the existing system will go on forever. In many countries there are political and economic challenges which lead to potential funding instability. In countries like the UK and Australia, where international students have been an important source of income, the development of high quality universities across the world, as well as political concerns about immigration, jeopardise that source of income.

We discuss these issues in detail in Chapter 8 but it is important to note here that, at the end of the day, the framework of university funding can only be created by government, and such a framework needs to foster and encourage the kind of university contribution to addressing a changing world that we have described earlier in this chapter. That will mean variability and flexibility of courses, teaching, modes of learning and research structures and modes of learning. Also there is no more certain way to ensure a mediocre university system than to underfund it.

We would also argue that, as far as possible, the funding systems should enable universities to be independent of government.

One danger of over-reliance on direct student funding rather than a mixed model with a component of government contribution from the tax base is that the student sees themselves as a customer, with almost a guaranteed academic grade. Put simply, it may be possible to buy a first class education but no student should ever be able to buy a first class degree. That should always be earned, despite the claims of some who have taken their disappointment to the courts.

Systems and structures

As we describe in Chapter 2, the university systems of every country have grown in rather haphazard ways, reflecting the education, training and societal imperatives of the time.

There are now about 160 universities in the UK. These have very different provenances. There are major mergers, such as that which created the modern Manchester University in 2004, while speculation about potential acquisitions, and also university closures, is perpetual.

New universities are regularly being formed as the private sector plays an increasing role. Since 2000, there have been regular government changes in the definition of the right to University title and degree awarding status.

The new UK Higher Education and Research Act of 2017 has as a key objective the establishment of a wider range of universities including more private providers.

In considering these important developments, the distinction between public and private universities may not be key but that between profit and not-for-profit providers may be more significant.

Great universities such as Oxford and Cambridge, Harvard, Stanford and Princeton are private institutions. Other universities, for example those stemming from the Land Grant in the US and the former polytechnics in the UK, are more 'public' in character but they are all committed to public service and the public interest and to charitable purposes.

However, the newly emerging for-profit private universities, such as BPP and the University of Law in the UK, should have to demonstrate their public service commitment and value and it is not evident that the new regulatory regime really enables this to happen in a transparent way.

The creation of new qualifications, such as foundation degrees and degree apprenticeships and the waxing and waning of new institutions like Sector Skills Councils, reflect uncertainties about the best institutional arrangements to meet the skills challenges that a modern economy faces.

And this fluidity takes place against a constant background of concern about the unfairness of the distribution of university opportunities, where it remains the case that a young person's chance of higher education remains sharply dependent upon their socio-economic background.

Change in the national structure of universities is certainly happening. It is for discussion what process of change in universities will best foster their contribution to national welfare.

The international context

Finally, none of these current changes, and consideration of those that are necessary in the future, can be thought about in a purely national context.

It remains difficult to explain why US, UK, Australian and Canadian universities have been so dominant in the world university rankings, in comparison with those in other OECD countries and the rest of the world. No doubt, part of the explanation is the shared English language, which helps to create networks, and the essential autonomy of universities in these countries.

And this dominance is beginning to be challenged, notably as a result of the enormous commitment in China and university reorganisation in Europe.

However, this book is not systematic in its analysis of universities throughout the world. Its main references are to the situation in the UK and, to some extent, in Australia and the US, but only to a very limited extent elsewhere in the world. A comprehensive analysis would certainly be valuable and would offer important insights. However, we decided that the challenge of doing this properly is beyond the scope of this book.

Universities are more international than ever before and, indeed, it could well be argued that the process of globalisation has moved faster in the field of universities than any other. It extends to research, teaching and knowledge transfer and it is accelerating.

An important component of the change is massive expansion across the world and travel of students around the globe.

Modes of study are changing with distance learning and online education and so different forms of pedagogy are now well established. New paradigms of learning are also inevitably becoming more international and less focused on traditional ways of doing things.

These changes will have an impact on the structure of universities and their funding.

We analyse these changes in more detail throughout the book.

Conclusion

This opening chapter sets out the overall challenges that we believe universities now face in a world that is changing increasingly rapidly.

We hope it is clear that we believe, and are confident, in the capacity of universities to make the contribution that the world needs them to make and that they have traditionally been able to.

But we also want to emphasise our view that to achieve that successfully will require universities to change themselves significantly, and to take the lead in so doing.

We conclude that this responsibility to meet the challenges of a changing world should be at the centre of universities' missions, and so:

Governments should regularly make a clear statement of the contribution that they hope universities will make to developing the society and economy of the country and indicate the ways in which they will support and promote that. They should incentivise and reward universities that place the addressing of change at the centre of their work, for example through:

- promoting the impact of research across the disciplines; and
- strengthening their local communities and economies.

▶

Universities should place the addressing of change at the centre of their own missions by clearly identifying the way in which they:

- understand and interpret change in the world;
- offer approaches to harness the process of change for general benefit;
- educate and train the specialists whose skills are necessary to address change;
- create an intellectually engaging climate and culture across societies.

They should clearly identify their strategy to achieve that mission.

The rest of this book addresses these issues in more detail and we hope offers an approach that can command widespread support.

Chapter 2

Historical perspectives and international comparisons

Why the history matters

In our exciting forward-looking world, history can sometimes be seen as boring or even irrelevant!

That is why one of the co-authors, Charles, ventures into this discussion with some trepidation. In 2003, he gave a lecture at Worcester University, trying to address some of the themes of this book. The lecture was badly misrepresented as his attacking the value of studying medieval history (which he didn't do, or imply). This gave rise to a lot of ignorant vituperation from some medieval historians. But when one complained about the reported remarks to their Vice-Chancellor (VC), a historian himself, the VC rightly responded that he thought the first rule for all historians was to check their sources. So we address the subject in that spirit.

Some might think that, in universities, the old adage that those who don't know their history are destined to repeat it may seem to have less relevance since the new world we are entering is so very different.

But we think that some understanding of how universities came to be as they are today is important to help understand not only the challenges they face now but also some of the obstacles they face in meeting them.

Of course, countless books have been written on the history of universities so all we intend to do here is to highlight a few pivotal stories that underpin the development of today's universities. We contend that throughout university history two of the four pillars of university roles identified in Chapter 1 have been central, namely:

- *understanding and seeking to interpret the process of change;*
- *educating and training specialist workers.*

We also contend that, over time, the other two pillars have become increasingly important, namely:

- *harnessing change for the general benefit of society;*
- *creating an intellectually engaging climate and culture across societies that promotes the virtues of understanding and science.*

We will look through the lens of those roles in order to tease out the ways in which societal expectations and needs have been met in a wide variety of environments over history and across the world.

Since their origins almost a millennium ago, universities have always served, shaped and adapted to society around them. The central contention of this book is that they must continue to do that. This means that, as well as telling their story better, universities today need to do things differently and be much more open to real change.

At a time when many argue that universities should go backwards to what they are seen to have been in the past, and some even urge that many recent innovations in university organisation should be reversed, we argue that, actually, the opposite is true – that universities need to move forwards to meet changes in society, and that such thinking is completely in line with the historical evolution of universities over hundreds of years.

The core of universities is the creation and transmission of knowledge. The four pillar roles of the university, which we have identified, all relate to one aspect or another of 'knowledge'. Their key role has been to acquire knowledge and understanding, to assist young people in attaining a higher level of generalised knowledge and to enable professions to acquire specialised knowledge they need. Understanding change is impossible without some idea of the societal forces at play; harnessing change for good requires firm knowledge-based foundations; education both for new and for existing skills requires a deep knowledge of the current lexicon.

The recording of knowledge, its transmission and, increasingly, its creation are closely linked to the communication technologies of the day. That couldn't ever have been more obvious than it is today when the creation of a new knowledge culture through the internet is the biggest challenge universities face. Forty years ago, the knowledge was hidden and had to be found. Now the knowledge is published and available, but needs signposts to be understood and used and this changes the character of modern universities. Knowledge is deregulated, almost anarchic, now.

The needs of 21st-century societies in a globalised knowledge economy are diverse and complex. An educated and informed citizenry is vital to sustaining a successful economy and a healthy civil society and democracy. The responsibilities of universities, therefore, are vast not only in supporting these needs but in playing a role as key civic institutions in crafting the type of world most people want to live in.

How have universities evolved? The changing European model

The incredibly complex university world of today has developed from a rich and multifaceted history of societal evolution which universities both contributed to and adapted from. There are rich university traditions in many parts of the world which have now converged on the model that began in Europe. But it is important to recognise that quite distinct university models existed elsewhere in earlier centuries which were equally intellectually valid in meeting local expectations and their own societal needs.

In this short analysis, we feel that concentration on the European tradition is justified, at least in part, by the linear ancestry of today's global university model to developments in Europe 1,000 years ago. Even more so, it is justified by the scientific revolution, the High Enlightenment and the rise of the knowledge-creating institutions closely associated with these momentous historical paradigms such as the amazing strength of the Scottish universities and their contribution to the Scottish Enlightenment, which then culminated in the launch of the University of Berlin as an institution devoted not only to teaching but also to discovery.

University traditions in other countries were heavily influenced by these developments. Moreover, in all historical periods, universities needed to meet the aspirations of three key 'stakeholders' – staff, students and wider society (external interests) – and to enable them to flourish. We believe that, in the main, they achieved this, though they very much reflected the culture and mores of the societies in which they were located. In some eras and countries, universities were the strongest bastions of existing conservative power. In others, they were the source of intellectual and political challenge. And sometimes both simultaneously.

Early years

While the term 'dark ages' is less fashionable than it was, it cannot be disputed that there was a catastrophic collapse of civilisation in Western Europe with the fall of the Western Roman Empire. A society that had embraced the critical thinking developed in Athens centuries earlier was swept away in just a few years in the early fifth century. In succeeding centuries, intellectual life was largely centred in monastic communities often following the Irish tradition. As Christianity grew in strength, the great monastic traditions flourished and formed the beginnings of universities in the West.

Many students were destined for religious orders and universities played an important role in training these skilled intellectual workers for their place in society. However, others wished to expand their horizons for knowledge as such, beginning the rise of the modern university and defining its key mission. Much intellectual effort went into theological and related philosophical issues. Aristotle was greatly admired. The evolution of Western Christianity was significantly influenced. Students were taught logic and critical thinking and exposed to the great minds of the day.

In an institutional sense, there was little drive or kudos in creating new knowledge by increased understanding of the natural world. Indeed, the church authorities of the day generally blocked any such endeavours. In spite of that, outstanding individuals such as Duns Scotus and Francis Bacon, three centuries apart, could shine like beacons in their success in probing the frontiers of knowledge and acted as role models for others. What knowledge was understood and harnessed was through these institutions, and indeed almost all education above the lowest levels was centred in them. Though we tend to think of these people as preserving fragments of lost knowledge rather than creating and harnessing the new, this is unfair as clearly movement occurred – albeit slowly. The Middle Ages did not begin in a single day when Charlemagne was crowned in 800 AD but through a slow adjustment over many years!

Scholars came to medieval universities in the main to extend the boundaries of religious understanding. They lived in a world with an average life expectancy of less than 40 years, with periodic breakdowns of social order and with waves of disastrous disease spreading through Europe almost every generation. Yet they made real contributions that kept the flame of human knowledge alive. The great Université de Paris came to prominence in a way that shaped much of Western thought as Europe emerged into the Middle Ages.

Those privileged few students who attended these great institutions in medieval Europe were mainly priests or monks, either ordained or in training. The university exposure was a great boost for many for church careers but many were less interested in ecclesiastical advancement than in teaching and knowledge, the drivers for academic life today.

Most of the great thinkers in the Middle Ages worked and thought in a clerical university environment – sometimes in a monastic setting. Copernicus (in Krakow, Bologna, Padua and Ferrara 1491–1503), Erasmus (Cambridge and Paris 1495–1515), Luther (Wittenberg 1513–46), Francis Bacon (Cambridge 1573–76) and Galileo (Pisa and Padua 1589–1610), among many others, shared this type of background to which universities were central.

The boundary between staff and students was blurred, given the religious background of most. Even then, as today, gifted students in turn became faculty and built their lives within the universities of their day. This was the origin of the concept of a 'community of scholars', which still persists in some institutional cultures, though is not typical of most modern universities.

Society intermingled religion and state in medieval Europe very closely and the university system was tightly aligned with the class and social structures that then prevailed. It was a much simpler world where little changed and life continued as it had done for generations. The medieval universities were fit for purpose for staff, students and society at large. They did trigger some change. Undoubtedly, it was little and slow but from small beginnings great oaks grow!

The first great leap

We now leap forward to Renaissance Italy when the world was remoulded. The first university had been founded at Bologna in 1088. Old ways of thinking were rediscovered, refined and extended. These tumultuous years led human thought to become as much centred on man as on God. This freed up the great thinkers of the day to engage in intellectual journeys which began to vastly increase humanity's knowledge of our place in the cosmos. So astrology gradually became astronomy. In creating a new climate, the artistic revolution explored humanity and its place in the world from a broad base rather than a purely religious base. Human anatomy was investigated by Vesalius and, in creating new intellectual paradigms, experimental science had its humble beginnings. Teaching both for the professions and of new concepts accelerated. All of this was underpinned by the acceleration of knowledge transmission made possible by the new communications technology, the printing press.

Much of this thinking occurred in the Italian universities which had grown out of the Middle Ages, notably Padua. Yet much of the intellectual explosion took place outside the church-sponsored universities through great sponsors such as the Medici and the Dukes of Urbino and an occasional irreligious Pope. Undoubtedly, there was a new intellectual vibrancy in the air – a spirit to learn, challenge and exchange ideas.

This was not welcomed by the authorities of the day. Giordano Bruno was burnt at the stake and Galileo would have faced a similar fate if he had not recanted his view that the Earth rotated around the sun. The religious and secular authorities of the day were threatened by universities as institutions exploring new knowledge in the natural world with conclusions not always in keeping with contemporary theology. It may be for this reason that, after a few hugely important decades, the Italian Renaissance petered out in a scientific sense and the energy of new ways of thinking moved to the Protestant countries to the north.

UK developments – the Scottish university story and Oxbridge

In discussing events on the European continent, it is important to acknowledge that the most enduring developments on the journey to the modern university took place in what is now the UK. The great English universities of Oxford and Cambridge now dominate this story but our journey will take us first to Scotland where the history was both similar to and very different from the predominantly clerical origins that had dominated earlier university foundation to the south.

The first Scottish university, the University of St Andrews, was founded in 1413 as a religious institution established by papal bull by one of the Avignon antipopes. The papal bull was issued to a group of Augustinian clergy who had come from the Université de Paris as a result of the schism in the papacy and also from the already established institutions of Oxford and Cambridge.

In 1451, the University of Glasgow was founded by a papal bull and was an ecclesiastical foundation. In 1582, the Edinburgh town council established the University of Edinburgh. It was subsequently granted a Royal Charter by the King of Scotland and was one of the first universities in the West not to be established through a papal bull.

The Universities of Edinburgh and Glasgow played central roles in the Scottish Enlightenment. They exemplified early on the Scottish tradition of educating young people from a range of economic backgrounds and not just the wealthy. The civic origins of the University of Edinburgh are particularly relevant to the need for modern universities to be very close to the civic institutions around them and have porous boundaries with their local communities. A strong sense of local ownership and civic obligation permeates the great Scottish universities, even today. Most of them are true civic institutions. From early times, all aspects of education have been at their centre, with a strong emphasis on the professional education role. After all, even Burke and Hare, the body snatchers who were selling corpses to the medical school at Edinburgh, were involved in educating medical students!

This more secular base perhaps paved the way for the Scottish universities to play such a crucial role in pushing the boundaries of scientific knowledge. Its alumni include some of the greatest figures in the humanities and in science in the succeeding centuries such as Adam Smith, who lectured in Edinburgh and was professor at Glasgow University from 1751 to 1764. In his *The Wealth of Nations*, he wrote: 'In the University of Oxford, the greater part of the public professors have, for these many years, given up altogether even the pretence of teaching.' And he complained to friends that Oxford officials once discovered him reading a copy of David Hume's *A Treatise of Human Nature* and they subsequently confiscated his book and punished him severely for reading it.

From their beginnings, these Scottish universities have led the understanding and harnessing of change. They have educated the creators and innovators of the time.

Rather earlier, one of the seminal events in the university journey was the establishment of Oxford University during the 12th century. It was given a boost when Henry II banned English students from attending the medieval Université de Paris. Academic discord, or at least disputation, was as prevalent then as now and the world benefited when, after a dispute between students and townsfolk about 100 years later, some academics left Oxford and founded the University of Cambridge, which was awarded a Royal Charter by Henry III in 1248 and a flourishing college system evolved.

Most of the key religious orders of the time developed branches in Oxford affiliated with the University and major private benefactors also established a number of colleges. Oxford and Cambridge established a shared monopoly of the English university world until the early 19th century when the great

University of London colleges and Durham University were established. Their monopoly was no coincidence. In contrast to the development of a network of regional and city universities across the rest of Europe no new universities were established in England in the six centuries between 1209 (Cambridge) and 1826 (University College London). For example, the exceptionally well-resourced Gresham College, founded in London in 1597, was never permitted degree-awarding powers. One historian explained this very clearly:[1] 'This long period with just two universities was not because of lack of demand. It was because of barriers to entry policed very forcefully' by Oxford and Cambridge.

Oxford embraced the new thinking that came with the Renaissance but was not as great a centre of Enlightenment thinking as the Scottish universities.

In the mid-19th century, the Oxford movement associated with Anglo Catholicism was prominent. While having a major influence on the Anglican tradition, the ongoing influence on the development of universities was less. John Henry Newman himself concentrated more on the development of individual students in a moral and intellectual sense and was not wedded to the idea of universities as institutions primarily involved in the development of new knowledge. The German tradition of the research university was already beginning to strengthen elsewhere and was starting to be taken up in Oxford in Newman's time.

The University of Cambridge, like Oxford, continued as an ecclesiastical institution. Following the dissolution of the monasteries between 1536 and 1541, the University disbanded its faculty of canon law and moved its curricula towards the classics, biblical studies and mathematics. Many Cambridge graduates came from the nonconformist tradition. From the 17th century, the University has had a strong emphasis in arts and sciences including mathematics. Out of this a wonderful scientific tradition developed, with many of the greatest scientists of the ages having studied and worked at Cambridge University.

When one looks at the history of the English and Scottish universities, even in a superficial way, it is apparent that the individual institutions differ in very significant ways. The balance of the religious and the secular, the move from a canon law or theological bent to a wider knowledge base embracing the natural sciences, the strength of local civic links and the source of their funding, especially underpinning foundations, are all points of difference.

Why is this? Knowledge is universal and the intellectual foundation in which these institutions operated from their beginnings, although altering dramatically over the centuries, were very similar at any given time.

A possible answer is that, even in much simpler times than the world today, society and national economies were very diverse. To meet their needs required some diversity in the university system of the time. How much truer is that today with a degree of complexity in educational, research and societal needs unimaginable in the 17th and 18th centuries.

Indeed, there was a general decline in European universities in the 17th and 18th centuries (except in Scotland) and they were ready for reform. In France and then more widely, Napoleon had swept aside the traditional universities, and replaced them with the Grandes Ecoles, still dominant in France.

Humboldt and the University of Berlin

Spectacular examples of new knowledge creation can readily be identified earlier in the university story, witness Galileo in Padua and Newton in Cambridge, both of whom made contributions of the highest order and rank among the very greatest scientists of any age. Universities prior to the early 19th century certainly concentrated on better understanding but, in the main, through existing texts and concepts rather than creating new paradigms. Newton and Galileo were the exception rather than the rule. This all changed rather dramatically in Berlin probably as one of the modernising responses to Prussia's crushing defeat in the mid-years of the Napoleonic wars.

Wilhelm von Humboldt (sometimes confused with his more famous brother, Alexander, the explorer) played a key role in establishing the University of Berlin between 1809 and 1811. Its initial faculties were law, medicine, theology and philosophy.

Some of the greatest thinkers in modern European history studied and worked at this University. The intellectual environment from the beginning was quite different from the traditional university of the time. The creation of knowledge was as important as the passing on of knowledge, loosely referred to as the freedom to learn and the freedom to teach wherever knowledge takes you. This was quite a different ethos from that developed later by Newman at Oxford. There were some similarities to the philosophy underpinning the Ecole Polytechnique established in Paris in 1804 by Napoleon. The liberal ideas characteristic of the time led to recognition of the importance of seminars and laboratories and an increasing concentration on science. Religious studies as an influencer on the extent of new discovery in science no longer operated as they had in the past.

This is sometimes referred to as the Humboldtian model of higher education. At its very centre is the combination of study and active research. It is the beginning of the concept of the researcher as a teacher and of the student as a researcher. The humanist principles of the High Enlightenment underpinned Humboldt's thinking. All four of the university roles described in Chapter 1 can, for the first time, be seen fully in Humboldt University in Berlin.

Working and studying in an environment of this type was quite a different thing to the heavily religiously influenced institutions still operating at that time in most parts of Europe. It was less different perhaps from the University of Edinburgh where, as described earlier, civic influences had been so strong from the beginning. Certainly the aspirations of staff and students were met. The University became renowned throughout the world as did the wider German university system and, for several generations, the aspiration of many of the most gifted students in the English-speaking world was to spend some time studying in Germany.

And in cities throughout England, the German model and the challenges of the industrial revolution deeply influenced the establishment of new, primarily technical, universities and other educational institutions such as the polytechnics which were founded in the late 19th century in London[2] and the Mechanics Institutes established in cities of the industrial revolution such as Liverpool, Manchester and Bradford, which later became universities or further education colleges providing higher education courses. At various points, the Christian religious denominations founded colleges of education to train teachers including for their own primary and secondary schools. Many of these too have now become universities.

This has enormously expanded the nature of the UK university system away from their Oxbridge and Scottish origins. Moreover, during the late 19th century, significant efforts were made to reform Oxford and Cambridge universities, through government intervention. For example, between 1854 and 1880, there were 10 reforming Acts of Parliament. The government certainly played its role in those changes!

The quality and achievements of the academic faculty speak for themselves. Much of the knowledge that underpinned the scientific, agrarian and industrial revolutions came out of immensely strong German universities. As to society, expectations and needs were largely met with a range of studies in health, biology and the natural sciences and with knowledge outputs that had real practical applications to the world outside universities. While still a community of scholars, these ideas of what a university should be led to a paradigm shift in contributing to massive societal change. Undoubtedly, in a scientific sense, the strongest universities in the world in the early decades of the 20th century were in Germany. Just look at where the Nobel Prizes in physics and chemistry were awarded in those years. Yes, some went to the Cavendish laboratories at Cambridge and some to Paris but large numbers went to Gottingen, Heidelberg and Freiberg.

In recent decades, European university reform has been strongly influenced by the Bologna process which was commenced by a declaration signed in 1998 at the 800th anniversary of the foundation of the Sorbonne in Paris and then formally launched by 29 European education ministers in Bologna, Europe's first university, in June 1999. Forty-six countries are now members.

The Bologna process is intended to create coherence and a more strongly harmonised European university system. It is intended to make it more possible for academic credits to be transferred between universities across the continent. In practice, it has spread the current British model of university education. Its standardisation of European higher education specifies an undergraduate degree of at least three years called the 'licence' or bachelor's degree, followed by a two-year diploma called the master's degree, then a doctorate, meant to be obtained in at least three years.

Jo Ritzen, the Dutch Minister of Education from 1989 to 1998, and then President of Maastricht University, has written comprehensively about the successes and challenges of this process.[3]

Developments outside Europe

US

Nine 'colonial colleges' were the first universities in the US, founded well before American independence and, in some cases, to provide university education for those excluded from study in England because of their 'dissenting' religious beliefs, such as Puritans at Harvard (1636), Yale (1701) and Dartmouth (1769), Presbyterians at Princeton (1746), Baptists at Brown (1765) and the Dutch Reformed Church at Rutgers (1766).

It is not surprising, therefore, that the more freethinking and dissenting history of these first American universities, combined with the model of the research university that had developed in Germany, rather than the more backward-looking Oxbridge model, spread rapidly across the US.

Quite rightly, the establishment of Johns Hopkins University in 1876 is regarded as being of huge importance. Gilman, the first President of Johns Hopkins, promoted a model of integration of teaching and research taken directly from Germany which, in turn, revolutionised higher education across the US. The concept of the graduate school was taken from the University of Heidelberg and the ideas of research-led teaching and of an institution where new knowledge was explored as well as taught – first developed in Humboldt University in Berlin – were fully adopted and indeed extended. It is an interesting historical fact that the resounding success of this integration then returned to Europe and was taken up quite rapidly by almost every significant university in Western Europe. When one thinks of Cambridge in the early decades of the 20th century, the pivotal work at the Cavendish laboratory stands out. This would not have sat so well in the predominantly ecclesiastical institutions of previous times. When Rutherford split the atom at the Cavendish, it led directly to Oppenheimer, Los Alamos and the atom bomb only a few decades later.

China and East Asia

In China, the history of education is significantly longer than in the West. Confucius and others set directions almost 3,000 years ago and respect for education and career advancement prospects of a more advanced education underpinned the Mandarin system in Imperial China. This respect lasted until the Cultural Revolution, in the 1960s and '70s, whose impact on China's universities cannot be overstated, with academics driven from the workforce or worse and universities essentially closed for significant periods. A generation was largely lost to a higher education.

With Deng's reforms in the 1980s, and with stable leadership since, China's university system has improved and strengthened year by year. The importance of world-class universities to a leading world economy is fully understood by the Chinese leadership and there has now been unprecedentedly heavy investment in universities for several decades.

There are some 2,000 universities in China supported at city and provincial level in the main. A small number of some 30 institutions report directly to the central ministry in Beijing and have been identified as China's great research universities for the future. The aim is to make sure that some of these universities are at Oxbridge level in the not too distant future.

While China has encouraged great diversification, the university system has moved towards more all-embracing university models. For example, previously independent medical universities have been amalgamated into more comprehensive structures.

There is some discussion and controversy about the extent to which university presidents in the People's Republic of China have genuine autonomous control of their universities.

However, it seems that Chinese universities have considerable autonomy in setting curricula, and have control over their own budgets in a similar way to what is seen in state-sponsored institutions in the West. China graduated some 7 million university students in 2010 and this continues to increase. For some years, China has been the major exporter of international students to other countries, adding to the capacity of national institutions.

In structure and in mindset, Chinese universities have become quite close to the Western model and have fully embraced the view that teaching and research are best combined in single institutions. There is also a high commitment to interdisciplinarity and to collaboration with other institutions both within China and more broadly. The best Chinese universities rank among the most improved in Asia on most rating scales in recent years. It is likely that at least two of the world's top 20 universities will be China-based within a decade.

The educational models of Hong Kong and Singapore, global cities that have strong economies, parallel that found in Western countries, most notably the UK. The quality of education is outstanding and there is uniform adoption of research-led teaching with major research carried out in educational institutions. Similarly, Taiwan, Korea and Japan have first-rate university systems that are now solidly based on the Western research and education model.

As in China, university entrance standards are extremely exacting for the top universities and the students who gain entry receive a first-rate education. Pedagogy is still rather more didactic than in the West with teachers doing most of the talking and dialogue less accepted.

India

India has the third largest university sector in the world by number and a vast array of types of institution. Higher learning in one form or another goes back in India for millennia. Over the centuries, more and more education was delivered in religious institutions and a formal university system was only developed in British India in the 19th century.

In that era, many wealthy Indians sought education in the UK, especially at Oxbridge, a prerequisite to a leadership role in British India. Both Gandhi and Nehru illustrate that.

A number of local universities were established by the British and continue to flourish, including the University of Calcutta, the University of New Delhi and the University of Madras. India now has a small number of universities overseen by the central government and some 300 universities overseen by provincial governments as well as a vast number of colleges of higher education.

Higher education in India has a technology and science focus and many of the best institutions, especially in the postgraduate space, have a STEM orientation. Prominent among these are the Indian Institutes of Technology (IIT), which excel both in research and education and attract absolutely outstanding students. There are a number of other specialist colleges in India that excel in different aspects of engineering or the sciences and are highly regarded.

The public university system, by contrast, struggles a little for institutions to reach the level one might expect in a country with India's massive intellectual firepower. This may, in part, be due to many outstanding Indian academics being attracted out of India by Western universities or to high-level science research colleges such as the IITs.

India graduates more university students than China does but with a wider range of quality of institutions.

Universities such as Ashoka are leading the way, educationally speaking, for a thriving private sector that is now developing. The Indian Government has been loath to allow unfettered entrance by international education providers, which are still held at arm's length. The range of private college offerings provided by domestic for-profit operators is considerable and varies widely in both quality and price. Almost as many Indian students as Chinese students now study outside India, with a tendency for some students to seek residency in the West at the conclusion of their studies. The attraction of brilliant young people from overseas to study and, where appropriate, to contribute to the workforce is a huge boon for many Western economies.

It is relatively unlikely that India will have universities in the top 20 within a decade in the way that China will but it may well have institutions in the top 100.

Africa and Latin America

Across the African continent, the research quality of universities is very patchy and – especially in sub-Saharan Africa – the availability of student places tends to be low for the size of population. South Africa has some excellent universities that are continuing to adapt to much larger student numbers after the end of apartheid. The development of effective alternative pathways and the challenge of getting more students ready for university are important in South Africa.

In Latin America, the university system has taken inspiration from both the Iberian peninsula and the US, the latter to a greater extent in more recent decades. There are a number of first-rate institutions and a range of provider types including, in many countries, a well-developed private university system. The Laureate private university group has a specific role in Latin America in providing first-rate education in a non-research-intensive setting.

The past 70 years – equity and 'massification'

Culture, traditions and pedagogy

University systems outside traditional English-speaking countries and outside Europe bring much from their own cultures and traditions as well as simply copying what has worked well in the traditional West.

Of course, in these countries, their local and national traditions hugely enrich the educational experience and, in significant part, guide research direction notably in the humanities and social sciences. This adds to the diversity and strength of any university system. In serving local communities, universities must understand their traditions and their history in a way that is not subservient to a wider view of human knowledge. Students exposed to this approach benefit greatly from it as both local and global citizens.

It is equally interesting to observe how both the philosophy of education and pedagogical approaches are altering in Western societies that have become multicultural, such as the UK, part of the US and the major Australian cities. Here we are seeing a move from approaches developed and centred in the traditional West to a richer model where learning and insights from across the world are incorporated in a way that is truly global in its orientation. This process has quite a way to go and it is noteworthy that student bodies and employers operating in a global context generally support such an approach.

This overview of the historical evolution of universities outside the traditional West shows that, in the main, universities have merged with the research/education model that came out of Europe, albeit with unique local aspects. The research-intensive model originating largely in Germany some 200 years ago still dominates almost everywhere. Changing societal needs have driven a steady evolution in approach and structure.

The beginnings of differentiation that were evident in the Scottish universities from early days had become quite marked by the mid-20th century. Some institutions specialised in a very small number of themes, science or medicine or the humanities, while others were comprehensive entities encompassing the humanities and sciences broadly. A small number of institutions, notably in the US, continued to have a very heavy teaching focus with little active research but the great majority of universities fully embraced the co-location of research and education side-by-side and the value of research-led teaching. Most universities were secular institutions, supported by civic authorities at either city, regional or national level but institutions with religious affiliations were and are still not uncommon, for example William and Mary university in Virginia and many more. It was clear that diversification of the university sector was important in meeting individual and national needs. This theme of diversification is one to which we will return.

The UK since the '50s

The UK was an exemplar of a country with a diversifying and high quality university sector in 1950. What did universities look like at that time? Firstly, very few students went to university. In Britain before the Second World War there were only some 50,000 students enrolled in universities. Only a tiny proportion of these were women and most students came from an upper-class or upper middle-class background, including a high proportion from the private schools which educated only a tiny minority of the population.

It is not true to say that all students were from well-off families. Less well-off professional people, recognising the value of a university education, might shoulder fees for their children. Board of Education and local authority grants were available which were often taken up by bright youngsters from working-class families – hence the significant number of schoolteachers from that background. A small number of state scholarships were available with some diversity in economic background even in Oxbridge institutions.

There continued to be something of a class divide between Oxbridge and the civic universities in the UK, which developed over the past 150 years, originating in the University of London and their external degrees.

Universities had long taken on much of the responsibility for the continuously expanding professional training. Medicine was well established as a university discipline. Strong engineering departments were found in most universities, although most engineers were not educated in universities at that time. Many universities had law departments. Most postgraduate professional education took place within the professions through a variety of apprenticeship models. Technological education was offered by a range of different institutions, some in the university sector, others not.

A strong tradition of the value of a broader education persisted strongly but, in contradistinction to the liberal arts tradition of the US, tended to stream into either an arts/humanities or science direction. The school leaving and university entrance qualifications, controlled as they were by the universities, reflected these differing strands. This led to the narrowness and specialisation of British school education which is a significant weakness for the country and contrasts with many other education systems across the world.

It is legitimate to ask how well this worked both for the individual and the country. Clearly, it was not terribly effective for young people with the capacity to complete a university education who were not given a reasonable opportunity to do so. While high quality education was certainly available for the few, the wider social responsibilities of the university role were not being adequately met. Many of the bright working-class students who became schoolteachers may have preferred another career but teaching was often the major opportunity for them.

The social exclusivity of universities meant that they played a considerable role in ensuring class division persisted longer than was necessary, and that history is still all too present in some areas. Education remained the key mechanism of crossing social divides for those who could access it at university level.

For society, the more limited university system at that time had largely met general needs in terms of professional graduates and the number of graduate-level jobs then available. It was clear, by 1950, with the expectations of society at large much higher after the Second World War and with the needs driven by a much more rapidly developing economy, that the highly restrictive universities at that time were no longer fit for purpose in terms of student intake and numbers of graduates. The society and economy required far greater numbers of students at university level.

'Massification'

It is interesting that both in the US and the UK, the elite institutions (Oxbridge and Ivy League) initially failed to expand rapidly to provide adequate new places and this was left to the civic universities in England and to the public land grant universities in the US. The next stage of university development was one of huge energy as universities expanded in number, interdisciplinary range, in size of student bodies and in equity programmes at an unprecedented rate. This saw, at its fullest extent, the development of what the great American educator Clark Kerr has referred to as the multiversity. These institutions have tens of thousands of students, encompass every faculty, have graduate and undergraduate schools, are huge employers in their regions and contribute in a major way both through the students they educate and their research and innovation outputs to regional and national economies. In essence, most of today's great public universities are institutions of this type. All four pillars shine out in them.

Equity

As the modern university has developed, two trends, both beneficial, have become enhanced. Firstly, equity in intake and staff composition has advanced considerably.

Women students in particular have gone from a vanishingly small percentage of all commencing students to more than half in many universities, reflecting the composition of society at large.

Representation from underprivileged and minority groups has lagged behind this and in many countries it is still nowhere near where it needs to be. This is best seen in the US in the very low participation rates in students from working-class families belonging to the lowest socio-economic tier and in the UK by the very low participation rates among young working-class men. In academic staff workforce composition, imbalances have improved but are still marked the further one goes up the academic ladder. The proportion of women full professors is still woefully inadequate and that pertains even more to minority ethnic groups. Nevertheless, an absolute imperative of continued improvement in these areas is now generally, though not universally, accepted,[4] a real step forward in itself, though with continuing massive underrepresentation of women and minority ethnic groups at the most senior university academic and leadership levels.

The second area where real change has been seen has been the broad embracing of the concept that universities not only can but must contribute to the wealth of society at large[1]. This is through the research they do and its applications as well as through the achievements of their graduates.

The most spectacular example of this in modern times is the development of Stanford University as one of the world's greatest research institutions and the spawning by Stanford of Silicon Valley with huge wealth creation for California, the US and the world. Although not so spectacular, numerous examples of universities contributing very actively to job creation and to national economies now exist. These include the technology industries in the UK around Cambridge University, the massive Boston clever industry hub, the new industries in the University of North Carolina and Duke university triangle, the Rhine Necker developments in Germany and the new biotech industries in San Diego. And it is not all about their precincts! Both university research and development and gifted graduates flow everywhere and drive the global economy wherever one looks! Creating entrepreneurial environments has truly become core business.

This has led to a general acceptance of the view that a crucial component of successful modern high-tech economies is the working together of industry, government and universities.

As this progress has continued, Clark Kerr's multiversity has evolved even further with increasing 'massification' of many institutions. University participation rates are now well over 40% of all young people in entry age cohorts in a number of countries. What a change from the situation in the 1950s! As this has happened, the diversification remarked on earlier has increased even further.

A major development in relatively recent times has been the entry of high quality for-profit private providers in many parts of the world, exemplified by the Laureate group established by Doug Becker in the US, which runs private universities through much of Latin America and Asia. Laureate offers high quality education with limited or no research productivity. Becker has now sold his interest in the Laureate group and is launching a new business helping universities to increase efficiency and productivity in administrative systems.

Indeed, in terms of our four pillars, the mission of many such universities is heavily biased towards teaching. It is clear that in a differentiated university model, individual institutions might contribute unevenly to our four pillars. (By contrast, the private Ivy leagues make a major research contribution, supported by massive foundations.)

An even more major change, with both public and private uptake, has been the development of distance learning, for example through the pioneering Open University and its imitators, and e-education, with wide provision of both undergraduate and master's degrees that can be taken electronically in many countries. Some of these are offered across continents. Arizona State University in the US has been particularly active in this area and King's College in London and Monash University in Australia are among a number of institutions that have partnered with a private provider, the Pearson group, in high-level e-master's provision.

This overlaps with the development of Massive Open Online Courses (MOOCs), a high-volume modular provision offered by a number of providers and universities at sub-degree level and we discuss this later. The university world today is much more diverse than it was at the turn of the last century. It is evolving rapidly in how it delivers its core missions of education and research with very different approaches from different institutions.

Universities have always changed in response to external pressures, but it is also evident that, before the 20th century, change was quite slow and there was a period of relative stability in the first half of the 20th century when very little change occurred. The research university model then evolved considerably with the development of institutions on a greatly increased scale, encompassing a wide spectrum of professional training and with enrolment of a much higher proportion of younger people than previously.

Superimposed on this change in response to societal need, the technological changes following the information revolution included an increasing presence of distance education. It is relatively straightforward until we get to recent times to map these changes against societies' demands both for education of talented graduates and university knowledge creation through research.

Historical overview and the situation today

When looking at earlier centuries, we can pinpoint a close alignment between universities' ethos, outlook and contribution to the wider world and the needs of the world around them. The ongoing evolution of our four pillars (understanding change, harnessing change, education for change and creating a facilitating environment for change) characterises this journey.

This is important because, seen in this way, the massive changes that are looming can be seen as an intrinsic part of this historical enterprise rather than completely new and alien. The monastic universities thrived in a world with limited knowledge and virtually no technology as beacons of light. They provided students with access to libraries and the ability to interact with gifted teachers and peers. They contributed very significantly indeed to the stability of medieval society.

It would be an overstatement to claim that the massive re-orientations in human thinking that are called the Reformation, the Renaissance and the Enlightenment were driven by universities, but at the very least one can say that universities contributed to them and massively benefited from them.

This phase of history was characterised by a transition that was almost certainly more gradual than the above account suggests, from rather rigid religious institutions to institutions where new knowledge was valued both for itself and to pass on to others. As this happened, the monastic ethos was gradually replaced by a guild ethos, a type of thinking that saw universities as beacons of rationality separate from the outside world, influencing yet strongly independent.

The 'ivory tower' view of universities dates from this time. It represents supremely a view of universities as having an absolute responsibility to knowledge as truth and to make that available to the outside world but perhaps not to be too influenced by the outside world. This type of institution is, perhaps, quintessentially represented by Newman's Oxford.

It is indisputable that, as universities have evolved, all of these earlier traditions can still be found within them sitting, at times uncomfortably, side-by-side. Even the monastic tradition is represented by strong theology departments in many universities, it has to be said very different from those of the 19th century in that they are influenced strongly by the academic traditions around them. The Guild tradition is still very strong in academic life, with many taking the view that universities should have quite a high degree of separation from society at large and not take on too many responsibilities that are outside their traditional preserve. This view is less prevalent than it was but can still found in some influential quarters of the leading universities and may even be the prevailing attitude in certain faculties.

Conclusion

This overview enables us to consider how some other more major probable changes over the next few decades are likely to play out. It can be seen that the evolution of our pillars from Chapter 1 can be seen in every age, albeit with varying speeds of evolution. The changes in modern times in this respect can be seen as nothing new but they are of greater magnitude.

Going ahead, the landscape is not so straightforward. Society is changing more rapidly than ever before. We are still in the early stages of the information revolution and how people access, use and even add to knowledge will, undoubtedly, undergo even more transformation in the decades ahead.

Many of the problems the planet faces require multidisciplinary approaches with gifted researchers from many disciplines bringing new approaches through multidisciplinary education in key areas as well as multidisciplinary research. All the global grand challenges require such an approach.

The capital investment and the running costs of major universities, especially those engaged in the natural sciences, engineering and in medical science, are enormous. These consume an increasing proportion of university budgets and even wealthy countries have increasing difficulty in funding costs solely through the tax base.

It is incumbent upon universities to respond to today's challenges by aligning with society's needs as they have done in the past. This will require not only consideration but implementation of different ways of doing things. What is needed is not only increasing diversification of an already diversified system but also a willingness by traditionally focused institutions to adapt more rapidly than they may feel comfortable with. Challenging times are undoubtedly upon us!

An analysis of the university journey through history sheds considerable light on the absolute necessity for today's universities to rise to the challenge of meeting societal needs much more broadly than they do at the moment. This is true generally but also applies to each individual university.

Is this too high an ambition, at a time when some in political leadership consider universities as a glorified finishing school where clever youngsters go before entering the real world and immersing themselves in their professional journeys and in a productive life?

Among many, respect for universities and those who teach and work in them is nowhere near what it was in earlier years. Indeed, in the UK at least, it has reached a real nadir in recent years, perhaps because the universities themselves are no longer institutions for the elite alone, and in the US, UK and Australia the public funding, such as it is, of universities has been under some scrutiny with downwards momentum. This has started to impact on the self-belief and confidence of the sector.

This book is about helping universities to regain their belief and confidence in contributing to the future strength and resilience of societies and economies around the world. To help that:

Governments should develop a narrative of the history and contribution of universities in their country and the way in which they hope to develop this to meet the challenges of the future.

Universities should develop a narrative of the contribution that the university over its history has made to the local, national and international community including the roles that they play most strongly and effectively.

Chapter 3

Universities and work

Why work matters

All of us worry about something a lot of the time but, in particular, occupational anxiety – getting a job that is suited to one's talents and holding it down and occasionally achieving promotion – is an important part of the human story for just about everyone. That's partly because of the 'work ethic', which is widely understood and is related to the contribution any individual makes to society. But it's also related to bringing in the income to pay for life's necessities.

Most of us experience employment anxiety at one time or another and it is particularly strong at times of transition. For most, this is most acute when they are reaching the end of periods of full-time study and beginning to look for career-building work.

The traditional university mission of creation, curatorship and transmission of knowledge certainly still exists and is a prime driver for many who work in universities but that doesn't of itself address students' worries about work.

Ed well remembers in his own life the anxiety he felt about employment at each stage of career development and especially as he was leaving university after his undergraduate degree, and so he completely understands the increasing focus of young people on institutions that get them job ready.

Introduction

Almost every aspect of our world is changing increasingly rapidly. That means that we all – individuals and communities – face increasingly deep and complex challenges as we live our daily lives. The central thesis of this book is that high quality universities have to be the essential means of addressing those challenges and enabling us to live well.

There are many descriptions of the kind of economic and societal change that we are undergoing, but this summary,[1] written in early 2016 by Klaus Schwab, the founder of the World Economic Forum, is typical:

> The First Industrial Revolution used water and steam power to mechanize production. The Second used electric power to create mass production. The Third used electronics and information technology to automate production. Now a Fourth Industrial Revolution is building on the Third, the digital revolution that has been occurring since the middle of the last century. It is characterized by a fusion of technologies that is blurring the lines between the physical, digital, and biological spheres.
>
> There are three reasons why today's transformations represent not merely a prolongation of the Third Industrial Revolution but rather the arrival of a Fourth and distinct one: velocity, scope, and systems impact. The speed of current breakthroughs has no historical precedent. When compared with previous industrial revolutions, the Fourth is evolving at an exponential rather than a linear pace. Moreover, it is disrupting almost every industry in every country. And the breadth and depth of these changes herald the transformation of entire systems of production, management, and governance.
>
> The possibilities of billions of people connected by mobile devices, with unprecedented processing power, storage capacity, and access to knowledge, are unlimited. And these possibilities will be multiplied by emerging technology breakthroughs in fields such as artificial intelligence, robotics, the Internet of Things, autonomous vehicles, 3-D printing, nanotechnology, biotechnology, materials science, energy storage, and quantum computing.
>
> Already, artificial intelligence is all around us, from self-driving cars and drones to virtual assistants and software that translate or invest. Impressive progress has been made in AI in recent years, driven by exponential increases in computing power and by the availability of vast amounts of data, from software used to discover new drugs to algorithms used to predict our cultural interests. Digital fabrication technologies, meanwhile, are interacting with the biological world on a daily basis. Engineers, designers, and architects are combining computational design, additive manufacturing, materials engineering, and synthetic biology to pioneer a symbiosis between microorganisms, our bodies, the products we consume, and even the buildings we inhabit.

The first of these industrial revolutions was mainly located in the UK. The fourth is mainly located in Silicon Valley, in the US, and increasingly in China. It should be obvious that countries and universities need to be educating people for the Fourth Industrial Revolution and not the first.

Most commentators would consider the above analysis uncontentious but the purpose of this book is not to discuss the detailed rights or wrongs of this assessment.

But we do argue that universities across the world have the duty to understand, interpret and prepare for a world in which such change is taking place. And, indeed, that universities are better placed than any other institution or organisation to be able to do that well.

And nowhere is the dramatic impact of such change more evident than in the world of work and so the kinds of skills and knowledge that will be important in the newly evolving economy. Universities play a central role in educating people for the work and roles that they will play in this new economy and new society in precisely the same way that they have done in preceding industrial revolutions, during which, as described in Chapter 2, many of our modern universities were founded.

As the economy has globalised, the physical locations of industrial production have changed. Traditional geographical areas for the production of, for example, coal, steel, ships, cars and an enormous range of products have moved across the world, leaving whole communities without their traditional sources of employment and prosperity. And, quite apart from the economics, this is having significant political consequences.

In addition, the nature of the production process has changed dramatically and continues to do so, for example in the decline of massive production plants, each employing thousands of people, and the rise of automation for more routine tasks together with far more complex networking relationships.

The working population has changed dramatically as women have joined the labour market and people live and work longer as 'retirement' retreats further into the future. Most countries of the world continue to experience a major shift away from agriculture and, thank goodness, child labour is increasingly challenged and curbed.

More and more jobs require the ability to use technology effectively, from the simple laptop computer or phone to highly complex systems of production.

This is all set out very well by Joseph Aoun, the President of North-Eastern University, in his book – *Robot-Proof: Higher Education in the Age of Artificial Intelligence*.[2]

The challenges of these changes are deep and wide-ranging. They are not only technical, but also philosophical and ethical, as the nature of work, and its dominant place in our society, changes.

And the changing nature of work and employment patterns at the same time poses important questions about individuals' incomes, almost all of which derive from work. So, as work changes, income changes and new means of financial self-sufficiency and sustainability need to be established.

This chapter addresses the ways in which these changes in the nature of work are changing our society, assesses the ways in which universities could be contributing to change and then looks at the ways in which universities themselves have to change in order for that to happen.

The change that is all around us

It is important to identify the particular changes in the nature of work that universities have to consider. Universities need to address a number of specific aspects of this process of change:

1. 'Careers for life' are in steep decline. This means that the traditional single point of entry to higher education, at around the age of 18, has been replaced by a number of new entry points to learning, which requires unprecedented flexibility in courses and modes of teaching.
2. There is now a different pattern of skills which almost everyone needs in most areas of employment. CP Snow's 'Two Cultures'[3] is even less defensible now than it was 60 years ago. In addition to 'Maths, English and Science', most people need a variety of technology and communication skills. The move to a service economy has led to a weakening of basic mathematical skills. This de-emphasis on maths continues into the university years and has led to a workforce that may well be ill-prepared for the technological demands of the new century and even the analytical capacities needed for effective citizenship. These problems are particularly acute in the narrow English system of 16–18 education and training as a number of studies have identified.
3. Aoun's book,[4] which considers the importance and impact of the development of artificial intelligence, suggests that the particular attributes that humans have, and need to develop, to distinguish their capacities from those of machines are their creativity, mental flexibility, sociability and imagination. Universities can and do help teach those qualities.

4 Professional skills, which needed little updating during a working life are now changing very rapidly, partly, but not only, due to technological change, so those working as doctors, engineers, teachers and the whole range of professions need to be able to update their competence regularly. This means that universities have to work more closely with businesses and professions than has been the case in the past.

5 The balance between 'employment' and 'self-employment' is changing as the 'gig economy' develops. This too means that individuals need networking and collaborative skills, and to be entrepreneurial in their attitudes.

6 Entirely new skills and types of work are emerging, which requires much more open consideration of how labour will be educated and trained to do this work.

7 A far greater number of jobs require higher-level technical and analytical expertise, which may well need to be acquired through postgraduate education. This is illustrated in work by think tanks such as the Royal Society of Arts[5] and the Chartered Institute of Personnel and Development[6] and consultancies such as the Deloitte 2019 Global Human Capital Trends.[7]

   This highlights the dichotomy, discussed in Chapter 2, between the UK and the North American system. In the US, a broad undergraduate experience is often supplemented by graduate school whereas much of that graduate school training is encompassed in UK first degrees.

8 It is now the case that workers for almost any organisation can and do come from throughout the world, via 'outsourcing' and other means. The world offers a potential workforce and the supply of education is no longer fundamentally national but more international in nature. Migration is a very substantial political challenge but this reality is unlikely to change and the mobility of labour will become increasingly important.

These are the challenges that universities and university systems have to address, all of them highly significant. Many universities are already facing up to these now, at least to some extent. But most are not.

University relationships with the world of work

Universities have always had a vocational dimension to their institutional mission, as we explored in Chapter 2. In medieval times, they trained theologians and priests, the intelligentsia and civil service of their time. By the

19th century, they were training engineers and scientists, lawyers and doctors and, in more modern times, they train the whole range of professional and technical workers.

An illustration of the range of vocational courses currently taught in the UK can be seen in the Times and Sunday Times Good University Guide[8] rankings. This includes 67 subject tables.

Of these, 38 might be considered predominantly 'vocational':

Accounting and finance
Aeronautical and manufacturing engineering
Agriculture and forestry
Animal science
Archaeology and forensic science
Architecture
Art and design
Building
Business studies
Chemical engineering
Civil engineering
Communication and media studies
Computer science
Creative writing
Criminology
Dentistry
Drama, dance and cinematics
Education
Electrical and electronic engineering
Food science
General engineering
Geography and environmental sciences
Hospitality, leisure, recreation and tourism
Land and property management
Law
Librarianship and information management
Materials technology
Mechanical engineering
Medicine
Nursing
Pharmacology and pharmacy
Physiotherapy
Radiography
Social work
Sports science
Subjects allied to medicine
Town and country planning and landscape
Veterinary medicine

And 29 might be considered predominantly 'academic', though of course with significant vocational implications:

American studies
Anatomy and physiology
Anthropology
Biological sciences
Celtic studies
Chemistry
Classics and ancient history
East and South Asian studies

Economics
English
French
Geology
German
History
History of art, architecture and design
Iberian languages
Italian
Linguistics
Mathematics
Middle Eastern and African studies
Music
Philosophy
Physics and astronomy
Politics
Psychology
Russian and Eastern European languages
Social policy
Sociology
Theology and religious studies

Of course, these classifications are somewhat arbitrary but we set this table out in full to convince the reader that a huge amount of technical and professional education already takes place in universities. It is necessary to do this since the view is gaining traction in some places that modern universities are 'academic' rather than 'vocational'. We do not share this view and think the facts are compelling. The perception that universities are principally academic builds the idea that universities can contribute little to 'apprenticeships' and educating in the skills that the economy needs.

Most employers would say that good degrees in many of the 'academic' subjects would be an important and valued qualification for work with them. Indeed, many so-called non-applied disciplines now include a lot of vocational type training.

But what this list of subjects studied at UK universities illustrates beyond question is that the vocational element of university education is an absolutely central part of universities today, as it has been throughout their history.

'Purely' academic subjects are, of course, an essential component of university education, but 'vocational' subjects are at least as important, irrespective of some ill-informed criticisms of 'Mickey Mouse' degrees and the like.

The institutional structure of universities reflects that history. Following the 1963 Robbins report,[9] the then colleges of advanced technology were turned into universities in 1966. The 1992 Further and Higher Education Act then entitled polytechnics and some other bodies to be designated as universities. In 2004, the criteria were further relaxed, so that many former colleges of education (primarily teacher training institutions, colleges of arts and design and similar institutions) could become universities, and the requirement that awarding research degrees was a fundamental requirement for any institution to be able to call itself a 'university' was removed.

Then, under the Coalition Government in the 2010s, we saw the emergence and growth of private for-profit higher education institutions, many of which successfully attained the university title and degree-awarding powers. The government encouraged such for-profit private, mainly teaching, universities so that they could be challenger institutions, which they believed would create more choice for students. They are highly vocational in character and focused in particular on more business-related programmes like law, accountancy and business studies. They are sometimes monotechnic institutions like the University for Law, though some are seeking to develop as multi-faculty universities.

In parallel to these institutional changes, further education colleges have played a major role in educating people for work, often through offering higher education degree qualifications in partnership with universities.

Over the past 50 years, professions such as nursing, the paramedical subjects and accountancy have started to get degree-level status for their qualifications, which in turn are themselves acquired at universities.

It is noteworthy that, in some areas, notably nursing but increasingly primary education, some argue that universities are not the right place to educate professionals. It is suggested that this should be done predominantly in the workplace. In our view, this attitude does not sufficiently take into account the additional status of university qualifications and the importance of broad thinking skills in all areas of work.

But the concerns about overly 'academic' qualifications in such professions do make the case for strong collaborations and relationships between universities and the related places of work. It may well be that there should be a stronger work component of such professional and vocational university courses.

In order to deal with such concerns, some leading educationists urge 'bringing back the polytechnics' and lament their becoming universities. We reject this approach as it would recreate the unsatisfactory and disruptive 'binary' divide between universities and other parts of higher education. This vein of argument also tends to reflect and perpetuate social and economic class division.

And we note that some who make such arguments would reject, for their own children and grandchildren, the corollary that they should not aspire to university with all that implies.

The key is not creating new divisions but establishing true differentiation, including in the relationship between work and education, within an envelope of equal esteem.

Universities, including strong 'academic' universities, are of course already doing this. Different qualifications led to different course structures and modes of study. Architects, doctors and vets, for example, normally had to study for five or six years to acquire their degrees, and a significant part of that time was not spent in the lecture theatre but 'on the job', working in hospitals, architects' practices or similar institutions.

There is usually a close relationship between the requirements of employers and professions in the relevant field of study and the content and assessment of the courses studied.

In many universities, the forms of study were themselves designed to integrate the university with the place of work. So-called 'sandwich courses' and then 'foundation degrees' were intended to emphasise that relationship and to give employers a direct stake in the nature of university education, the curricula for the courses and the ways in which they were taught.

A recent example was the UK Government announcement in March 2015 of nine new industry-designed 'degree apprenticeships'. These combine a full degree with professional training, with the cost covered by the employer and the government. The Skills Funding Agency estimates that between 1,500 and 2,000 students enrolled on these programmes in 2016 across 40 universities. A further tranche of new degree apprenticeships is currently under development. That said, however, current strategies to achieve a transformative scaling up of this form of provision, including the apprenticeship levy, are operating in a sub-optimal way and are being rejected by some of those employers upon whom the system relies if it is to succeed. It may well be that a more effective way of developing this idea is through strengthening university/further education partnerships.

To address these points, different course structures were evolved including part-time study and home and online learning. New, different modes of study were developed, notably at the Open University, with its use of modern technology to enable students to study at different times and in different places to suit their own convenience. Such models opened the opportunity of university education to millions who previously had not had that chance, and has been copied by major universities across the world.

One of the tragedies of the new funding system is that it has rendered Open University courses economically unviable. New forms of support for this approach are needed, as for part-time education of all types.

Of course, the development of online university education is expanding rapidly and that trend is likely to continue.

Over the past 50 years, these trends have often been accompanied by controversy. Many academic commentators bemoan a number of the changes described above, for example the decision in 1992 to allow polytechnics to become universities (as previously noted), or the development of 'online' university degrees.

However, the basis of such criticisms is not at all clear. It is certainly the case that some of the institutions that became universities experienced 'academic drift' as their focus moved away from high quality vocational education and towards the research element of their university's mission, sometimes at a not very high standard of research. We address some of these issues in Chapter 6.

It is also the case that a number of non-university institutions felt disadvantaged in competing for undergraduate students with universities, which actually had a worse record of providing good quality undergraduate education, including good potential post-university employment opportunities, than they did. This was in an era where the entitlement to the 'university' title depended upon the quality of research and not teaching.

But some of the criticism came from straightforward snobbery and a concept that some forms of vocational education were 'appropriate' for universities and others were not. This went with an inaccurate perception, felt by some in universities, that their universities were the places where the most intelligent people in the country could be found, rather than in business, the civil service and professions or other areas of national life. While some of the most brilliant people in the country do indeed work in universities, there is a danger that inappropriately high self-esteem can contribute to an ivory tower mentality.

It is far better to acknowledge from the outset, as this book does, that a central part of the mission of universities is vocational, to prepare students for working life, both in specific professional disciplines and in general skills, abilities and characteristics.

It follows that universities should have as porous a boundary as possible with the outside working world whether public or private, and that policies should be fashioned to encourage such strong relationships within the constraints of propriety (for example in cases of commercial competition). Such porosity cannot be taken for granted – for some universities it can be more challenging to develop a valuable base of partnerships with industry partners and other key institutional stakeholders.

Research is also, of course, a central part of the mission of many, though by no means all, universities and is a vital part of national university life. We address this in detail in Chapter 4.

In Chapter 2, we describe the great effort that has taken place over several decades to give as many as possible the opportunities of university education. The Robbins Report in 1963 was seminal in the UK as was the commitment of the Gillard Government in Australia that 40% of young people should achieve a full university education.

These efforts have consistently been opposed by a small but politically significant group of ideologues who simply assert that 'More means worse', as long as their own families and social class are guaranteed university places.

However, if this 'roll back the clock' school of academic comment on the role of universities is not right, as we believe it is not, the question then becomes how to ensure that universities can themselves change in order to meet the very rapidly changing nature of work in the modern world and it is to this that we now turn.

How should universities now change?

There are a number of ways in which universities can and should change to address these rapidly changing patterns of the nature of work, of which the most important is for universities to acknowledge explicitly their key role in preparing students for the world of work.

We focus upon three, all of which require good partnership and collaboration with both public and private sector employers:

- the need to examine courses from the point of view of preparation for modern work, with the related development of new courses and new modes of study, mainly part-time, throughout life with a variety of entry points for study;
- improving students' preparation for work;
- developing the international dimension.

The timing of study and courses, in preparation for work

In most countries, including the UK, the EU and China, university education has developed principally on a 'front-loaded' model, though the detail of this varies between different systems. About 90% of university students are aged between 18 and 24 and the culture of the developed OECD economies mainly expects young people with the school qualifications to go straight to university, usually for a three-year course. This same approach largely holds in the US graduate school model, where many students leave university after college as undergraduates and others leave after (post)graduate school.

After they graduate, some students may study for a year or two for a master's degree but, after this, in almost every system, most will have little or no practical contact with universities for the rest of their lives.

The theory upon which this 'front-loading bias' is based is straightforward and obvious: entrants to work need their training at the beginning of their working life so that they can be properly qualified to work well. In many cases, the university degree accreditation is sufficient to entitle the graduate to work in the professional discipline that they have studied. In others, it may, in addition, be necessary for the student to pass a formal professional qualification, separate from the degree, in order to go on and work in that profession.

More generally, very many employers will see a degree, and sometimes a 'good degree' (meaning a 2.i pass grade or above), as a qualification to apply for certain job vacancies in their organisations. They may very well be prepared to be flexible about the exact subject of the degree that is studied but they will want evidence of the application and study that a degree is presumed to offer. And they, broadly speaking, have confidence in the quality of the university that has awarded the degree.

However, the rational reality upon which this 'front-loading model' was originally conceived is changing dramatically.

A far smaller proportion of graduates will now leave university to start a job that they can expect will last them for the rest of their lives – that is to say for about 40/50 years until they reach 'retirement age', probably some time between 65 and 75. And those that do stay in the same occupation will find that the way in which their profession is carried out will change almost beyond imagination, over the time of their working life.

This absolutely fundamental change alone poses four significant challenges for universities, which at the moment only few address seriously.

The first is what form of courses, if any, should they be offering to enable those who already have university degrees to more easily acquire the professional and technical qualifications that they need to enter a new career or profession at a later point in life, for example between 35 and 45? And what should be the structure and methods of teaching of those courses? A retaken full degree course is not at all the only option and some universities are offering more imaginative possibilities, but such alternatives need to be strongly developed. In general, universities are not vigorous enough in developing these possibilities. In particular, universities have been very sluggish in developing part-time educational qualifications that would be of benefit throughout life. An additional key aspect, only becoming more widely available relatively recently, is e-education master's degrees, which can be studied flexibly while people are working.

The second is should universities be offering retraining/updating/continuous professional development to enable those who have graduated, particularly in 'vocational' subjects, to keep up to date in their field over their working life?

The 'continuing competence' and 'continuing professional development' (CPD) requirements for lawyers already mean that lawyers need to get regular CPD credits in order to be able to continue practising. Some big employers, for example BT, do the same in their areas of professional competence. This will be an increasing trend for all professions, and universities ought to be in a position to offer the training needed, usually part-time, not full-time. Part-time courses and online education offer particularly good modes to do this. A good example is E-Learning for Health which is a Health Education England programme, in partnership with the NHS and professional bodies, though participation in such courses is not a formal requirement.

A particular opportunity for universities might well be the accreditation of shorter course units and material in a way that could jointly contribute to recognised postgraduate qualifications. This requires creative thinking about the modular structures of qualifications.

The third is can universities be flexible enough to meet such challenges by offering new modes of study, structure of courses and systems of delivering education? This would probably require a better system of benchmark testing for admission to courses, which would itself have important pedagogical benefits, especially if viable alternatives to the current final academic school performance tariff come into play.

Another very important issue with flexibility is the willingness or otherwise of the academic staff to permit course structures that allow more flexibility in relation to the timetables of the academic year. One has only to observe the massive university facilities that are wasted and empty for half the year to understand the current lack of flexibility. They could easily and beneficially be used for part-time CPD and master's qualifications at the times when they are not being used for current purposes.

The fourth challenge is to what extent can universities agree with the relevant professional bodies a system of accreditation that makes the courses themselves valuable to potential students and enhances their employment opportunities? For example, could a qualification be agreed that would permit potential head teachers to apply for posts on the basis of possessing a qualification that accredited their readiness for the role?

It ought to be possible for universities to pursue agreement with major business and industrial partners in order to co-design and fully accredit their own in-house lifelong learning and professional development activities.

And a more general issue arises – which is, what wider range of skills and talents should a university degree be offering, in order to enable students to prepare themselves better to flourish in a more fluid labour market? And what measures should universities be taking in general to enhance the 'employability' of their graduates? There has been some recent movement in this area but a great deal remains to be done. Universities should be far more ambitious and innovative in this sphere.

In each of these areas, the outdated 'ivory tower' approach has held universities back. To some extent, universities have been resistant because they believe – understandably and in many ways rightly – that they shouldn't be seeking to 'power steer' their students towards particular careers, but instead focusing on helping them become independent learners.

If universities are to move with the times, it is crucial for academics developing and designing courses to appreciate that key individuals working in business, industry and the professions have valuable ideas about ways in which an optimal course structure can be created and delivered. The work of Kumar Bhattacharyya and his colleagues at Warwick University's Warwick Manufacturing Group is an excellent example of what can be achieved but it is the exception rather than the rule in areas other than medicine and related health fields.

But, particularly in some economic sectors and at some universities, it seems that there is insufficient meaningful industrial engagement in the academic university world, for example in relation to course options and work placements, yet surprise is expressed when employers complain about the graduate skillset.

There is a range of possible solutions to these challenges, all of which are already being carried out by some universities but are not at all widespread. These include:

1 Offering a 'skills and profession update', with a variety of modes of study, to last throughout life, for example through refreshers every two or three years. This could be offered generally but might be offered particularly to the university's own alumni, perhaps as a 'life membership package'

to which they become entitled on graduation. Such an approach would have the additional benefit of really offering professional substance to the relationships with alumni, whom universities are increasingly wanting to contact almost only for fundraising reasons.

2. Offering a wide range of postgraduate degree packages, again with a variety of course structures and modes, to allow graduates with undergraduate degrees to develop particular professional specialisms, which could be taken up as desired throughout an individual's professional life. Again, such courses could be generally offered and also particularly targeted at the university's own alumni.

   One really interesting possibility here is the award of microcredits which allow accumulation to a master's degree accreditation while still in the workforce.

3. A particular example of this category is developing a wider range of 'Year 4' master's courses, tailored to particular vocational and work-oriented qualifications. Sadly, in many universities, the postgraduate master's degree is seen as either the first year of a doctorate, prior to entering academic life professionally, or as a money-spinner little integrated into the life of the university. A change of attitude is needed. To really maximise the utility of postgraduate study, there should be a greater degree of cross-sector focus on developing closer partnerships with employers for some postgraduate master's courses, most of which would be part-time and extend over a number of years. These partnerships could involve not only course design and adjunct teaching, but also mentorship and secondment opportunities.

4. Establishing a benchmarking system, beyond the 'A' Level, which is the current 'front-loaded model' requirement for university entrance, to assess the potential of students later in life to benefit from the chance to study a particular vocational university degree. This already exists in part but needs to be substantially developed in order to create a genuinely flexible and open means of studying for a new career later in life.

   The key thing is to ensure that young people who have the capacity to complete the course are enrolled in university, without compromising the level of difficulty offered.

All of these ideas are intended to enable universities to respond better to the changing demands of the world of work. They would be more effective if the courses and qualifications could be developed in close collaboration with the relevant employment and professional bodies, most of whom have a fairly well-developed infrastructure that could easily facilitate more effective working together with universities.

In the UK, the Sector Skills Councils, of which there are now 21, were established from 2001 onwards. They are the employer-led skills organisations that cover approximately 90% of the UK workforce and work with over 550,000 employers to define skills needs and standards in their industry. And in many localities there are strong Local Enterprise Partnerships that bring together all those working for local economic development.

This network provides the sectoral reach that could help universities to work to address skills needs within and across sectors and to develop innovative skills solutions.

The challenge of constructive change in this area has also been a major focus for the Australian Government but, as in the UK, a great deal more needs to be done if universities are really to succeed in transforming their relationships with work.

Improving preparation for work among students

Over recent years, 'employability' has been given greater priority among universities in the US, UK and elsewhere. The Times Higher Education (THE) 2018 Global Employability Ranking[10] sets out a current world ranking of universities from the point of view of employability. The introduction to their 2016 edition stated, quite rightly, that:

> **The idea of employability is full of paradoxes. The most striking is that, while universities and employers agree that it's increasingly important for graduates, there's little agreement on what it means.**

But there is no doubt that it remains an important university ambition.

Despite this lack of clarity, the Higher Education Funding Council of England in the past encouraged universities to focus upon measures that make their students more employable. And its successor body, the Office for Students, is developing this approach even more vigorously.

The new Teaching Excellence and Student Outcomes Framework explicitly requires 'employability' to be demonstrated and gives significant weight to success in this field in the overall rating of the university.

In the UK, the success rate of individual universities varies from about 55% succeeding in getting work to about 90%, which is a pretty wide range.

The Higher Education Statistics Agency publishes regular data that reveals how well individual universities do and how likely particular courses of study are to achieve professional employment.

The THE Global Employability Ranking suggests that institutions at the top of the rankings, like the Massachusetts Institute of Technology, the California Institute of Technology, Stanford University and the Technical University of Munich (TUM), are well known for their industry connections and entrepreneurial environment. For example, TUM credits its success to the deep relationships between the university and industry in Bavaria where the university's academics also work for companies such as BMW, Siemens and Lindner, which gives students an immediate insight into the work environment.

The depth of this university–employer relationship is an important factor and some institutional structure can often improve these relationships, for example through the establishment, at the level of an academic school, of an advisory board of eminent external stakeholders who represent that school's disciplinary make-up.

Though most examples in this area relate to private sector employers, it is just as important for public sector employers such as schools, hospitals, police and so on to engage in such joint work with universities. A good example is the programmes to involve students in helping to teach maths or languages in local sixth forms.

There is a range of policies and approaches that operate in this field and that are used by different universities. These include:

1 *Embedding and integrating work experience through the undergraduate placement and pre-registration year*

This is a very effective method for students to acquire the knowledge, skills and attributes that are valued by employers. It is already being carried out by a number of universities.

For example, over 70% of Aston University students take a placement in the third year of their course, or engage in the equivalent through clinical practice and the University has the objective of reaching 100% by 2020.

An international example is the University of Waterloo, Canada's leading engineering university, where very many students have a one-year placement in an industrial environment. Waterloo University prizes this as its key distinguishing feature.

At Aston, every student on placement has a contract or learning agreement with their employer, and job descriptions are jointly agreed with the employer and the University. All students are required to keep a reflective workbook, as well as submitting an academic assignment based on their experiences. Placement tutors provide ongoing academic support throughout the placement year, coupled with regular contact with the university's careers service. Preparation and returner sessions are held to support the transitions from study to workplace and back again.

Such placements can include international opportunities, for example through Erasmus+ funding.

2 *Enhancing student employability through a one-to-one professional mentoring scheme beyond the placement year*

This matches business professionals with second- and final-year students. This can be supplemented by a peer mentoring programme, which enables current placement students to mentor second-year students on their upcoming placement journey.

3 *Developing work-related course modules*

Courses can include compulsory modules that provide insight into industrial sector trends and challenges as well as the nature of working life. For example, Aston University has a module called 'Introduction to Organisational Behaviour', which has been developed in conjunction with Unilever, a major recruiter of graduates.

Most universities have entrepreneurial support schemes to encourage and develop the enterprise skills of students and graduates, including programmes to take original academic work into practical business opportunities.

There are many other examples that can be developed.

4 *Offering a good range of master's and short-term postgraduate courses, mostly part-time and online*

Some master's and short-term postgraduate courses are available but universities could develop these far more widely. Access to student loans to finance these should be extended and broadened. These should also enable students to prepare better for an increasingly international labour market.

5 *High quality careers advice*

Most universities now offer a more comprehensive careers advice service than they traditionally did. They regularly seek and advertise graduate and placement opportunities and they increasingly offer personalised one-to-one support. In most institutions, the days of a university careers service being a portacabin with two to three staff are long gone. Some universities provide timetabled sessions for all second-year students, covering skills such as CV writing and mock interviews. They organise assessment centres, employer-led webinars and live chats.

University careers service professionals emphasise the need for personal reflection and self-development and think that students need time and space to review, analyse and learn from their experiences. This helps to provide clarity in decision-making, as well as enhancing skills in all areas, which is essential as students prepare for the world of work.

It is also important that students engage early with the career development process so that they can focus their professional development efforts on building connections, attending career-focused programmes and pursuing internships and other experiential learning opportunities.

Depending on the particular relationship with employers, the careers service can organise on-campus company presentations and job fairs, guest lectures and workshops and off-campus activity for students, perhaps including employment as appropriate.

The international nature of work and the market place

The final, enormous, change in the nature of work for which universities should be preparing their students is its acceleratingly fast international nature.

One illustration of this is that the just over 2 million internationally mobile students around the world in 2000 had increased to more than 5 million by 2014 and a more than doubling of this number is currently under way. As employers receive ever more international applications, it becomes yet more important for ambitious students to graduate from a university that has a 'global brand'.

The most successful universities are beginning to address these needs by a number of means:

1 *Language teaching and cultural awareness*

A precondition of successful working abroad is to understand the culture and customs, and ideally to speak the language. Even though English continues to strengthen its position as the world language, individuals will gain respect by speaking more languages. English speakers have been, and will continue to be, in a privileged position as English is by far the most common second language, though the inexorable rise of China means that fluency in Mandarin is likely to be an increasingly valuable commodity.

Provision of language courses, and encouragement to take them up through provision of course credits and other means, is an important aspect of a university education, and may be particularly useful in Year 1. Development of appropriate accreditation is also worthwhile.

2 *Course alignment, study abroad and student exchanges*

The European Union's Erasmus programme[11] is probably the most developed student exchange programme in the world and it has proved extremely successful for developing student experience within the Erasmus countries.[12]

Many Australian and UK universities have the ambition for as many students as possible to study abroad, even for a short summer placement. The Warwick–Monash relationship is an example. Most are a long way from achieving this for a majority of students and it is even less common for students to spend a significant time in another institution.

This failure is driven by lack of alignment of course content and of credit arrangements. One way of overcoming this is through special university partnerships. It is early days in the development of courses that are compatible and would permit and encourage students to spend terms, semesters or years studying abroad at partner universities.

This could be an important and valuable improvement in international education opportunities.

More generally, student exchanges are long-standing, remain extremely valuable and can be developed. Undergraduate exchanges are relatively uncommon for students from the UK and Australia while they are increasingly common for students from parts of Asia. UK and Australian students could be at a cultural disadvantage unless such approaches are strongly developed.

Australia's New Colombo Plan,[13] which is managed by the Department of Foreign Affairs and Trade and not the Department of Education, enables Australian students to go to countries in the arc Pakistan to Fiji (perhaps seen as Australia's sphere of foreign affairs influence) and, apart from its educational benefit, is an exercise in soft power and geo-politics.

3 *Work/Employability opportunities*

This is addressed above in a national context, but the international component adds to their educational value.

Little of this international awareness is intrinsically difficult to provide but it is dependent on having staff who can help mould an internationally-oriented curriculum and mindset in the classroom. It is not always easy for universities to attract and retain this skillset across all programme areas. But it will be easier if there are strong international university partner organisations that can facilitate these possibilities.

Conclusion

We suggested at the beginning of this book that universities have four major essential contributions to make in helping the world deal with the changes we are considering:

- *understanding and interpreting the process of change;*
- *offering approaches that would harness the process of change for general benefit;*
- *educating and training to high quality the specialist workers whose skills are necessary to address change properly;*
- *creating a general intellectually engaging climate and culture across societies that promotes the virtues of understanding and science.*

In this chapter we, have focused upon the third of these contributions, which is universities' fundamental role in educating and training the young people of the world. Of course, while preparedness for work is absolutely crucial, this is not the sole role of university education. The fundamental role of the university in preparing its students for the fullest possible intellectual life remains central. Success cannot simply be defined by a student's first job after university. But it is an important step to independence.

However, the other three contributions are also very important, and use universities' key research and thinking strength.

We need more research into, and understanding of, approaches that will ensure that these changes in the nature of work can take place in a way that is of general benefit. Hopes here have inspired utopians such as HG Wells[14] for over a century as they see a world in which machines do all the work while people enjoy the leisure with the opportunities it offers. More pessimistic visionaries like Kurt Vonnegut,[15] for example in *Player Piano* as early as 1952, illustrate how difficult it is for a society to adapt itself to the challenges of these changes. Again, universities have the important role of convening thinking and leading opinion in the hope of influencing the course of events in a constructive direction. This is particularly important as the fears of change among the population, justified or unjustified as they may be, are growing.

At the moment, the nature of work is changing with very little public understanding of how and why it is happening. The 'gig economy', 'globalisation' and 'artificial intelligence' are all enormous changes that are happening but are not understood, let alone properly prepared for at either an individual or a societal level. Universities need to do more to help people understand what is happening to the foundations of their world.

So, at this time, the fourth university responsibility that we identify, to create an intellectual climate that promotes understanding, faces particular challenges. When a senior government Minister in the UK can talk contemptuously about 'experts' and the President of the US is expressly contemptuous of scientific facts, universities are clearly facing an uphill struggle. Nowhere is this struggle more important than in relation to the world of work, which is why action is needed:

Governments should establish a proper comprehensive framework of post-school education and training which covers the vital 14–19 years and then promotes lifelong learning for all. This requires a buoyant funding basis.

And they should promote systematic and constructive dialogue between employers (private and public) and universities and the wider education system about the ways in which they can support each other and meet each other's needs.

Universities should form strong relationships with both local and national employers in their fields, for example in the way that medicine and related health fields have done for many years.

They should develop their courses with future employability and work in mind, including commitment to preparation for modern work and new modes of study, structure of courses and systems of delivering education throughout life with different entry points. They should systematically amend their course structures to improve students' preparation for work.

They should offer a range of courses for professional updating, with a variety of entry points and a wide range of postgraduate degree opportunities and continuous professional development. These will probably be mainly part-time and online and it should be possible to take them at all stages from immediately after graduation to much later in life. This would probably require a better and universal system of benchmark testing for admission to courses.

And universities should develop stronger international components of their courses and student lives, at both undergraduate and postgraduate levels, including education in languages and cultures.

Chapter 4

Research: understanding and transforming the world

Why research matters

Ed's academic career developed in a world where universities both teach and do research. That was the worldview, which he accepted. But as he moved on in his chosen profession, he realised that many people in most universities did not both teach and research at a very high level. Some were dedicated researchers, many were dedicated educators and some were really great at both, perhaps at different points of their working life. Yet this lack of comprehensive skills in everyone was not always reflected by clear differentiation of institutional mission. He came to consider that the view that all universities should both teach and research, and that the mission of almost any university should not differ significantly from that of Oxford or Cambridge, does not reflect reality.

Different universities need to meet social and community needs that vary enormously with the geography and history of institutions, ranging from the responsibilities of small regional universities that provide local needs and support local economies to the output of a massive research university that collectively powers much of the national and international economy.

Ed began to realise that clarity of purpose, so well recognised in the business world, was a bit patchy in his own. This realisation helped him work with like-minded colleagues to clarify the mission of both great universities he has led, Monash and King's.

In this chapter, we argue that we all need great research to flourish and that a clear-headed mission and focus is necessary to achieve that. That's what this chapter is about.

Introduction

At a time when Greta Thunberg and her colleagues in the school strike for climate movement are highlighting by their action the existential debate about the future of the planet, the President of the US and a British Cabinet member decry the value of science and knowledge in our public debate. On one side of the argument are those who fear the irretrievable exhaustion of the planet as a result of the environmental and resource problems associated with growing populations, which demand ever-higher standards of living. On the other is the more optimistic group that feels, on the basis of experience over the past 50 years, that the pace of human advancement in technology and science will continue and will be able to envision, develop and implement effective solutions to these challenges.

However, whichever view you take, the challenges ahead are immense and science and knowledge need to contribute to solving them.

It should be self-evident that we need a very high quality understanding of our world if we are to master the increasingly rapid process of change through which all dimensions of our lives are passing.

Not everyone appreciates that universities are the single greatest engines of research and so can and should play a vital role in addressing these grand societal and global challenges. It is crucial not only that they perform at the highest level in addressing these challenges but that they co-operate fully with government, industry and the rest of society to address and focus on the very specific challenges that our world faces.

This truth about the future of our planet applies with equal and compelling strength to a whole range of issues. It applies to the structure of the human being, our DNA and our cells, to the nature of our universe in all its unfolding complexity, to the human, artistic and cultural achievements of our civilisations over history, to the basic rules of mathematics and law and indeed to any of the enormously varied aspects of our society and civilisation, which determine how we have lived, live now and will live in the future.

The need for us to understand the world around us is the principle argument for the place and emphasis given to research in our universities, and for governments' support for that role. Not all research, and extension of our knowledge, stems from universities, of course, but high quality university learning is at the centre of our society's efforts to maximise our capacity to understand, interpret and then act upon the knowledge that we steadily acquire.

That is manifestly the case today and has also been the case throughout much of history. It is the reason why universities began to be formed in the first place and it is why the great historic universities have the very high reputation that they do. It is why the whole world gives such high respect to institutions that recognise these achievements, such as the Nobel prizes. The importance of this aspect of university work is very widely understood and supported across populations. It is significant that almost every Nobel prize in science has been awarded to a university researcher. The rare exceptions are occasional government-funded research centres and islands of industry focus such as Bell Laboratories in the US.

That said, however, the reason for the enormous growth in the numbers of both students and of universities across the world is not simply the need to maximise our ability to extend the knowledge of the world around us.

As we have argued earlier, it is also the need for far better educated and trained populations, and in particular workforces, as the complexity of our economies increases.

And it is also the need for our economies and societies to be stimulated and enhanced by the insight and experience that universities can bring to the society and economy around them.

These varied explanations for the increased importance of universities in our societies mean that it is necessary to think carefully about how best to maximise the capacity of our university system to expand the boundaries of our knowledge as quickly and systematically as we can, and to explore the parts of our civilisations and cultures that we most need to understand.

This is difficult in any case, and raises profound philosophical and organisational questions that are not easy to resolve in the best of circumstances.

But the process has been made more difficult because university research has not historically been aligned with national and international priorities but has been driven far more by individual curiosity. Such curiosity has, of course, been an immensely powerful and welcome force – essential for many vital areas of scientific advance – but, combined with the outdated ivory tower philosophy discussed in Chapter 2, has often served to inhibit effective collaboration between universities and other key entities such as government, industry and business. This has reduced the possibility of the types of game-changing research discoveries and applications that transform our society.

Individual nations, and the wider world, can no longer afford to predicate the funding of research in universities predominantly on a 'let a thousand flowers bloom' model. We need to align all efforts to maximise our capacity to understand how our world is developing and to drive social and economic success. Research in the humanities and social sciences is more integral than ever to this objective, largely because of the fundamental importance of human behaviour. These academic disciplines should never become the poor cousin of the global research endeavour, which some fear it is becoming.

In the UK, this ambition is being promoted by the establishment of the new UK Research and Innovation (UKRI),[1] which was established in 2018. It is a new body that works in partnership to try to create the best possible environment for research and innovation to flourish. It operates across the whole of the UK and brings together the seven Research Councils, Innovate UK and Research England. It states:

> We will be measured by the impact we deliver, and this will have three elements:
>
> - We will push the frontiers of **human knowledge** and understanding
> - We will deliver **economic impact** and social prosperity
> - We will create **social and cultural impact** by supporting our society and others to become enriched, healthier, more resilient and sustainable.

UKRI's funding is substantial: £7 billion in 2019. This is principally attached to the REF process, which reinforces the research predominance of a small number of institutions to which we refer elsewhere in this chapter.

Confusion about the roles of universities as research engines has made it more difficult to achieve the alignment that is necessary. The widespread insistence on the crucial importance of the research-teaching nexus for students to thrive has contributed to this confusion and inadvertently diminishes the importance of the research engine.

It is not straightforward to achieve the alignment and focus upon research success that we urge. The acquisition of understanding is a very complicated process that is not at all linear in nature. It is usually necessary to explore a wide range of blind alleys and theories before reaching a reasonably accurate and truthful account of what we know. Great breakthroughs can occur from unexpected directions. Therefore, a simple value-for-money metric is certainly difficult and probably impossible to establish.

This chapter addresses four main issues:

- Where research is done: its concentration.
- The relationship between research and teaching.
- The global higher education system and international university networks.
- How useful is the research that is done?

A note on league tables

We make some reference to the national and international university 'league tables' and ratings against which universities often measure themselves. Their impact on the dynamics of global higher education has been well analysed by Hans Peter Hertig,[2] and we comment later in this chapter on some of his points.

At the global level, the three longest established, and undoubtedly most influential, are those produced by Shanghai Ranking Consultancy (the Academic Ranking of World Universities, ARWU), Times Higher Education (THE) and Quacquarelli Symonds (QS). All of these, along with other global rankings, primarily measure the research performance of universities rather than their teaching or other attributes. The ARWU is based solely on research-related criteria and was devised because of China's desire to match and replicate the successes of the West, as the Chinese Government understands their importance in nation-building.

All of these look at a subset of the world's universities, in fact the most research-intensive ones, and then use varying combinations of metrics to create a ranking. Rankings are created on a continental or geographical basis, and in particular academic or professional disciplines. These all stimulate interest and comment and sometimes offer insight.

In the UK, three ranking systems tend to predominate: The Times and Sunday Times Good University Guide, The Complete University Guide and the Guardian University Guide. However, for UK universities themselves, the REF is the most important research ranking.

These are marketed to help students choose which universities they will apply for, and they measure a wide variety of aspects of university life. In particular, they do not measure only research. They include efforts to measure teaching quality, student satisfaction and other indices. They also try to include data from all universities in the UK.

All of these ranking systems are rightly subject to controversy as all efforts to measure hard-to-evaluate characteristics are bound to be. And, in addition to the problems of actual measurement of some university qualities, each ranking system has made its own choice of the weightings to give each index in achieving an overall ranking, and so those weightings are obviously subjective in nature.

Nevertheless, we consider that there is some value in these rankings, and they certainly play a significant role in driving university behaviour. It's also important to acknowledge that the international league tables, though they are based on research, are significant factors in influencing student choice as to where they study for undergraduate degrees. By that process of choice, research excellence therefore itself becomes part of a virtuous economic cycle which draws significant wealth into a country through sustaining the international student market

This current reality may change as better measures of teaching capacity and quality are developed.

A valuable recent development of the rankings is the THE[3] University Impact Rankings, which assess universities against the United Nations' Sustainable Development Goals and generate an interesting group of universities leading in this field.

In this chapter, we have mainly used the Times and Sunday Times Good University Guide rankings to inform some of our discussion.[4] The other rankings could equally have been used and would produce similar results.

Where research is done: its concentration

Across the world, research excellence is, in general, highly concentrated upon a subset of universities, relatively small in number.

The reasons for this concentration of research lie in the widely accepted explanations of what makes successful world-class research, which really does extend the boundaries of our knowledge. Two main requirements are generally thought most likely to lead to research success.

The first is the bringing together in one place of the most successful researchers and the focusing of resources upon them. The development of the internet, the enormous network of e-communication around the world between top-class research and the vast range of international conferences around particular research themes has hardly weakened at all the view that it is important for top researchers to be physically located near each other. Proximity engenders serendipity and synergy.

The second requirement is the need to co-associate researchers in different academic disciplines, particularly those in neighbouring fields of study, which can stimulate original thinking and experimentation, building on the experience of others.

These two requirements help explain why so many research achievements in a wide range of disciplines, and therefore so many resources, are focused at a very small number of universities across the world.

Almost all of the world's great research universities are multidisciplinary, bringing together great research strength in humanities and social sciences in close proximity to strength in the natural and biological sciences. Paul Wellings[5] has analysed the THE academic disciplinary rankings[6] and concludes that most of the top 50 universities do very well across the board. The only ones with strengths in only a limited range of disciplines are those that could be defined as 'monotechnic', such as Imperial College London and LSE. The leading UK universities founded in the 1960s all have similar top 100 strengths in humanities and social sciences except for Warwick which has 'broken the mould' by exhibiting wider strength. In sharp contrast, universities of similar ages in the Eastern hemisphere have top 100 strengths in computing, engineering and other sciences. Paul suspects that this has been driven by policy intervention and investment in the Eastern hemisphere, in contrast to institutional autonomy in the UK.

Research strength in humanities and social sciences should not be equated to relative research income (not least because this research is significantly cheaper than in the hard sciences!) but the contribution of both humanities and social sciences is central to addressing the world's current challenges.

In this section, we illustrate this concentration by focusing on the UK.

However, as we discuss below, similar foci of research excellence undoubtedly also exist in other countries. For example, the US's Carnegie Classification[7] in 2018 designated 131 universities (out of about 5,000) as 'R1: Doctoral Universities – Very high research activity'. Australia's focus is around the 'Group of 8' (out of about 40) and in China the 'C9' (out of around 3,000).

We present the UK as a detailed case study that illustrates the point that even a wealthy Western country can support only a limited number of absolutely world-class comprehensive research universities.

The danger for countries is that human capacity and available resources will be spread too thinly if they follow too much of a 'level playing field' approach to university research. There is evidence[8] that, in modern times, some concentration of research capacity and expertise is needed, at least in most disciplines.

This may be one reason why the great continental European universities don't shine in the league tables. Consequently, the governments of France, Russia and Germany are all considering carefully how to create national centres of research excellence and a small number of great research universities.

The German government is completing a second round of anointing a small number of super-universities such as Gottingen and Heidelberg that will attract federal funding.

It is instructive to consider where, in the UK, good quality research is mainly done.

The Times and Sunday Times Good University Guide measures the overall quality of research based on the most recent Research Excellence Framework (2014), based upon data from the Higher Education Statistics Agency (HESA) and the Higher Education Funding Councils. These rankings offer a percentage rating of research quality.[9] Their ranking of UK universities[10] is as follows:

Rating over 50% (5 universities)	
*Cambridge	57.3
*Imperial College, London	56.2
*Oxford	53.1
*London School of Economics	52.8
*University College, London	51.0

Rating 45–50% (1 university)	
*Bristol	47.3

Rating 40–45% (5 universities)	
*Southampton	44.9
*King's College London	44.0
*Edinburgh	43.8
*Warwick	44.6
St Andrews	40.4

Rating 35–40% (23 universities)	
*Glasgow	39.9
*Manchester	39.8
*Queen's, Belfast	39.7
Lancaster	39.1
*Durham	39.0
*York	38.3
*Exeter	38.0
*Queen Mary, London	37.9
*Nottingham	37.8
*Newcastle	37.7
Strathclyde	37.7
*Sheffield	37.6
Bath	37.3
Essex	37.2
*Birmingham	37.1
*Leeds	36.8
Heriot Watt	36.7
Reading	36.5
Loughborough	36.3
Royal Holloway	36.3
East Anglia	35.8
Kent	35.2
*Cardiff	35.0

Rating 30–35% (8 universities)	
Swansea	33.7
Goldsmiths, London	33.4

▶

Rating 30–35% (8 universities)	
Leicester	31.8
Sussex	31.8
Ulster	31.8
*Liverpool	31.5
Dundee	31.2
Stirling	30.5

Rating 25–30% (7 universities)	
Aberdeen	29.9
Surrey	29.7
Aberystwyth	28.1
SOAS, London	27.9
Bangor	27.2
Aston	25.8
Brunel	25.4

Rating 20–25% (4 universities)	
Roehampton	24.5
St George's, London	22.2
Keele	22.1
City	21.4

Rating 15–20% (3 universities)	
Hull	16.7
Staffordshire	16.5
Plymouth	15.9

Rating 10–15% (2 universities)	
Oxford Brookes	11.4
Lincoln	10.3

Rating 5–10% (33 universities)	
Westminster	9.8
Middlesex	9.7
Huddersfield	9.4
Bradford	9.2
Liverpool Hope	9.2
Bournemouth	9.0
London South Bank	9.0
Northumbria	9.0
De Montfort	8.9
Liverpool John Moores	8.9
West of England	8.8
Portsmouth	8.6
Salford	8.3
University of the Arts, London	8.0
Bath Spa	7.9
Brighton	7.9
Manchester Metropolitan	7.5
East London	7.2
Bedfordshire	7.0
Glasgow Caledonian	7.0
Queen Margaret, Edinburgh	6.6
Nottingham Trent	6.5
Chichester	6.4

▶

Rating 5–10% (33 universities)	
Sunderland	5.8
Winchester	5.8
Harper Adams	5.7
Central Lancashire	5.6
Hertfordshire	5.6
Norwich University of the Arts	5.6
Anglia Ruskin	5.4
Sheffield Hallam	5.4
Abertay	5.1
Kingston	5.1

Rating <5% (37 universities)	
Edge Hill	4.9
Greenwich	4.9
Edinburgh Napier	4.6
Falmouth	4.6
Canterbury Christchurch	4.5
Birmingham City	4.3
West of Scotland	4.3
Worcester	4.3
Chester	4.1
Leeds Beckett	4.1
York St John	4.1
Robert Gordon	4.0
St Mary's Twickenham	4.0
South Wales	4.0
Cardiff Metropolitan	3.9
Teeside	3.6

Rating <5% (37 universities)	
University for the Creative Arts	3.4
Coventry	3.8
Gloucestershire	3.8
London Metropolitan	3.5
Northampton	3.2
Bolton	2.9
Newman	2.8
Derby	2.5
Arts University, Bournemouth	2.4
Glyndwr	2.3
Bishop Grosseteste	2.1
Leeds Trinity	2.0
West London	1.6
Buckinghamshire New	1.5
Cumbria	1.2
Royal Agricultural University	1.1
Southampton Solent	0.5
Buckingham[11]	–
Highlands and Islands	–
St Mark and St John	–
Suffolk	–

Or in summary:

	>50%	40–50%	30–40%	20–30%	10–20%	<10%
Number of universities	5	6	31	11	5	70
Proportion of universities	4%	5%	24%	9%	4%	55%

58 out of 128 universities (45%) have ratings greater than 10% for research quality; 70 (55%) have ratings of less than 10%.

This is a highly skewed distribution of university research quality and contribution which immediately makes it crystal clear that, as most people understand very well, internationally leading and world-class research in the UK is concentrated in a relatively small number of universities.

This assessment is complicated a little by the rankings of some less research-intensive UK universities in other international research-based rankings. For example, 78 UK universities feature in the QS top 1,000 world university rankings and 93 are in the top 1,000 of the Times Higher Education 2018 rankings.

However, the same concentration of research is demonstrated by all these analyses of the distribution of research, classified, for example, by research spending, number of research-active staff, value of research projects, amount of external research, and so on.

The overall picture is that, in the UK, this world-class research is concentrated in about 40–60 universities, out of 167.[12] Similar analyses of the structure of research funding, and its location, can be made in countries across the world.

It is important to emphasise that there is also value in the 2* (internationally recognised) and 1* (nationally recognised) research, which is done throughout the university system, though it does not receive significant resources from the funding councils. It does contribute to local economic and social strength and enables those universities to play a highly significant role, which we address in Chapter 5.

We can draw the following lessons from this:

- Firstly, in the UK (as in Australia and the US), there are a relatively small number of universities that shine across many research fields. These carry out research for the nation. Other countries are urgently seeking to replicate that model.
- Secondly, well over half of the universities themselves do little internationally excellent and world-class research. They struggle if they ever seek to present themselves as research-intensive institutions. In most cases, the quality of their university teaching is good or excellent and several get gold status in the Teaching Excellence Framework ratings. Clear national recognition of the prestige and importance of high quality university teaching might well make the life of such institutions a great deal easier. They should not be forced to compete in league tables on a terrain that is loaded against them.

- Thirdly, it is difficult to draw the line when considering the intensiveness of research. There are a lot of institutions where some good research is done but it is not excellent across the board. The key is for those institutions to recognise that they are hybrids, often with widespread teaching excellence and islands of research excellence on which they should concentrate in the knowledge that their standards of excellence in these areas may well be every bit as good as those in broader research universities. It may well be worth those islands of research strength joining stronger research-intensive universities.
- Fourthly, we fully acknowledge that the distribution of world-class research funding, and universities, doesn't allow for regional needs as it should and we discuss this in Chapter 5.

As we have stated at length in this book, we firmly believe that the destiny of universities should be in the hands of universities themselves. It is therefore crucial that each university defines for itself what it wants to be, taking full account of its actual and potential research and teaching capacities.

Academic staff will be appointed in such universities who are committed to a research career. We believe that effective academic, professional and industrial networking, particularly around the large cities in which the overwhelming majority of universities are currently located, can be established. This is actually not so dissimilar to the University of California system designed by Clark Kerr half a century ago.

Greater university differentiation almost inevitably means a greater degree of regional university planning. In the UK, such a better joined-up regional strategy could and should be shaped by universities themselves, perhaps encouraged and incentivised by the government in terms of certain funding incentives or signals.

One example is the government support in 2004 for the merger of the then Victoria University of Manchester and the University of Manchester Institute of Science and Technology to create a new University of Manchester with much greater research weight. Another is the N8 Group[13] initiative for regional research collaboration.

Though of course it is for universities themselves to define their own clarity of mission, there might be a case for designating between 40 and 60 universities in the UK as 'research universities' (a terminology already used in some countries). This might be done by government and its agencies allocating resources, or it could be done more informally by a process such as the independent Carnegie Classification in the US.

The reason for doing this is to bring much greater clarity, transparency and understanding into public debate about the roles and strengths of universities. As we discuss below, the research/teaching confusion leads to many dishonesties which both mislead potential students and harm universities. We can understand the fear of creating a new binary line division of 'research universities' and 'universities' which might be damaging. But, in our view, it is more destructive for two thirds of British universities to claim that research is a central part of their mission when that is not, in fact, the case.

Charles floated this idea when he was Secretary of State but dropped it as a proposal when it was met with almost universal opposition by academics worried about letting light into the mystery of the research–teaching relationship. And it is to this that we now turn.

The relationship between research and teaching

The Humboldtian form of organisation of research, which has evolved and, over time, has proved very resilient, does, however, raise significant questions about the relationships between research and the other functions of universities, notably teaching. The overwhelming majority[14] of undergraduate university students are, in fact, not being taught in universities that are carrying out high quality research.

The fundamental reason for the very large numbers of universities in the UK that have relatively low research ratings lies in their history, as discussed in Chapters 2 and 3. They were intended to recognise the importance of high standard undergraduate degree education and they reflected a wide range of teaching disciplines. They drove the expansion of undergraduate student numbers in the UK, which has been common across the developed world.

But, crucially, none of these changes in the number and nature of universities was principally driven by the ambition of raising standards of research in this country.

So, as these new universities expanded in number, research was not the main driver of their missions. In some cases, what was conventionally called 'academic drift' set in as new universities began to develop a research capacity and to move away from the technological and industry-based roots to look more like their predecessor conventional universities. This 'academic drift' was criticised by many as weakening the important original mission of the new universities, notably in relation to technical and vocational education and the relationship with work.

In other cases, institutions desirous of gaining university status, for the purpose of attracting undergraduates, developed a small research capacity purely to enable them to gain the right to award research degrees and then to call themselves universities – all in order to help recruit undergraduates.

This unsavoury process was entirely understandable but did nothing whatsoever to improve levels of research quality overall. It has caused a great deal of confusion about the role of universities which infects a good deal of public debate on the matter.

'Apprenticeships' and 'vocational education' have been thrown into the mix as some call for the changes in university status of 1992, 2004 and later to be reversed.

The best way to clarify this situation is to acknowledge the reality, which is unlikely to change, that high quality research is concentrated in a minority (say 35–40%, as above) of UK universities and that is why we make the proposal that university naming should reflect the reality of research practice and resources.

But this approach comes up against one important quasi-ideological perception: the proposition that research and teaching are intrinsically interdependent in the spirit of a classic Humboldtian university. It is argued that the presence of high quality research is a necessary, though not sufficient, condition for the existence of high quality teaching.

This view is very deeply held in the university world but it needs to be challenged. In many principally teaching universities, a key driver for the development of research was regulatory rather than philosophical. Another key driver for co-location of research and teaching has also been pragmatic since many academics are attracted to academic life by research more than by teaching. And the current ethic means that, in general, teaching only happens if the job includes a significant research component. It fails to acknowledge that many of the most outstanding teachers never were research-active but they are well able to understand and engage with intellectual development in a way that enables them to impart new knowledge to students.

The greatest research universities are already recognising this by the development of staff whose roles focus on teaching. There is no reason why this cannot also apply to whole institutions. It is interesting to note that Universities UK, the umbrella group for UK universities, estimates that of the 212,000 academic staff in the UK, 29% are working purely in teaching, 23% purely in research and 47% in both teaching and research.[15]

The skills and mindset needed to be a great researcher and great educator often overlap (and many people do both) and are not always the same. But the great researcher may not shine in the lecture theatre while a great teacher may not shine in the laboratory.

Anecdotal evidence of the inability of many brilliant researchers to teach well is legion. For example, the different phases of the lives of Crick and Watson illustrate how the balance can change over time.

However, the conservatives are often vehement in stating that there is only one really effective model, which is that teaching and research co-exist and reinforce each other.

This model has now, undoubtedly, become dominant in the Western university. But there are exceptions, such as very successful alternatives like the Scripps and Salk Research Institutes where research is world-class but with little or no undergraduate teaching, but also Notre Dame and many others which are highly successful teaching universities and are often better known for their education than their research.

A distinguishing characteristic of the Open University (OU), from its foundation, was its focus upon the quality of its teaching materials, on- or offline, which addressed the varying academic backgrounds of their students. This meant that the OU was the most successful innovator of its time, bringing the university experience to the nation in previously unforeseen ways. And, of course, it has been copied in many countries, even though it is now under pressure.

The development of the private university sector has been strong, notably in the US but also now a little in the UK. The largest private group, Laureate, runs universities around the world. New university providers, such as the BPP University and the University of Law, mainly targeting the classic professions, have focused their offer, and successfully, entirely on the quality of their teaching for undergraduate degrees and not at all upon their research contribution, if any. For these universities, the model is centred around teaching and education. Research is offered where it is a prerequisite of course recognition but is regarded as an expense on the bottom line to be minimised in accordance with regulatory requirements concerned with awarding degrees.

The fact is that excellence in research and teaching can be achieved through a variety of models and the subject should be considered from that point of view.

A university needs to select its own mission carefully in a way that is fully appropriate to its own stakeholders and recognises its own existing and potential strengths and weaknesses. It should eschew ambitions that are very difficult, possibly impossible, to achieve. Universities should do really well by leading in the areas where they have strength rather than lagging behind in fields where they can't achieve at the highest level.

This necessitates reaching the recognition, and getting it accepted far more widely than it actually is, that there is not a national or international hierarchy of universities, of the type implied by the various league tables with their focus on research. Research should not be seen as the top of the tree. Each university is valuable through its own, differentiated, mission including in research and teaching, independently.

And for those who argue that the relationship between research and teaching is fundamental, it is instructive to compare the university rankings[16] for Research Quality[17] with those for Course Completion,[18] Graduate Prospects[19] and for Teaching Quality.[20] The correlations are revealing.

The correlation between Research Quality and Course Completion is high: 0.73. As it is between Research Quality and Graduate Prospects: 0.69.

These high correlations simply confirm the commonly held views that universities with high quality research ratings succeed in keeping their students, so that they complete their courses, and are then relatively successful in securing good employment prospects for their graduates. These are good achievements, a tribute to these universities, though of course they open the door to an interesting discussion, which we do not pursue in detail here, about what it is that makes them successful in these regards. The next correlation shows that it may not be the quality of their teaching.

This is because, significantly, the correlation between Research Quality and Teaching Quality shows no such success. Indeed, the correlation is even very slightly negative: –0.15.

This inverse correlation is very striking, particularly given the fact that the research-intensive universities are significantly wealthier and better resourced. In addition, the students at these universities generally have higher university entry exam grades and should therefore be better able to benefit from good teaching quality, while the students from the less research-intensive universities include many who need far stronger teaching support to enable them to do well and possibly to overcome relatively disadvantaged educational backgrounds.

On the basis of this negative correlation, it should not therefore be surprising that the rankings based purely on teaching quality suggest that non-research-intensive universities do pretty well and some of the research-intensives not that well. An extreme example is that Cambridge and Oxford, 1st and 2nd (by a long way) in both the overall and the research quality rankings, are 26th= and 41st in the rankings of teaching quality.

Such results naturally lead some to challenge the ranking methodology for teaching quality, as we discuss later in this book. But whatever the explanation, and education research doesn't give many useful answers about the ways in which teaching quality can be increased, these results should both stimulate serious debate about and challenge the conventional wisdom about the interdependence of teaching quality and research quality.

But a corollary of these findings may be that the success of the research-intensive universities in keeping the students they admit, and helping them to gain good employment later, may well be down to their status (deriving from research quality) and the quality of the students they admit (based on school exam performance), rather than on any achievement of high quality teaching at the university itself.

All that said, an important attribute of any university, research-intensive or not, in its approach to creating high quality teaching is the promotion of an atmosphere of scholarly interest and endeavour. That has to include ensuring that university teachers are themselves at least familiar with developments of research and knowledge in their particular academic field.

There is a range of ways to achieve such a positive teaching environment, but the most important is establishing networks that bring top-class researchers into regular and productive engagement with university teachers more widely, and also with schools. Such approaches should be promoted (which would be a change in practice for many top academic researchers) but it is not the case that high quality teachers need at the same time to be high quality researchers.

There is one further important suspicion felt by many. It is that, in the research-intensive universities, and also others, a proportion of the money that is received by universities for the purposes of teaching (ie the student fees of around £9,000 per year in the UK) is, in fact, being diverted to support research independent of teaching. Measurement is difficult here as the kind of atmosphere of scholarly engagement mentioned above does promote teaching quality and has to be paid for.

A HEPI report[21] in November 2018 suggested that most universities spend somewhere between 40% and 45% of their income on the direct costs of teaching. Despite the heterogeneity of the higher education sector, this appears to be a fairly stable figure across a range of institutions. Much of the rest is also spent on student-facing priorities, so the inclusion of teaching buildings, IT and library facilities can take the total closer to two-thirds of fee income. Including all student-facing expenditure (such as welfare services and the students' union) can increase it further to around three-quarters of fee income.

In almost all countries, research infrastructure costs are not fully recovered from research funding sources and so finance has to be found elsewhere. In the ancient universities, such as the Ivy League and Oxbridge, this comes from their considerable foundations. Some universities achieve substantial support from benefactions and endowment. In others, notably in Australia and the UK, the resources come from the margins developed from the international student market. Often, domestic fees cover the costs of teaching but international income subsidises research.

We consider that there is a strong case for clearly separating universities' research and teaching budgets in order to provide the kind of transparency that would enable students to know where their money is going, eliminate unwarranted suspicions and promote good decision-taking. We also agree with the recommendation of the Education Select Committee report in November 2018 that: 'Every higher education institution should publish a breakdown of how tuition fees are spent on their websites.'

The global higher education system and international university networks

The global higher education system

Of course, the exact structure of research, and its exact relationship with universities, varies across the world. It reflects the varied and different histories of each national research and university system.

Research spending is concentrated upon a number of world-class specialist research institutions, as well as the universities at the top of the world research rankings.

Nevertheless, international relationships are an essential dimension of the quality of world research and, in recent decades, a system of global higher education has developed.

This[22] has opened tertiary education up for parts of the world that had only very limited access in the past. It is increasingly networked and cross-linked using the power of the internet very creatively. It is highly competitive for students, researchers and research funding. It is seeking to deal with strongly interconnected world research challenges, precisely those that this book has identified from the outset. It is seeing a slightly weakening hegemony of the US and Western Europe as new key players are arriving onto the scene at the top level, notably from China and East Asia. This university system has a lingua franca, which is English, is developing new forms of global and online teaching models such as MOOCs, and it champions globally active research universities.

There is, thus, an international elite of high quality research universities, which compete among themselves for research funding, talent and prestige. Universities from a particular country are helped if their own country's government gives priority to research spending, and in the European Union there is substantial competition for EU research resources, which are increasing and where the UK does particularly well.

The 31 UK universities that are in the top 200 of Times Higher Education 2018 global rankings compare and compete with 62 in the US, 20 in Germany, 13 in the Netherlands, 8 in Australia, 7 in China and Switzerland and 6 in France.

China is an interesting case as its universities continue to rise up the research rankings following a commitment in 1995 from its central government to invest billions of dollars to raise its top universities to world standards. For example, in 2013–16 Tsinghua University (the alma mater of many of the country's leaders, including Xi Jinping and Hu Jintao) produced more of the top 1% most highly cited papers in maths and computing, and more of the 10% most highly cited papers in the STEM subjects, than any other university in the world, according to Simon Marginson of Oxford, who says Tsinghua is on track to be 'number one in five years or less'.[23]

The truth is that, in the major research countries, the world-class research universities in this elite group have more in common with each other than they do with the other universities in their countries which are far less research-active.

It is probably for that reason that a number of countries use the terminology 'research university' to describe those universities that are most research-intensive. Hans Peter Hertig calls these 'World Class Research Universities'. He suggests the following 10 criteria that a university needs to obtain or defend to be able to compete among the best in the world, of which he thinks the first 3 are the most important:

- A politically, economically and culturally favourable local context
- Abundant funding
- Excellent leadership
- World class faculty
- High quality students
- A research portfolio adapted to the major global challenges of the 21st century
- Adequate structure and governance
- 'Global spirit'
- Excellent links to off-campus stakeholders
- Efficient and successful reputation management

A detailed analysis of these 'success criteria', which we generally accept, is beyond the scope of our book, though we address a number of them. However, for the purposes of this book, the central point that we wish to emphasise is that there is, in practice, a profound institutional distinction between the universities in any country that are part of this system of global higher education, and those that are not. This distinction needs to be taken fully into account when considering the future of universities, and the various policy issues that flow from that.

How useful is the research that is done?

Evaluation of the products of research

The hypothesis that encourages governments, corporations and charities/non-governmental organisations to fund and otherwise support research is that the research bears economic or social fruit. That is to say that human knowledge is extended, and then applied, in a way that will enhance the human condition.

If research is only funded 'for its own sake', as some maintain should be the case, then society as a whole is entitled to ask itself what value the research is bringing to society. Indeed, the overall effect of such an approach would only be to reduce the amount that societies spend upon research.

The fruit of some research can easily be seen, for example in dramatic increases in the understanding of conditions of ill-health, and what can be done to address them. In other areas it is less clear. The case of education is discussed below.

It is certainly true that any benefit to society will come only after chasing down a whole range of unproductive cul-de-sacs, or may offer real fruit only after a very long period of time, in ways that could not have been predicted at the outset. Blue sky research certainly has value.

But, nevertheless, society is entitled to look for the fruit, in terms of the knowledge extended and benefits gleaned.

That is why the Research Assessment Exercise (RAE) was established in the UK in 1986. It was followed by similar exercises in 1989, 1992, 1996, 2001 and 2008. The RAE evolved rapidly after the unification of the university sector in 1992 and this morphed into the current Research Excellence Framework, which was first published in 2014. The next REF exercise will be in 2021.

The actual assessments are conducted by the academic world itself and they do have an impact on the direction of research funding, the overall amounts and the overall research impact of the resources that are spent within the framework of guidelines set out by UKRI.

This process has been controversial throughout, partly because the statistical processes and judgments were bound to have some subjective elements, and partly because some researchers were concerned about the increased scrutiny of their work (a concern that has been shared in all other professions as public accountability has increased). As a result, the system has evolved over the 30 years of its existence and continues to do so as changes have been made to try to address at least some of the concerns.

The REF process has been carried out by the UK's four HE funding bodies,[24] and describes itself[25] as having the key three purposes of providing accountability for public investment in research, and producing evidence of the benefits of this investment; of providing benchmarking information and establishing reputational yardsticks for use within the HE sector and for public information; and informing the selective allocation of funding for research.

The REF assesses the quality and impact of research outputs and the environment that supports them.

The major change in this process, which took place in the 2014 REF, was the specific inclusion, for the first time, of a measure of research impact, which had been prepared over some years.

'Impact' is defined by the REF as follows:

> **For the purposes of the REF, impact is defined as an effect on, change or benefit to the economy, society, culture, public policy or services, health, the environment or quality of life, beyond academia.**

It emphasises the importance of impact being 'beyond academia'.

It is fair to say that the publication of the results of the 2014 REF was met with shock in some academic quarters as it became clear that, even in some very distinguished corners of the research world, 'impact' was not sufficiently understood and applied, and so the consequent rankings reflected that. Maximising 'impact' is now taking on more importance as the 2021 REF proceeds.

A detailed analysis[26] of the 'impacts' of the research in the 2014 REF was commissioned by the four UK funding councils and its results are very much worth considering in detail, though such detail is beyond the scope of this book. HEFCE[27] also describes the associated Impact Study Database[28] which permits more detailed consideration of the impact element of the REF.

The analysis considered the 6,679 impact case studies submitted to the 2014 REF by Higher Education Institutions in the UK. The report provides an initial assessment of the nature, scale and beneficiaries of the impact of UK universities' research and highlights four high-level observations:

- **The societal impact of research from UK Higher Education Institutions (HEIs) is considerable, diverse and fascinating. Over 60 unique 'impact topics' were identified.**
- **The research underpinning societal impacts is multidisciplinary, and the social benefits arising from research are multi-impactful. Over 80% of the case studies included underpinning research that was multidisciplinary.**
- **Different types of Higher Education Institution specialise in different types of impact. Over 3,700 unique pathways from research to impact were identified.**
- **UK Higher Education Institutions have a global impact. Research undertaken in the UK has made a contribution to every country in the world.**

This type of analysis strengthens the case for the funding of research and so the extension of our knowledge and society. It is necessary to develop and expand this work and to analyse more deeply the level of impact that research in different academic disciplines can achieve.

An important positive approach to strengthening impact is the What Works Network,[29] which encourages structured dialogue between researchers and practitioners. This should be developed further.

For example, while there is a clear acceptance of the potential positive contribution of research in the field of health, the potential contribution of research in other fields is far less clear-cut and it is necessary to appreciate why that is the case and to understand what needs to be done.

So, for example, it is fairly well accepted that research in fields like information and communications technology, and engineering are similarly strong across the range and there are others.

But an interesting contrast is the field of the environment and climate change where university research has successfully identified the reality of climate change and its challenges, and has influenced most (though not all) leaders of government and public opinion of the need to address the threats. However, a clear path to changing our behaviour so that these threats are effectively mitigated remains to be clearly identified.

Different considerations obviously apply in each field of research, and clearly not all fields of research have pathways to 'ready-made' end users in industry or policy customers in government in the way that health does.

Nevertheless, the growing emphasis on impact is a welcome feature of the UK research environment, and is an example of where the UK has been a trendsetter that other research systems are increasingly looking to follow.

The example of education research

In contrast with the highly visible impact of research in medicine and health we have selected the field of educational improvement.

The subject itself is complicated. Some argue that all you need to improve educational outcomes is money. But the truth is that more resources are, at best, a necessary and not a sufficient condition for improving educational outcomes. Indeed, extra resources may not even be necessary to improve outcomes.

At the same time, some adopt the pessimistic, deterministic and self-defeating view that educational outcomes are predetermined by economic, national and class origins.

But whatever the background and environment of the children and whatever resources are available, decisions have to be taken as to the best use of those resources: which levels of education to focus upon, whether to spend on more teachers, better-trained teachers, better equipment and facilities or other approaches.

Educational decision-takers at all levels and in all countries are wrestling with these issues every day. Research in education should be an important part of providing answers to such questions. There is enormous potential for properly focused educational research and many organisations are ready to commission it, including governments, global charities and non-governmental organisations, professional associations and employers. But, to do so, they need to feel that the research will be worthwhile, of high quality and provide useful pointers as to what policies are likely to be successful.

There are many questions that still need answering. These include straightforward pedagogy: Does class size make any difference at all? To what extent, if at all, does individual tutoring improve results, inside or outside school? Do innovations like a focus at primary level upon literacy and numeracy improve outcomes? What is the best way to teach English and reading, maths and science? What are the roles of parents, teachers and pupils working together to help children's educational performance?

And how can different technologies, for example PCs, laptops, electronic interactive whiteboards and mobile phones, be used to improve educational results? Do they make any difference at all and how should they best be used?

The same is true for the curriculum and the nature of assessment.

And, in most countries in the world, the burning question is how to improve the quality of teaching. There is little consensus about the best methods of initial training nor the best form of continuous professional development. How can leadership be improved on a systematic basis and head teachers be more consistently effective?

And what is the best way to drive improvements in performance? What is the best form of accountability? What is the place of inspection regimes, of reporting through 'league tables' or similar methods?

And how should schools be organised? Does selection at 11, 14 or 16 have a role to play? Do different types of schools, like 'academies', specialist schools', 'free schools', have a purpose? What, if any, is the role of the local education authority? Should classes be streamed by ability? Should the school day be longer – or shorter? Should the school year be differently organised – for example should terms last for more weeks of the year?

There is plenty of room for 'gut feeling' on questions such as these, but what is really needed is judgments based on real research and understanding. This is the challenge for educational researchers. There's no doubt that, across the world, policy-makers are actively looking for answers to questions like these, but not finding them in university departments of educational research.

The answers will vary, of course, from country to country, region to region, society to society. But there ought to be reasonable objective answers to at least some of these questions, based on high quality research analysis.

It sometimes seems that educational research is addressing minor or introverted research interests, rather than offering answers to the questions that preoccupy policy-makers.

Of course, the often rapid timescale of political decision-taking does, in practice, significantly limit the extent to which research can inform policy and practical decision-taking. This is a persistent tension, particularly in a political climate where governments are under great pressure to raise educational standards for the whole population.

These subjects are also controversial and it is necessary for researchers to be ready to engage in the types of controversy and polemic that characterise a field of policy in which public interest is so strong and opinions so forthright. Every parent, teacher and pupil has a point of view, based on personal experience.

Educational researchers should seize the initiative by conducting research that addresses the kinds of questions that are of concern to policy-makers around the world. The overall approach of educational research needs to be driven by a desire to understand the best ways to improve educational outcomes for people throughout the world who are seeking to improve the quality of education.

The best way to do this is to enhance the quality, as well as regularity, of dialogue between the educational research and policy-making communities. The research community should initiate discussion with practitioners around the 'future of education' and 'educational improvement' agenda, accepting that things can be changed and improved.

Education researchers need to understand the agenda of policy-makers in countries throughout the world and to offer their services to help analyse what needs to be done and how best progress can be achieved. A completely different level of engagement is needed. Such dialogue, difficult though it is, is certainly the best way to proceed.

This approach and engagement is necessary for all areas of research and, most particularly, in the fields of the global challenges, which are shared so widely across the world.

Conclusion

This chapter has focused almost entirely upon the first two of the four major essential contributions that universities can make in helping the world deal with the changes we are considering:

- *understanding and interpreting the process of change;*
- *offering approaches that would harness the process of change for general benefit.*

Though success in these areas also helps in the fourth:

- *creating a general intellectually engaging climate and culture across societies that promotes the virtues of understanding and science.*

The pressure for universities to do more to help people understand what is happening to the foundations of their world and what should be done has never been greater. That is why action is needed:

Governments should directly target a greater share of research funding upon the strongest research universities (about a third of UK universities) and should encourage their definition as 'research universities'. The self-selecting Russell Group should be deprioritised in government policy on the basis that it does not comprise all of the most highly rated research universities in the UK and there are many strong research-intensive institutions outside the Group.

The agreement between research funders and universities should recognise the importance of 'blue skies research' but also recognise that research is not funded simply as an end in itself but as a means to inform and transform the world. They should continue to reward research that can demonstrate a strong societal impact and promote research on how impact can be improved on a discipline by discipline basis in order to increase understanding of the ways in which research can more successfully bring about positive change.

Structured dialogue between researchers and practitioners should be encouraged in order to increase the impact of research, for example through the What Works Network, which should be strengthened and widened.

▶

The doctrine, which some promote, that all universities are broadly the same, should be explicitly rejected and governments should promote and support strong research universities. Governments should consciously seek to develop them in those parts of the country that have disproportionately low levels of research funding, for example by encouraging university mergers and partnerships. High quality research teams, which do exist in universities that are not research-intensive, should be encouraged to move to those that are. Barriers to their success, such as unnecessary immigration restrictions, should be removed.

Universities should focus research on problem-solving and knowledge, which illuminates how we address change, particularly in disciplines where evidence of this is weakest.

They should develop local research and 'knowledge transfer' to strengthen local economic development and proactively organise researcher networks to engage in the research work that is being done with teachers at other universities, further education colleges and local sixth forms.

They should develop stronger systemic international research partnerships across the world including in developing countries.

And they should take steps to separate clearly their research and teaching budgets, in order to increase transparency and develop confidence about their missions.

Chapter 5

The local economic and social impact of universities

Why the local impact matters

Ed's experience of promoting the merger of Monash University's Gippsland campus with the University of Ballarat to form a new regional economic powerhouse, Federation University, was that the merger was inspirational. Gippsland was one of Australia's most disadvantaged regions but the new university has already proved very successful in better meeting regional economic and social needs.

He continues to believe that, though universities do best when they have strong international partnerships, these are greatly strengthened in terms of institutional support when they bring manifest benefit at home. Research can lead to positive community outcomes and supporting jobs. It is possible to increase educational opportunities across university degrees or international study opportunities and it is local impact that is more noted and is most crucial.

His passionate belief is that it is as important as ever for universities to be both local and global and for the global to benefit the local.

Charles had experience as the Member of Parliament for the constituency of Norwich South, which included both the University of East Anglia and the city and civic centre. This showed the immense benefits of a wide variety of types of partnership that could be achieved when they worked together but also the often substantial difficulties in getting practical agreement on joint strategies.

These experiences led us to believe that the local economic and social role of universities really matters.

Introduction

Chapters 3 and 4 of this book address the importance of universities for work and for research, and their importance in facing the big national and international challenges in those areas.

However, in very many ways, the principal impact of universities is local. In Chapter 2, we saw the ways in which many universities, for example in Scotland and the civic universities of England and their successors, were the explicit product of civic economic and social commitment, and that is also the case across the US, Europe and Australia. That history has, ever since, been at the core of their existence.

In this chapter, we discuss the nature of their local impacts, which extend across the economic development of towns and cities to the civic and public engagement, that universities should bring with them.

That is the context within which we address the particular importance of local university action for the last three of those pillars we identified in Chapter 1:

- *offer approaches to harness the process of change for general benefit;*
- *educate and train the specialists whose skills are necessary to address change;*
- *create an intellectually engaging climate and culture across societies.*

Of course, different localities vary immensely, as does the importance of their universities to that community, with the different roles that they have and that we have described.

This is not the place to develop a general theory of the local role of universities but we think that there are a number of common points that can be developed and that will guide both university behaviour and government approaches to stimulating local university interventions.

We begin with the importance that some commentators have recently given to the positive role of the university in contesting the negative effects of globalisation, and then discuss the more general local impact of universities.

We then consider the important local civic and intellectual role of universities promoting an intellectually engaging climate and culture across societies.

Universities and globalisation

The central theme of this book is the need for universities to help the world to deal with the challenges of increasingly rapid global change. They have already played a major role in the scientific, technological and economic breakthroughs that have enabled globalisation to happen. That will continue and intensify.

Of course, this globalisation has happened on a global scale but, as it has, it has left hundreds of individual localities around the world floundering in its wake. It has brought well-recognised local downsides in parallel with global upsides.

As we have seen, the steady expansion of world trade and destruction of tariffs and protections has led large parts of our populations to lose faith in the capacity of the whole post-war system to meet the problems they experience, whether economic, social or cultural in nature.

Whatever the economic successes of 'globalisation' in the round, it did not answer the widespread concerns of individuals and communities about economic desolation in some geographical areas, such as the US rust belt and the former coal and steel communities in the UK, France and elsewhere. Nor did it sufficiently address worries about control of the immigration, which was a significant side-effect of globalisation as individuals moved, as they have always done, from economically less successful areas to build a livelihood in more prosperous parts of the world. It's been true since Dick Whittington went to London in the 14th century to find the streets that he hoped were paved with gold.

However, the speed of current change has no historical precedent. It is disrupting almost every industry in almost every country and the possibilities of billions of people connected by mobile devices, with unprecedented processing power, storage capacity and access to knowledge, are unlimited. And these possibilities will be multiplied by emerging technology breakthroughs in fields such as artificial intelligence, autonomous vehicles, nanotechnology, biotechnology, materials science, energy storage and quantum computing.

Among the many implications of this accelerating process of economic and technological change is the transformation of entire systems of production, management and, importantly, governance. In addition, it highlights the critical importance of higher quality education and training and spotlights the further decline of traditional communities.

This highlights the relatively weak position of those who don't have the education that would have helped them deal with what have become threats to their whole way of life.

Analyses of both the Brexit referendum and the 2016 US Presidential election point to the importance of education in explaining voting behaviour.

An analysis by Adam Jacobs[1] concluded that education was a remarkably strong predictor of voting outcome in the EU referendum, and that that statistical relationship is not much affected by age or ethnicity.

A Brookings Institute study[2] observed that 75% of voters with a post-secondary degree voted to remain in the EU while 73% of voters without one voted to leave the EU, and demonstrated similar divergences in the US 2016 Presidential Election.

It should have been no surprise that those who believed that they had lost out from that very process of globalisation turned towards those populist political leaders, of both right and left, who spoke out against the status quo rather than just going along with it.

Tens of millions of people moved away from their support for the economic and social model that had served so well for decades and towards the challenges represented by Brexit in the UK, Donald Trump in the US and similar movements in a number of other countries.

There has always been some social division between those with post-school education and those without but the circumstances have now changed so much and the numbers of those with post-school education have increased so greatly that the dangers of divided, even polarised, societies have become a real threat to economic and social stability.

The challenge posed by those opposed to globalisation and the post-war system is existential. But the central point is that the main responsibility for this state of affairs lies less with Trump and the Brexit supporters themselves than with those who did not use their economic and political power well enough to address the concerns that those people had before they fell for the snake-oil offers put forward by the new 'nativist populists' as they have been called. Brexit and Trump only exploited a failure by the governing 'establishment', which had failed to reinvigorate the very institutions and system that had the responsibility for dealing with these issues.

And universities are at the core of that challenge. So the question arises, can universities do more to deal with the perceived downsides of globalisation rather than just, in effect, creating the conditions for, and to some extent benefiting from, the upside?

The answer turns out to be a qualified yes.

Two recent books have emphasised the important roles that universities can play in helping local communities recover from the economic devastation that globalisation has forced upon them.

The first, *The Smartest Places on Earth: Why Rustbelts are the Emerging Hotspots of Global Innovation*,[3] by Antoine van Agtmael and Fred Bakker, shows how 'rustbelt' cities such as Akron, Ohio and Albany, New York (eg the SUNY Poly NanoTech complex[4]) in the US and Eindhoven in

Holland are becoming the centres of global innovation, and creating new sources of economic strength though coming from 'rustbelt' areas that had been written off.

They identify a series of cities – Dresden in Germany, Lund-Malmö in Sweden, Oulu in Finland, Batesville in Mississippi, Minneapolis, Minnesota, Portland, Oregon and Raleigh-Durham in North Carolina, and also others in the US, Canada, Mexico, the UK, Germany, Sweden, Switzerland, France and Israel – where a combination of forces – local universities, visionary thinkers, regional government initiatives, start-ups and big corporations – have created what they call 'brainbelts' that are transforming and creating industries that have turned the tide from cheap, outsourced production.

Their list does not only include purely 'rustbelt' areas, but also includes some well-known university-industry centres. However, a lot of them are globalisation losers. There are other examples at places like Wollongong, Australia's tenth largest city and a traditional centre of heavy industry with an ambitious university.

Other than the crucial role of the university itself, these authors emphasise the entrepreneurial importance of the 'Connector'. This is usually an individual who has sufficient vision, energy, networking capacity and drive to assemble the working partnerships and engagement that bring together university, industry, government and others to make change happen. They emphasise that the 'Connector' can come from any one of a range of places but must have the ability to make the connections that are essential.

They also emphasise 'the pragmatism ambition and the collaborativeness of local and regional politicians, entrepreneurs and scientists' who were ready to come together, and the importance of a wide variety of types of initiative that promote interdisciplinary collaboration.

They are clear that today's innovation is more bottom-up than top-down and that support, for example in the form of incentives and rewards, can help, including guidelines and articulation of best practice.

For the purpose of this book, however, what is important is the critical significance of the university itself in this process of regenerating a local economy, sometimes devastated by the collapse of traditional industries, and the related importance of high quality university leadership that can stimulate and engage with such a process, a point to which we return in Chapter 9.

A supplement to this view comes from John C Austen writing from the Brookings Institute,[5,6] who notes how important the university system has become to the economy of the Great Lakes rustbelt region. Universities in this region date back to the beginning of the 19th century and 'are, in many ways, the foundation of the Midwest's society, economy, and identity. No meeting of state business, civic, or political leaders in Michigan is held without the requisite nod to these university allegiances.' This area of the Midwest boasts no fewer than 20 of the world's top 200 greatest research institutions, including institutions such as the University of Chicago, University of Pennsylvania, Carnegie Mellon and the University of Pittsburgh. With 31% of the nation's population, Rustbelt states produce 35% of the nation's total bachelor's degree holders, 33% of its STEM graduates and 32% of higher education degrees awarded.

Austen goes as far as to say that the university efforts are resulting in a rebooting of local economies for a post-rustbelt era. Austen makes the point that, as well as providing superb education for locals and inculcating an entrepreneurial mindset, these institutions are massive employers of labour and serve as anchors for new business development. He notes the economic development of areas such as Green Bay, Wisconsin and Kalamazoo, Michigan.

And a further reinforcement of the importance of universities in post-globalisation local regeneration comes from *Our Towns*,[7] James and Deborah Fallows' more quirky account of five years of journeys across the US to look at a wide range of communities hit by globalisation.

These are their conclusions about what made towns succeed in finding a prosperous post-globalisation future:

1. People working together on practical local possibilities.
2. Picking out the 'local patriots'.
3. Making the phrase 'public-private partnerships' something real.
4. A well-understood civic story.
5. Having downtowns.
6. Being near a research university.
7. Having and caring about a community college.
8. Having distinctive innovative schools.
9. Making themselves outward-looking and open.
10. Having big plans.

Again, the significance of the university, the partnerships and networks, the history narrative and the innovatory approaches stand out.

And, in fact, the importance of universities to the regions desolated by the decline of traditional industries such as coal, steel, shipbuilding, cars and tyres should be clear.

These areas cannot be regenerated by economic protection and trade barriers to try to bring back the old industries. Even if that approach might ever have worked, and we doubt it, the stable door was open and the horse has well and truly bolted.

Nor can these areas be regenerated by state actions, or a series of welfare protections, important though they may well be in the short term. They all need to find again the competitive advantage that coal, steel, mass industrial production or transport gave them in the past and that brought them the prosperity that lasted for perhaps 150 years before it declined.

That is the meaning of the process of economic change we have discussed earlier in this book. The old industries will not provide a sustainable economic and social future for the communities we are considering. That will only come from the industries and economics of the future, whatever they may be. It is universities, working locally, that give the best possibility of helping that change to take place, and building the new community.

The most likely source of resilient competitive advantage in the future comes from the creativity and innovation in new industries that universities are best placed to offer, properly stimulating and properly stimulated. And, in addition, the universities, possibly with associated schools and colleges, such as further education colleges, are best placed to provide the education and training those communities need to provide the new workforce that will be required.

That is why we believe that universities should adopt a strong local approach and play a very important role in counteracting the impact of globalisation in those localities that have suffered most from it.

This seems to us an absolutely central question for universities seeking to address the challenges of change.

We would encourage more systematic analysis of what could be achieved and believe that further work in this field is worth doing.

And, of course, there are already excellent local examples of work in this field (outside the immediate context of globalisation) that demonstrate the impact that universities can and do have upon the economies of their communities and it is to this that we now turn.

General economic impact of universities

The most obvious example of the economic impact of world-class research comes from the US.

At the end of the Second World War, on the advice of Vannevar Bush, President Truman decided not only to increase massively government investment in research but to make it almost exclusively through the university system because of the manifest excellence that was there.

This accelerated the development of about 50 universities in the US that have contributed enormously to the economy. There are many examples, such as Boston, North Carolina, the incredible medical research development with massive industry spin-offs in San Diego, Silicon Valley in the bay area of San Francisco with contributions from Caltech and Berkeley. Most of the world's modern great companies, including Hewlett Packard and many more, were directly spawned from these university centres. They drove the information revolution, the 'third industrial revolution'.

A key figure was Fred Terman, the Provost of Stanford University, who, in the mid-20th century, conceived the value of close-proximity industrial engagement and the importance of the university helping spin-offs and graduate start-ups.

He had a vision, revolutionary at the time, but widely accepted today, of the value of a knowledge cluster on the doorstep of his institution, and he pursued it with vigour. The result today is Silicon Valley, which has had a tremendous impact on the world.

This big story is supplemented by a large number of smaller stories. Almost all universities have a significant impact in the communities around them. This happens in many ways and it is always amazing to see the incredible impact that a university can have in supporting and improving local economies in so many different ways. Scope and responsibility vary considerably from institution to institution. A great research university in a small town is likely to be the key supporter of the local economy yet the main mission of the university is likely to be international scholarship at the highest level. A great research university in a megacity may also play a significant role in the local economy but it is likely to target a range of industries and services globally too. In this chapter, we concentrate on the university that is central to the success of a city or region.

The best way to illustrate this is by looking at a series of examples.

Let's start with the UK where the University of Newcastle upon Tyne is a high quality research university. While established just over 50 years ago after previous affiliation with Durham University, its origins are much older in an engineering college, Armstrong College, and a medical college, King's College, both established about 150 years ago. Since that time, it has gone from strength to strength and is now one of the strongest institutions in the UK. It sits alongside a high quality, more technically and educationally focused institution, the University of Northumbria and, together, these institutions provide a home for tens of thousands of students in the city of Newcastle upon Tyne.

Only a few decades ago, the economy of the North East of England was dominated by heavy industry including steel, shipbuilding on a grand scale and coal mining. All of these heavy industries, including the coal mines, fell into a precipitous decline with the result that heavy industry jobs largely disappeared from an area that had been dependent on them. The universities sought to step into the breach and Newcastle today is a transformed post-industrial city dominated in large part by its leading universities which offer great education for both national and international students. The universities together provide a wide range of courses in almost every conceivable area for local students and it is noteworthy that a high proportion of local students go to university in their own backyard. The universities also draw international students into the city, generating considerable wealth. They employ a large number of staff and draw other activities into the city, which essentially underpins the economic wealth of the area. Indeed, without the university presence, the city would be greatly diminished.

This is only one example and this model has been replicated in a range of other great post-industrial cities such as Liverpool and Glasgow. Of course, budding industry, including high-tech industry, tends to grow alongside universities in part because of spin-offs and in part because of intellectual synergies and a number of these cities show evidence of increasing activities of that type.

Around the world there has been a tendency for smaller cities and towns, previously lacking a university, to try to develop, attract or grow one because of this wide recognition of the accelerated effect on economic development. This has often been done in the past through branch campuses. These may continue to thrive as branch campuses (of which there are some examples in Canada) or may transform into full-scale universities in their own right. In the UK, one of the most successful examples of the latter is the University of Lincoln, which has continued to expand in recent times. While the city is ancient and has had an educational presence for many centuries, the University is relatively new. The University of Humberside was approached to develop a new campus to the south-west of Lincoln leading to a new entity, the University of Lincolnshire and Humberside, launched in 1996. The first few hundred students rapidly expanded to many thousands and eventually the University changed its name to the University of Lincoln in 2001. This was accompanied by a massive new development involving more than £150 million, transforming the city of Lincoln from an old city centre brownfield site to a vibrant retail leisure and property development centred around the University. The University is credited with creating at least 3,000 jobs within Lincoln and generates almost £0.25 billion a year for the local economy. These achievements led its VC, Mary Stewart, to be recognised as the Guardian Vice-Chancellor of the year in 2018.

Following the 2003/4 legislation in the UK, universities were established in places such as Bournemouth, Derby, Gloucester, Ipswich, Northampton and Worcester, which previously had had no universities at all, and this has led to similar stories, some of quite outstanding success.

Looking to Australia, the impact of the university sector on the country broadly is immeasurable. The sector provides high quality education for local graduates as well as a massive international student market and it underpins much of the smart industry in the country . Perhaps in contradistinction to the UK, even some of the largest Australian cities depend on higher education to sustain their economy. Victoria in Australia's South is dominated by the city of Melbourne, a metropolis of over 5 million people. According to the Victorian State Government, which has analysed the economic value of Victoria's international education effort from year to year, the educational service sector in Victoria (and this is predominantly tertiary education) generated $9.1 billion in export revenue in 2016–17, representing the state's best performance to date and growth of well over $1 billion from the previous year. This supported almost 60,000 jobs and was the most important export for the great city of Melbourne. This was supported by a range of institutions with 7 out of 10 universities figuring in significant rankings of the world's best. It is noteworthy that this international student market is embraced by the local population as well as both major political parties and figures in Australia's economic planning for the future in a major way.

Regional Australia includes a number of smaller towns and cities, typically long distances away from metropolitan centres. University education is crucial for many of these as a factor in the local economy. The role of satellite campuses of leading public universities in smaller centres is also significant.

Bendigo, one of Victoria's largest regional cities, has long since developed a branch campus from Latrobe University, a Melbourne metropolitan institution. This campus has grown to acquire most disciplines and is now a very significant entity in its own right. The poorest area of the state of Victoria is the regional area of Gippsland. This contains a string of smaller towns and developed a Technology Institute years ago which was taken over by Monash University as a regional campus. This branch campus grew to a significant size and Ed promoted the merger of Monash University, Gippsland campus, with the University of Ballarat to form a new regionally based powerhouse, Federation University, which plays a huge role in sustaining the economy in regional Victoria. This role includes educating young people for a range of jobs relevant to working in the country, close partnerships with businesses and government and the employment of large numbers of staff who are regionally based. There was much local resistance to this in Gippsland, one of Australia's most disadvantaged regions, but it has proved very successful in better meeting regional needs. Almost all regional universities in Australia underpin the local economy.

This phenomenon of revitalisation of an economy through university activity, whether gradual and incremental as in the case of the great northern cities of the UK or accelerated and planned as, for example, with the University of Lincoln, is becoming ever more prevalent around the world. While crucial at local level, the university system in any advanced nation is becoming increasingly relevant to its economy. In the age of AI, the pivot of human activity and thought towards high-level jobs and intellectual activity is irreversible. Universities are central to this story. Society has been transformed more rapidly than ever before and knowledge is doubling every few years. Out of this knowledge comes new technology, business and industry transformation and indeed a new world. The university system, that part of society that specialises in knowledge, is at the heart of this process, reinforced by wide and complex linkages across government and industry. While recognised at an intellectual level by government in most countries, national university policy does not always reflect the need to nurture and develop the country's university sector at this pivotal time.

We've concentrated to date in this chapter on some of many thousands of examples of regional impact. However, it's also worth mentioning the impact great universities have in megacities. Nowadays, even the most elite research university in a great city generally has an important role locally as well as globally. This always involves the employment of many thousands of people, with local economic benefit. It almost always involves supporting local industry through partnerships and through high-tech start-ups and spin-offs. Generally, there will be collaborations with major industry also, such as the pharmaceutical industry. This leads to the concept of the high-tech precinct as a collaboration between great universities, industry and government.

There are many of these around the world and, of course, the San Francisco Bay Area and Silicon Valley always stand out. Other great examples in North America include the city of San Diego – a critical mass of medical research and pharmaceutical industry activity, developed in just a few decades underpinned by the presence of the Scripps Institute, the Salt Institute, the Burnham Institute and the University of California San Diego. This is undoubtedly now one of the major medical research localities on Earth and, together with strengths in Los Angeles and in the Bay Area, contributes to the massive overall strength of the Californian knowledge production system and of the Californian economy. The North Carolina Triangle and the Rhine Necker Triangle in Germany are other examples, as is the thriving industry park around Cambridge University in the UK. Interestingly, the major new development areas of China tend to be based on a similar model. Ed had the opportunity to help establish an international postgraduate university in the Chinese city of Suzhou in the industry precinct, which had been created by the government of Singapore and the national government of China. A thriving city of several million people has been developed in just over a decade with several great universities, both Chinese and branch campuses of international universities, and thriving smart industry. This surely is an example of the city of the future and China is developing many more!

Well, what about the old world? The world's megacities tend to be rather comfortable with their universities which have often been there for many centuries. Yet still these institutions have the opportunity to develop impact, complementing and enhancing their education and research as a key part of their mission. King's College London's new strategic plan for the next 10 years gives global, national and local impact equal significance to absolute excellence in education and in research. A new Vice-President has been appointed to lead this initiative, which ranges from environmental awareness to equity and diversity programmes to direct interaction with local government and industry.

THE recently published its first ranking of impact across a range of measured parameters for the world's universities and King's ranked 5th in the world on these parameters, some way above its already high ranking in the main table. Worcester also does exceptionally well. Both New York University and Cornell are involved in major new projects in New York City, in the case of Cornell a massive research development with the Technion in Israel following an initiative by Mayor Bloomberg.

Perhaps the most striking example of inner city rejuvenation by an American university was initiated some years ago by the Ivy League University of Pennsylvania. Under President Amy Guttman's leadership, Penn launched a massive new development in downtown Philadelphia called Penn Connects,[8] based on 24 acres of land purchased from the US postal service. The ambitions of this project were enormous in boosting not only educational and economic, but also social, capital in the city of Philadelphia which had become rather rundown in its central precincts. This project has expanded with increased ambition to nurture start-ups and is now a central part of the Philadelphia economy. This has proved attractive to major industry as well as start-ups, a particular win being the creation of Johnson & Johnson's new research laboratories.

So, the story of university local economic impact is already strong and productive. We turn now to what the government and others could do to help.

Government and local university development

Most of the economic impact of universities described above has come as a result of the efforts of the universities themselves, and the partnerships that they have built. Among these is a vital partnership with all levels of government from the very local to the international (eg the EU).

Governments at all levels – international, national, regional and local – recognise the importance of local economic development, acknowledge that universities have a significant contribution to make and offer strategies and resources to encourage that contribution.

But at least as important as the actual resources offered by government, which are usually fairly small-scale, relatively speaking, is its contribution to the university's strategic thinking and wider collaborations as the university develops this kind of approach. It is these collaborations that can generate really significant resources for new investment, for example in new infrastructure which may be decisive in making change happen.

Most governments now have some form of funding support, usually pump-priming rather than substantive, to assist and incentivise universities to extend and develop their local economic role. The current UK examples are the Higher Education Innovation Fund,[9] which provides funding for knowledge exchange to support and develop a broad range of interactions between universities and the wider world; a Connecting Capability Fund,[10] which supports university collaboration in research commercialisation and aims to encourage university external technological, industrial and regional partnerships; and University Enterprise Zones (UEZs),[11] which are intended to generate and commercialise innovation and deliver skills that best serve the key sectors in their local and regional economy. In 2015, four pilot UEZs were established in Nottingham, Liverpool, Bradford and Bristol.

Such programmes can help universities in this area but there is a question about the extent to which such regeneration strategies do in fact engage universities at more than a formal level. National government can support, but not usually successfully initiate, engagement, although local or regional government, for example through a mayor, may be able to play an initiating role.

In the UK, there is also a significant issue about the overall geographical distribution of research funding, which is also a major contributor to local economic growth. For example, in 2015–16,[12] the proportion of the then £3.1 billion spending of Research Councils UK in each country or region of the UK was as follows:

National research spending received (%)		
South East	23	
London	21	57
East	13	
Scotland	10	10
Midlands	9	
North West	7	
Yorks/Humber	6	24
North East	2	
South West	5	5
Wales	2	2
North Ireland	1	1

Thus, the London, East and South East regions received about 57% of national research spending whereas the North East, North West, Yorkshire & Humberside and Midlands, with about the same total population, received about 24%.

This is, of course, a massive reinforcement of the acute regional economic divisions in England and contributes to the sense of social division to which we referred earlier in this chapter resulting from the impact of globalisation's winners and losers.

Perhaps it is also worth mentioning here that the proportion of that research money that goes towards the programmes to incentivise universities' local economic development is absolutely tiny and so will not feature highly when a university comes to think strategically about the sources of its government funds.

Governments need to recognise the need to plan appropriately to be able to spread research funding more equitably in a geographical sense. We acknowledge that this is not straightforward, both because of the academic independence from government of the new funding body, UK Research and Innovation, and because of the need to support research at the world-class level which is already geographically distributed in a heavily weighted way towards London and the South East. We would recommend identifying a small number of already research-intensive universities across the country where resource will be focused. This has already happened to some extent in Manchester, for example with the development of the highly innovatory material graphene, but it could also be done in other universities, perhaps having in mind the kind of potential local economic development that we have described earlier in this chapter.

University in civic community

Most of this chapter has focused upon the local economic impact of universities but we now turn to the important local civic and intellectual role of universities promoting an intellectually engaging climate and culture across societies.

A central reason why we have set this university role as one of the four pillars that we have identified as important university contributions at a time of very rapid change is the growth of disdain for facts and realities and their replacement by 'fake news' in the public discourse. This is itself one product of the increasingly divided, even polarised, post-globalisation society that we discussed earlier in this chapter. This 'anti-science' culture is, of course, inimical to the whole university ethic as it has developed over centuries and it is very dangerous for societies as it challenges a central premise of the ways in which we should be addressing change, that is through understanding correctly what is happening and then trying to deal with it in the best way possible.

There are important national ways in which universities can promote such a rational approach. But the local role is perhaps even more significant and important. It can be done in a number of ways, for example:

- engaging with local schools and colleges;
- looking to the future with local private and public sector employers;
- examining the way that local societies are developing, including engaging civic leaders;
- promoting equality and opportunity for the least advantaged people in the local society;
- considering ways of building social cohesion and eroding social divisions;
- developing strong civic and historical public narratives of the locality;
- looking at the ways in which grand challenges, such as environmental sustainability, public health and technological change, apply to the locality;
- promoting debate about, and looking at ways in which, cities and communities can be made more sustainable in general;
- engaging with local government upon their strategic priorities for the locality, for example in relation to education, health, crime and transport, including examining innovative means of delivering high quality public services;
- encouraging students to be active in local communities;
- promoting discussion and debate in local communities.

These are only examples and there is no national template that can simply be applied locally. The most valuable activity can only be determined by local universities engaging directly with the priorities and concerns of their local community, whatever they may be.

One UK organisation that promotes this kind of activity is the National Co-ordinating Centre for Public Engagement.[13] Based at the University of Western England and the University of Bristol, and funded by UKRI and Wellcome, it seeks to support a culture change in the UK higher education sector so that the sector makes a vital, strategic and valued contribution to 21st-century society through its public engagement activity. It supports excellent public engagement practice, creating the conditions for public engagement to thrive in universities and build strong networks and partnerships to amplify their impact.

As one Vice-Chancellor put it, universities have a choice between being '*engines of equality*', through strong local community engagement and promoting the public benefit and common good, or '*engines of inequality*',[14] keeping the poorer people out and standing aloof from their community. The choice should be obvious and we believe that the course of public engagement is the path for the future role of universities.

One final point for local university discussion is the most appropriate future pattern of university organisation in a city. For example, there are five higher education institutions in Leeds: University of Leeds, Leeds Beckett University, Leeds Trinity University, Leeds Arts University and Leeds College of Music. They all have their own distinctive, distinguished histories, going back a century or more. And they all have their own missions and individual strengths and weaknesses, serving a local as well as national community.

This pattern of university provision in Leeds may or may not well reflect the needs of the future, either in research or teaching. And the same could be said of other cities both in the UK and the rest of the world.

Local co-operation and integrated planning at regional level are more advanced in Australia probably in part due to the state system. In Victoria, for example, the eight universities meet regularly in a formal committee at Vice-Chancellor level and plan collectively on issues relevant to the state – that is to say local issues.

A discussion worth having in a given locality is what is the best form of organisation of universities in that locality to meet local needs. This is a discussion that it is far better to have locally than resulting from some national 'rationalisation'.

So we would suggest that universities in particular cities should give active consideration to the most rational pattern of university research and teaching in that locality and consider what steps should be taken to enable that to happen. And government should consider what incentives it can offer to encourage a more rational pattern of universities across the country.

Conclusion

We have given attention to the relationship of universities to their locality for two reasons. The first is the critical need for society to address the adverse consequences of globalisation, where we think that universities have a very important, positive role to play. The second is that, in contrast to the obvious impact of the great university drivers of research and teaching, it is often difficult to get a real focus on universities' immediately local impact. And indeed, very many academic staff, students and sometimes university leaders do not give this any form of priority in their thinking.

And that is why:

Universities should develop a clear strategy for their interrelationship with their local communities, including establishing strong relationships with local business and industry and civic leaders to take the relationship forward.

And they should discuss with these partners and other universities in the locality the best future form of university provision in that area.

Local and regional governments should develop their strategies for engaging with universities in their area to develop strong and productive partnerships.

National governments should commit to durable policy approaches to promote and support local university economic and social engagement.

Chapter 6

Who benefits from a university education?

Why it matters who benefits

In his political life, Charles met personally a very large number of people who would have benefited enormously from, and who would have been able to contribute more if they had received, a university education. They would have welcomed the opportunity, but never had the chance. At the beginning of the 1987 election campaign, he saw first hand the power, for millions of people, of Neil Kinnock's rhetoric about 'the first Kinnock in a thousand years to go to university'.

He saw what his wife Carol gained as a mature student, having not had the chance of a university education until she reached the age of 28.

Much more recently, he witnessed at Arizona State University the power of its link-up with Starbucks to provide degree opportunities for Starbucks' employees.

Ed's family moved to the smallest Australian state, Tasmania, when he was a teenager and the university there (UTAS) was the first he attended. It was very small but of high quality. It was the only university in a small state and has gone from strength to strength in recent decades. It provides broad-ranging educational opportunities and it makes immense contributions sociologically and economically to the community it serves.

He cannot think of an institution that makes a greater contribution to its community than UTAS. This experience reinforced his belief as to both the centrality of universities as civic institutions and their differentiation of mission to meet local needs.

Our experiences led both of us to believe that the question of who gets a chance to go to university is central to the economic and social welfare of any society.

That's why it matters.

Introduction

In Chapters 3, 4 and 5, we have discussed the key functions of universities if they are to play their role to full effect in meeting modern world challenges: in relation to work, to research and understanding the world and to their locality and community.

In this chapter, we turn to the difficult questions of who should best be studying in universities if they are to make their contribution well, what that means for the ways universities should seek to form and develop the values of the new generations and the importance of high quality teaching to achieve that. Consideration of these matters encompasses a range of cultural and practical issues that underpin wider policy discussions about the operation of universities. Public attitudes create an important political environment that makes decisions by both universities themselves and by governments more complicated.

We address first the demand for university places and their supply at a wide range of universities with different qualities, and then we consider the ways in which this demand and supply is resolved and how places are and should be allocated.

We then look at the importance of universities' overall benefit to society.

The demand for university places and their supply

Just about every middle-class or aspirational family puts a high value on their children going to university. In Japan, the stakes are so high that there have even been reports over the years of some young people committing suicide if they fail to get into a prestigious university. In some families in the UK, the whole household invests huge time and resources over many years to focus upon a child's path to Oxbridge or a 'good university'. Even selection of a primary or private preparatory school at the age of five may be made with this goal in mind. There is fierce competition for both state and private secondary schools that have a strong track record in getting their students into leading universities.

At the same time, over many decades, there has been a push across the West for more people to have a university experience. Despite the argument of some that too many young people aspire to university, no one making that case volunteers that their own children shouldn't go to university if they can. And in countries such as Finland, 50% of young people are getting undergraduate degrees.

Here we try to look at this very emotionally fraught area objectively. Conclusions may well differ when viewed from the standpoint of the individual rather than society at large. It is further complicated both by the very different socio-economic outcomes of different levels of study and by the complexity introduced by the different levels of university qualification (ie sub-bachelor's, bachelor's, master's and doctoral programmes). So there is no easy answer, but some general principles can inform how universities should approach the dilemmas.

We begin by considering what different individuals gain from a university education and the job and career opportunities that flow from it, which of course ultimately depend on the aptitude and aspirations of the person themselves.

Poorer families

We start with the lowest socio-economic groups in developed countries such as the UK, US, much of Europe and countries like Australia or New Zealand. In these countries, the university system is well developed and generally living standards are high.

It is very widely believed that university education is the key way to improve both quality of life and socio-economic position and indeed to enter the middle classes for those who grew up in poverty. In the UK, this view was particularly strong from the middle third of the last century onwards and in the US through much of its history.

That is why Neil Kinnock's famous appeal, 'Why am I the first Kinnock in a thousand generations to be able to get to university?', resonated so very powerfully with parents and children from both working-class and some new middle-class homes. And that is why Joe Biden plagiarised this in the 1987 US presidential campaign.

For most people, university is seen as the only real route to improve their social class and life expectations. The importance of education to working-class families, for example as shown by the establishment of the Miners' libraries in the South Wales valleys, is central.

It is certainly possible for a self-made person to reach wealth without any university education, and there are many famous examples of that, or for a landed aristocrat to inherit their wealth and status. But the overwhelming majority of people, across the whole of society, who improve their position in society, do so through higher education which enables entrance to one of the professions, to managerial positions or to successful business start-ups.

Nevertheless, however outstanding individual achievements may be, even a cursory look indicates a far less satisfactory overall situation and that we are not doing enough to meet these needs.

There are very many examples of outstanding individuals from social and class backgrounds where there had been no possibility of high-level education who shine and rise to national leadership positions in all aspects of national life once exposed to real university opportunities. This happened in the UK, beginning just before and building up after the Second World War.

Their inspirational successes, often achieved through highly selective education systems, obscure the fact that the great majority do not do so well. With any system of selection some, perhaps many, fail the test. Those who succeed tend to grow up in families who support their aspirations and indeed help to build them. Those less fortunate are likely to be surrounded by family members and peers who do not value higher education (or indeed sometimes any education). They are doomed, in many cases, to fail at school level and so not achieve a level of accomplishment in their schooling years that makes university entry straightforward.

Where is aspiration going to come from if one grows up in a family where there is nothing to read and little ambition? The answer should be, and often is, the primary and secondary schools system. However, it is an unfortunate reality that there are geographical areas of low educational performance and attainment with poor outcomes, which can reinforce family lack of aspiration rather than contest it. This is usually not because of poor teaching but because of an entrenched culture of poor attainment and low levels of parental engagement. This can be very difficult to overcome, though the initial Academy School programme in the UK from 2000 to 2010 attempted to do that, with many successes.

However, the problem can sometimes seem intractable. Recent figures suggest that less than 5% of Oxbridge undergraduate entrants are from the lowest socio-economic band. This is by far the lowest percentage among UK universities and it is persistent in spite of many years of attempted remedies. In the UK as a whole, the rate of participation of young white men from the lowest socio-economic grouping has stagnated at around 5% while every other societal group has improved at a time when huge gains have been made in overall university enrolment rates. Similarly, in the US, university participation has risen over the past 20 years for all except the lowest socio-economic quartile.

These students from the lowest socio-economic band are from the group who have most both to contribute and to gain from fuller educational opportunities. Their failure to advance educationally is an enormous waste of potential for the country as a whole.

It is clear that interventions are more likely to work when made in primary and early secondary school and are supported by family members. If students have missed the boat early in their school life, attempts to get them ready for university in the latter years of secondary school are unlikely to succeed.

Though it is true that improved schools are the main contribution to progress in this field, universities can certainly play a very important part in improving this situation. For example, the exposure of secondary school students to university students, especially from a similar background, in a mentoring process, can be very powerful. Universities typically have supportive, though usually limited, arrangements with a number of secondary schools in their local areas. And offering opportunities to study university degrees at partnered further education colleges can make a contribution. Sadly, as a generalisation, the more prestigious the university, the less well developed all of these relations tend to be. They are certainly a key aspect of an effective civic university – that is one that has a special relationship with its local community. Too many universities do not do enough.

Middle classes

Moving up the socio-economic ladder, we now look at the children of the middle- and upper middle-class families. Whichever developed country one looks at, this group is the traditional preserve of the universities. The majority of university students come from a relatively privileged social and economic background. The expansion of the modern university system was driven largely by market forces to meet their needs.

Here families understand very well that achievement of university education consolidates both a career and a position at the same or better socio-economic level than that enjoyed by the parents. So families encourage their children to do well at school and to engage with a peer group with similar aspirations, and therefore they enrol their children in a school where most students have the expectation of a university future.

Many students from this background will aim for a career in the professions and see university education as the route to that. In the UK, the first degree is likely to be a professional entry degree whereas, in the US, it is equally likely that a liberal arts college degree will be followed by professional study in graduate school. The value added is clear, the financial gain enormous.

This will continue as middle-class parents do their best to ensure that their children get the chance of university life.

In the UK, the majority of such students will aim to study at research-intensive universities, of the type that we have discussed in Chapter 4.

In the US, most students in this category will study at a large and well-regarded state-linked university, sometimes referred to as a land grant institution. While many students who aspire to study at the highest ranked international institutions will come from this socio-economic group, academic or financial inhibitions will prevent most from aspiring to Ivy League or similar institutions. Nevertheless, the university will do its job for the students. They will leave ready to take up a profession and considerable personal development. The value again is clear.

At the perceived apex of the university world, Oxbridge and the Ivy Leagues represent a pinnacle perhaps now being reproduced by the C9 universities in China and represented in continental Europe by the Grandes Ecoles of France. The majority of students who attend these institutions have aimed (or been aimed) in that direction from early in their school years. Their schools may well have been chosen with that in mind. There may well be a parental history of attendance at such institutions. Many students from their schools will have succeeded in securing places at such universities. There will also be high-achieving students from a wide range of socio-economic backgrounds but, relative to the total number of places and the likelihood of achieving a place, a background of entitlement and relative affluence remains a crucial advantage. Some have commented that, in these institutions, students from 'non-traditional' backgrounds may feel out of place.[1]

In the UK, 7% of secondary school children attend the great 'public' (ie private, paid for by parents' fees) schools, while 42% of Oxbridge students come from those schools – very substantially greater than the proportion who go from the state school system. Indeed, pupils from just 8 schools filled 1,310 Oxbridge places over three years, compared with 1,220 places from 2,900 other schools.[2] Similar issues arise for Russell Group universities.

If one looks at leadership roles across the UK,[3] 71% of top military officers, 74% of top judges, 61% of the country's top doctors, 51% of leading print journalists, 42% of British BAFTA winners and 32% of MPs have been privately educated. Oxbridge graduates dominate these roles even more significantly.

Why is this so? Undoubtedly, the highest levels of academic achievement are necessary in the school years to achieve entry to the Russell Group universities but there is enormous overlap with the capacity of student groups in other first-rate universities. Considerations of ability alone cannot explain these variations.

Similarly, it is possible that the quality of education at these universities may be higher in terms of the quality of the ideas and scholarship the students are exposed to and the discussions they have with their peers (though data on teaching quality does not seem to support this view, as we say in Chapter 4). It may be that it is peer aspirations that are influential in final career outcomes.

Perhaps most influential in career terms is the cachet of having a degree, especially a 'good' degree (2.i or better), from one of the greatest international universities. This gets most students off to a fantastic start in a career sense and is especially influential if they aspire to work for firms where the leadership comes from a similar background. Cachet may not be everything but it is hugely important now as in the past.

It is possible to acquire cachet, and strengthen one's CV, by further study in a great university for a postgraduate master's degree, for example at one of the great London universities. For those who aspire to the highest level in France, it is more difficult if they fail to obtain a place at a Grande Ecole as 're-entry' opportunities are fewer.

The pressures on young people in Asian countries, such as Singapore, Hong Kong and mainland China, to succeed in getting a place in a top university are immense and it is known throughout the world that the pressure young people are under in Japan to succeed in university entry is often excessive.

It may be, at the end of the day, that very ambitious students, for whatever reason – self-driven, historical familial or parental influence or a combination of all of the above – set a pathway early for themselves to achieve at what society considers the highest level.

A recent illustration of the high stakes involved in university admissions is the Operation Varsity Blues bribery scandal in the US, disclosed by US Federal prosecutors and involving at least 50 people, a number of whom have pleaded guilty or agreed to plead guilty. Thirty-three parents of college applicants are accused of paying a number of prestigious universities, including Yale, Georgetown, Stanford and Southern California more than $25 million between 2011 and 2018 to get their children into the universities.

Taking all of the above into account, we acknowledge the vast intellectual contribution really great universities can offer. The world would be an infinitely poorer place without them. But, in parallel, we say that more steps must be taken to reduce the sharp differences in access to those universities on the basis of social and economic background.

It is an unavoidable fact that demand way exceeds supply for university places in the super elite institutions. These institutions undoubtedly offer a superb educational experience and the number of places relative to demand is still very restricted. Michael Crow[4] makes the point in many of his writings[5] that we define the excellence of our universities by exclusion, as opposed to inclusion. And many use the language of inclusion so that, in fact, we are at risk of systematically deceiving ourselves.

This perception relates to the existential discussion about whether the education system, including universities, exists primarily to bring out the best in everyone and enable them to fulfil their potential. Or whether it just offers a sieve to identify and develop the 'most talented' of individuals.

Crow argues, rightly, that the harder it is for a student to get a place in a university and the harder it is for a staff member to secure tenure, the more prestigious the institution becomes and so the more value its degree acquires in career advancement terms. He therefore argues that there is absolutely no genuine reason why education at this level is not more widely available.

And of course, in fact, an equivalent education to the high-level Ivy League or Oxbridge institutions is already offered by very many universities throughout the world. But historical kudos is so linked to a handful of institutions that their special place in the university world is as secure as Fort Knox, whether justified or not!

It remains to be seen whether these perceptions will survive the changes flowing with the information revolution and increased student expectations at all levels. However, the evaluation that we describe has so far been extraordinarily resilient and these universities act as reinforcing agents of an increasingly outdated and unmeritocratic social and economic class system.

Wider benefits to the individual of a university education

In the preceding paragraphs, we have looked at the value of university education in markedly reductionist terms considering career advancement and financial gain. However, there are other important advantages that in terms of the full, happy and well-lived life, are usually equally important for the individual.

These include the acquisition of improved analytical skills, the ability to argue one's case, tolerance and a capacity to cope with ambiguity, an ability to think laterally and, in the case of those students who enter universities as undergraduates, the opportunity to continue to develop their personalities and their moral as well as professional strengths in a place and time protected at least partially from the pressures of the wider world which they will encounter when they fully enter the workforce.

The wide range of co-curricular activities available at all universities and the opportunity to develop real expertise and interest in areas outside of their primary field of study are huge boons to the development of students' personality and their capacity to fully engage with the opportunities life offers. International experiences are extraordinarily valuable here also. The global economy and the global workforce are more international in both physical movement and mindset than ever before.

Finally, friendship sets that are developed at university often last a lifetime. Students are exposed to peers from a much wider range of backgrounds than they would have encountered at secondary school. For the first time, they may be meeting and mixing with students from many countries and from different ethnic and religious backgrounds. The richness of this experience in framing an open mindset for the rest of their lives is invaluable for many students and not only in career terms.

The expectations and the benefits of a university education are considerable for students from all socio-economic and ethnic backgrounds. It is also extremely valuable for society at large for universities to serve a wide cultural mix and, in doing so, become champions of equity and diversity.

Expectations may differ but the advantages in career development, socio-economic well-being and personal development are very real for the vast majority of students, regardless of family background. By the time they get to university, the great majority of students are truly self-starters in a study sense and have the capacity to benefit considerably from the intellectual stimulation that is on offer, both in general terms and in terms of professional development.

Those who believe that university education should be more tightly rationed, and numbers reduced, often fail to take into account this full range of individual benefits.

These are the tensions and pressures that lie behind the interplay of supply and demand that ultimately determine which potential students get a university undergraduate place and which do not.

Participation rates

In an ideal world, every student who has the capacity to complete a university education should be able to go to university. Rather than setting artificial thresholds, great countries should continue to strive to prepare their young people in the school system for university entry and to provide a university system devoted to further developing specialist and general skills in the young.

In advanced economies, we should aim for the highest university participation rates. Rates approaching 50% are entirely appropriate where the secondary school system is functioning well and where national aspiration in lower socio-economic groups for self-improvement is entrenched.

Of course, a student's capacity to earn and complete a degree is fundamental. Here the UK and Australia do well. The US does very badly (however measured) with large drop-out rates after the second (sophomore) year of study.

It is instructive to look at the percentage of people from the ages of 25 to 64 who have participated in university education in different countries according to UNESCO data[6] (which is restricted to OECD membership countries and one or two others) and to correlate that with national wealth and development. Of course, there is an issue here of which is the cart and which is the horse! A series of countries can be identified including Australia, Canada, the UK and the US where over 40% of the population have a university qualification of one type or another. UNESCO data also tracks this information through each decade from 25 on and one sees significant improvement in the extent of engagement in 25 to 34 year olds from that in 55 to 64 year olds in all of the countries mentioned.

There is, then, a significant number of countries with participation rates of 30–39%, including many of the European countries, which also showed improvement from older to younger deciles. The striking correlation between national wealth and development and university participation is in the countries that have participation rates of under 25%, such as Brazil, South Africa and Turkey. These countries also showed a less discernible increase from older to younger deciles.

According to a study from Harvard and the Asian Development Bank, 6.7% of the world's population overall are college degree holders. This has risen by 0.178% a year during the past decade with an average just below that for the second half of the 20th century. We are moving in the right direction but very slowly! The correlation between national prosperity and the percentage of citizens holding a university qualification appears to be a very clear one.

Clearly, prosperous countries spend more on education and more young people have the opportunity to participate at university level. Yet those countries with very high participation, such as Switzerland and South Korea, are more than maintaining their competitive prosperity in today's world. The evidence is very strong that a high level of university attainment in the population is one of the underpinning factors in national prosperity.

As stated earlier, one still hears comment at senior levels that too many people go to university and that more should enter vocationally orientated tertiary education programmes. But this is not at all an either/or choice. Clearly, the aspiration should be that almost all young people have a tertiary education appropriate to their potential and capacity. This should involve as many as possible of those who have the capacity for university-level education to experience it. Any other approach significantly devalues the human potential of great countries.

In countries where entry to tertiary education in prestigious institutions has significantly underpinned social stratification, there may be additional reasons for making sure that tertiary participation targets are internationally competitive at the higher level. Fortunately, the UK does well. Canada, Australia, Switzerland and the Scandinavian countries do better. Especially in countries without massive natural resources, a well-educated, flexible and adaptable workforce is their greatest asset, and one clear driver of success is an improved rate of university participation over time.

What should students study?

From their own point of view, the student should be able to study whatever seizes their attention and excites their passion. There is a danger here that broadening university entry, possibly with weaker entry requirements for some universities, might encourage some students to enter university who are not academically confident on leaving secondary school and not ideally prepared for the rigours of university education.

Such students in that position may end up attending lower ranking universities, which depend upon them for income, offer courses that are less demanding, impart less useful skillsets and are not so well respected in the employment world. Furthermore, drop-out rates may be high.

This is not only a theoretical concern. For example, in Australia, the first experiment with uncapping of commencing places saw exactly this scenario with a number of low ranked institutions almost doubling their places, admitting students to degrees of lesser worth and tolerating very high non-completion rates in the first year.

Nevertheless, the students who successfully complete even these degrees undoubtedly get some benefit, although the benefits in terms of the first job immediately post-graduation may not be as high as desirable. However, the lifetime benefits in terms of overall skills and widening opportunities are still likely to be considerable.

In an ideal world, full success in university enrolment would see students from all backgrounds widely enrolled in the most demanding professional courses. For some, this might require specialised approaches and the development of tailored pathways, which is where teaching quality is important.

This is one factor that supports the offering of a range of high-level professional degrees in a graduate school setting as in the US. In Australia, professional courses such as medicine and law are often offered by the same university at undergraduate and postgraduate entry level. For many students, a general experience for their undergraduate degree is the optimum choice, with specialisation at postgraduate level. This is the model of the liberal arts colleges of the US and provides a superb platform for life.

The conclusion is clear. What should be studied is driven in the first instance by individual preference and it may take two bites of the cherry for some students to get into the profession that they've set their heart on.

Where and when to go?

What type of institution should students go to? This is a crucial issue for the university sector in any country that organises itself sensibly. Students have a wide range of aspirations, as well as different levels of inherent ability and varied experience of school quality. Not all will be able to achieve top-level academic performance. Even if they were, many want to get on quickly with professional careers and their eyes are set on other peaks. As already discussed, countries need balanced workforces with clever people going into a wide range of disciplines. Moreover, students vary in the length of university exposure they desire. Some want to complete an undergraduate degree as quickly as possible and get into the workforce. Others are attracted by deeper or longer immersion in their disciplines. A still smaller group will seek to generate new knowledge in doctoral programmes. None of these options is intrinsically better than the other in terms of individual contribution or individual success. A good university system will offer a range of options that meets both individual and national need. It is also really important that students succeed in their endeavours and that they are guided in the right direction, ideally well before they finish their secondary schooling.

This requires good quality and informed vocational and career counselling. For the great majority of students, the path will be reasonably clear from relatively early in their university years, though some students may return and have more than one tertiary immersion before their final level of academic achievement is reached.

An increasing number of students study close to home in their undergraduate years and attend a local university. This was traditional in Scotland (as opposed to England and Wales) and in Australia. In some cases, this is for economic reasons and, in some cases, just the convention. However, significant numbers of students prefer to leave home in their university undergraduate years, supported by often a rather meagre maintenance grant, some parental support or part-time work. They will select a university that has strengths in their chosen discipline and that is well regarded for its general quality of education.

All of these considerations reinforce the case that we have made throughout this book for real variation in universities' missions and educational organisation. The important thing is that all institutions do really well in their chosen areas of excellence and nurture their students appropriately. These considerations are well understood by the vast majority of university leaders. Clark Kerr understood this well when he developed the University of California system with a range of closely interrelated institutions operating in different but complementary spaces within an integrated system.

The framework he created included the great research universities, notably UCLA, UCSF, UCSD and UC Berkeley. These carry out research in ways that redefine our world and they are linked with teaching-focused colleges that are also very strong in their mission. Clark Kerr's clarity is not always so clearly reflected in national tertiary education systems, which have grown more chaotically. It is crucial that institutions understand their space and play to their strengths. In the UK, there is also an important place for further education colleges, often linked to universities that can increase the offer and range of opportunities.

Where do national priorities fit into this?

It is entirely legitimate – indeed essential – for nations to set priorities for key workforce areas and professions, whether through subsidy of targeted places, targeted bursaries or other mechanisms of differential support. Inevitably, some professions will be more attractive than others and some places more competed for than others.

This is something that cannot be disregarded by policy-makers and institutional leaders. It is a real danger of the institutional university autonomy that we strongly support that sufficient diversity for national needs may not develop and this requires real leadership not only from university Presidents and governing bodies but also serious dialogue with governments, economic and social institutions and the wider society. This happens far too little.

Such dialogue is essential to ensure that any national university system is fit for purpose in terms of both individual and national needs. It is then crucial that each individual institution understands and plays its part in the national ecology.

In recent years, there has been considerable debate in countries with a more centralised approach than the US to university enrolment, such as Australia and the UK, as to how student numbers should be set in different institutions. The historic approach was to set this centrally with allocation of a fixed number of places built on various criteria including range of disciplines and past performance. Such central planning was initially a function of grant-based public funding, but for many years it carried over into the era of tuition fees.

However, in the early 2010s, both Australia and the UK began a huge experiment where the numbers of students were uncapped to create a 'demand-driven' funding system to reflect the transition to a market environment in higher education. Under this model, market forces were allowed to determine commencing enrolment numbers for each institution and the government gave an undertaking through guaranteed domestic loan pools to cover the costs in the short and medium term with long-term recovery from students, through the tax system, as their incomes passed a certain threshold. This experiment was brave in the extreme because it exposed governments to billions of pounds of potential additional cost[7] and indeed, in both countries, that has turned out to be largely the case, with very significant increases in domestic enrolments to a new threshold level.

The increase in enrolment rates took place across all universities. For individual institutions, this has posed a dilemma. Should they grow and, if so, should this be done by increased competitiveness in a relatively restricted student pool defined by high academic capacity, demonstrated through exam results or alternatively should they grow by reducing entry academic standards?

Interestingly, in Australia, the approach of different universities was completely divergent around this issue. A relatively small number – at the top end of the academic tree in terms of admission standards and with high international demand – decided not to grow. Almost all of them decided to maintain academic entry standards or even to gradually increase them. Any growth in domestic numbers would, therefore, depend on an increase in competitiveness against peer institutions. Without exception, this strategy has been successful for the institutions that adopted it.

Another group of institutions, almost all relatively low ranking in terms of admission criteria, made a decision to drop academic criteria for initial admission, sometimes dramatically, and with resultant massive increases in student numbers and high attrition and drop-out rates. This policy may have improved some university bottom lines but contributed little to their reputation or to the success of the societies around them. Poorly regarded courses with relatively low completion and high cost could be a definition of university failure in serving the societies around them. This will continue to be a contentious area.

In the UK, universities faced similar tensions, dilemmas and competition between each other. The UCAS[8] End of Cycle Report 2018[9] analysed patterns of admissions policies and the UK Government[10] pointed out that, in 2018, 34.4% of 18 year olds from England, Northern Ireland and Wales received a form of unconditional offer[11] whereas, in 2013, this figure was just 1.1%. In some universities, up to 70% of admissions offers were unconditional. It therefore took action to challenge the universities that were making 'conditional[12] unconditional offers' in order to pressure students to make that university their first choice.

These kinds of practices could best be changed if schools and universities slightly altered the cycle of their examinations and admissions timetable in order to permit students to apply for university after their secondary examination results are known, rather than before, as now. This currently happens in Scotland and it is tricky but not impossible and would have the advantage of giving more confidence and certainty to student applicants, which would benefit students from poorer backgrounds.

An alternative way of achieving the same end is to encourage students to take a year out between school and university, perhaps with short-term employment options for students who do this.

What, then, is the answer? Should governments set the number of university places in the raw Soviet-style central planning approach with tight control perhaps reinforced through a series of academic five-year plans? Should the market prevail with an uncapping of places and a range of providers offering courses with different structures and knowledge sets? Should this allow for private provider entry?

The tension here is about whether to uncap the volume of student admissions, or the price, or both. In the UK, the 2010 Browne review wanted to uncap price and not volume. The Coalition Government responded by tripling fees and then uncapped numbers. In Australia, the Gillard Labour Government uncapped numbers and then her Liberal successor, Tony Abbott, failed to win the debate to uncap price. It's not an easy problem for politicians selling a message to prospective students, parents and taxpayers.

We discuss some of these issues further in Chapter 8 but we think that it is difficult to see how a tightly controlled system governed and overseen by tight central planning and with enforced uniformity can perform optimally and fully reflect student choices in a modern economy. We think it is necessary to accept that the market does have a role to play in determining the final mix, even though this could cause a degree of chaos and would require toleration of some skills oversupply. And there may well be consequences for possible university bankruptcies and a university version of 'mergers and acquisitions'.

In Chapter 7, we address postgraduate master's and doctoral courses and degrees, which are a very important element of university life, not least for international students.

International students

Of course an exceptionally important component of this system of global higher education, notably in the English-speaking countries, is the increasing flow of international students, who provide intellectual breadth and vitality and also the funding which keeps some universities going. It is worth identifying some important trends.

The overall international student population[13] is rising rapidly, from an estimated 2.1 million in 2001 to 4.6 million in 2017.

Australia (23.8%) has the highest proportion of international students in comparison with its home population, followed by the UK (21.1%), Canada (15.2%) and New Zealand (15.0%). European countries vary from 6% to 12%. The US has 5.3% (though it has the largest absolute number at just over 1 million). Japan (4.7%) and China (1.1%) are much lower.

And the numbers are changing fast, with the biggest increases from 2016 to 2017 being Mexico (58.9%), Spain (24.9%), Canada (18.3%), Japan (12.5%), Australia (12.1%) and China (11.4%). These are all in contrast to the UK (0.9%) where the figure was stagnant because of its negative and nationally destructive policies.

The UK has long placed a great emphasis on the value of an internationalised student and academic community, and successive UK governments have done much between the 1990s and 2010s to encourage UK universities in their attempts to diversify their academic workforce. But that has changed significantly in the past nine years as a result of incoherent and ineffective immigration policies in relation to universities.

Of the 93 UK universities in the top 1,000 universities in the THE 2018 rankings, the average (mean) proportion of overseas students is 30% and the highest proportions are in three of the London universities: the London School of Economics with 71%, the School of Oriental and African Studies with 56% and Imperial College London with 55%.

Of the 35 Australian universities in those top 1,000, the mean proportion of overseas students is 26% and the highest proportions are Murdoch with 48%, South Australia with 41% and Melbourne with 40%.

In contrast to the UK, international students in Australia are not included in migration numbers, have significant defined post-study work rights and are recognised by the Australian people and government as significant contributors to the national society and economy.

American universities are, in general, significantly less international. Of the 157 US universities in those top 1,000, the mean proportion of overseas students is 13%. The highest proportion is 45% at Carnegie Mellon, with MIT on 34% and Columbia on 32%.

However, there's no doubt that many US universities are targeting international student recruitment, notably from China, to replace falling domestic income, though it remains to be seen how deteriorating US–China trade relations will affect this approach.

China is at the other extreme. Of the 63 Chinese universities in those top 1,000, the mean proportion of overseas students is 5% and the highest proportions are Jinan with 25% and Peking with 16%.

The major bar to international student recruitment in China has been that the universities teach in Mandarin. English has been developed across China as the second language. Some of the newer universities, such as SUSTEC, are offering courses in English and it is likely that we will see international student recruitment grow in China.

South Korea has recently launched an elite university, KAIST, which teaches only in English and is launching itself in the international market. KAIST is also heavily focused on developing strategic partnerships with world-class universities and businesses from other countries.

The fact is that the competition for international students is increasing. Even without the UK's visa complications, British universities cannot rely upon this as a reliable source of income in the coming decades.

Benefits to society

The economic benefits

In Chapter 3 and earlier in this chapter, we have addressed many aspects of the economic benefits of university education, both to the individual and to society. We assert that universities make an enormous contribution to the economic strength and resilience of our society, and that universities need to change significantly in order to do this really well.

In summary, any national workforce requires adequate numbers of young people who are well trained to enter all of the key professions and businesses. And sophisticated education will be even more important in the artificial intelligence world of tomorrow where AI may well have a deleterious impact on a range of highly skilled jobs across the whole economy.

Any workforce shortages have significant economic and social consequences including economic failure in particular localities and the need for substantial immigration to provide workers in key sectors.[14] For example, the current UK economy is suffering a deficiency of individuals with a sound grounding in STEM knowledge and skills, and a related paucity of high-level engineering graduates. For some professions, workforce planning requires a timeframe of decades and this is a major reason why countries, and so their governments, depend on an appropriate number of university graduates across a wide range of professions to populate the workforce in an optimal way.

A generation ago there was a broad acceptance that the main purpose for most students in going to university was to acquire an education at tertiary level that would include a more analytical and sophisticated mindset as well as specific professional training, if appropriate.

However, today there is an increasing view by many in government, notably in the UK, that the prime role of universities is to produce young people who fill 'graduate-level' jobs. These are defined in a highly technical way sometimes as crudely as by income at entry, rather than analytical or interactive skills or organising capacity, which are harder to quantify. We consider that the concept of 'graduate-level' jobs is difficult to define in a more intellectually valid way.

Such an approach can lead to an incredibly mediocre and simplistic, even dangerous and destructive, view that, if more graduates have been produced than are needed to fill so-called graduate-level jobs, too many people are going to university. This worldview sees universities simply as technical finishing schools, almost a sausage machine, which continue the school journey and churn young people out into the workforce.

The fact is that young people often take some years to find the career of their choice. When they graduate, they follow a range of journeys, not all of which are financially driven. For some time they may well do fairly unskilled jobs. This tends to generate populist headlines about 'graduates working in Costa' or 'graduate underemployment' that focus upon graduates who are in jobs that do not pay 'graduate salaries' or use 'graduate-level skills'.

This narrative fuels the argument for reducing university student numbers but the point of a university education is that it has increased individuals' degrees of freedom and the number of options they will have on their life journey. It should only be a good thing for society to have as many of its young people in this position.

This battle continues to be fought. One can only hope that the reductionists lose this battle to those with more insight and breadth.

Helping to form the new generation

Quite beyond the economic benefits of university education to both individuals and society as a whole, university education makes an absolutely fundamental contribution to the strengthening and development of a modern, liberal democratic society that empowers younger generations to take responsibility for, and build, the society of the future. From that point of view, the culture of universities is very important with a focus on debate, critical thinking and intellectual openness.

The extent to which this is true varies across societies around the world. There are many countries whose political systems and cultures could not accurately be described as 'liberal democratic' and that limit open discussion either directly or implicitly. There are others where study is strongly focused on, for example, the STEM subjects with a small or altogether absent focus upon the humanities and social sciences.

But whatever the nature of society, universities by their very nature challenge dominant cultures and doctrines as education, of whatever type, inevitably raises critical questions about the societies of which they are a part. Attempts to shut down dissent in universities, which a number of totalitarian regimes have sought to do at various times in history, have eventually been doomed to failure since the economic necessity of educated people cannot be isolated from the society as a whole. In addition, the necessarily international nature of academic study erodes the grip of any regime insulated from the rest of the world. And these challenges are not restricted to totalitarian regimes, as the histories of French universities in 1968 and US universities throughout the Vietnam war clearly demonstrate.

This approach ought also to guide universities' international contacts. Such contacts inevitably mean that universities work in countries that do not follow a Western model of democracy and human rights. This can throw up difficult working challenges, for example in relation to the position of women in Saudi Arabia, freedom to publish in China or restrictions on research in other countries. And some argue that universities should never work in countries where there are serious human rights violations, and so promote an approach based on boycott.

We do not share that view. All educational organisations, and indeed others, face the same challenges. But the university mission and core values are central and it is vital to ensure that they are applied, as they have been, in the work that universities do around the world. The underlying principles have to be set out, understood and defended as clearly and unambiguously as possible, even when it can seem difficult to do so, and of course that is usually the case.

But the extension of educational opportunity and the raising of education standards in every country represents an expression of the liberal values that are at the heart of the university. The wider extension of educational contacts, and development of educational capacity and critical thinking, is of itself a significant contribution to weakening the grip of oppressive and restrictive regimes of a variety of types. On that basis, such contact should be strongly supported.

This vital role of universities in strengthening democratic and human values as well as fundamental individual freedoms makes it particularly important that universities in their academic and educational practice protect and seek to extend the democratic values that are at their core. As they form the new generation, it is essential that these values are maintained and strengthened. In the same way that universities have the duty to build the capacity and competence of students to make independent and informed judgments and not to be swept along by ignorant and misleading 'fake news', they have to inculcate the values of freedom and democracy.

And the best way to do that is to try to ensure that society is comprised of a well-educated and broadly thinking citizenship, a citizenship who can understand the great issues of the time and make considered and meaningful contributions that may influence those around them.

This encompasses a citizenship able to contribute to the political discussion in their countries around both local issues and the global grand challenges so important to us all in the years ahead. A citizenship who understand the importance of civic contributions themselves and volunteering and generosity as a part of their life journey. This is, of course, not only a university responsibility but any university worth its salt should work actively to strengthen these dimensions in its students.

From this point of view, tertiary education is a huge change agent for the better not just for the individual but also for the nation. One just has to look at the quality of public discourse in nations with reasonably high proportions of graduates to those with very few university graduates (who inevitably have a small middle class and a large and poorly educated working or peasant class). This used to be the situation in the West and is no longer so. All countries in the world are somewhere on this trajectory.

So, in short, the widely held acknowledgement of the clear link between a well-educated workforce and national prosperity is not enough. The strong national contribution of universities is about much more than a precise alignment between the numbers of graduating students and those who fill graduate-level jobs. The full university contribution is a much richer and more complex proposition in terms of building nations.

Values, free speech and democracy

In this context, it is absolutely vital that universities maintain these fundamental democratic values, however difficult that sometimes seems. And, in recent years, there has been increasing concern about threats to free speech and democracy in universities as extreme groups of different descriptions try to enforce their own anti-democratic values upon the wider university.

In the UK, for example, successive Universities Ministers expressed concern. In December 2017, Jo Johnson MP claimed that books were being removed from libraries, 'undermining the principle of free speech'. The Department for Education was concerned that books by Holocaust denier David Irving were being moved within two university libraries. In February

2018. Johnson's successor, Sam Gyimah MP, warned of a 'creeping culture of censorship' on university campuses.

In March 2018, The Joint Parliamentary Committee on Human Rights published the report of its Enquiry[15] into 'Freedom of Speech in Universities'. The report rightly asserted that universities must, within the law, be places of 'open and uncensored debate' and highlighted concerns that 'intolerant attitudes' threaten free speech in universities and could result in stopping free debate. Red tape, 'excessive caution' and confusion over what is permissible are as much of a problem as banning controversial speakers. The Committee's Chair, Harriet Harman, said: 'Students must respect the right of other students to say things, no matter how unpleasant, offensive or insulting. They can protest, but they can't stop them.'[16]

In response to these concerns, in October 2018, the BBC published a survey,[17] to which 120 universities responded, about books being removed from libraries, changes to courses and speakers being cancelled.

It turned out that, since 2010, there had been no instances of books being removed or banned and there had been seven student complaints about course content being in some way offensive or inappropriate, most of which had been rectified.

Sixteen universities had received formal complaints about speakers and nine events in all were cancelled including with controversial Islamic cleric Haitham al-Haddad, prominent professor Tariq Ramadan and a planned mayoral debate. The debate was due to include panel representation from the National Front and BNP and was cancelled because of planned demonstrations that caused 'concerns for student, staff and public safety'.

Feminist writer Germaine Greer and LGBT rights campaigner Peter Tatchell both delivered talks despite complaints about their presence. There have been cases – like those of YouTuber Sargon of Akkad and Maryam Namazie – where talks at London universities have been interrupted by protesters or hecklers.

Universities tend to have external speaker policies for any event taking place on campus, even ones hosted by students or unions. The problem comes if anticipated protests lead to events being cancelled, as has happened on a small number of occasions, or if fear of protest puts off people from booking potentially controversial speakers in the first place.

Six organisations are on the National Union of Students' (NUS) official 'no platform list': al-Muhajiroun, British National Party (BNP), English

Defence League (EDL), Hizb-ut-Tahir, Muslim Public Affairs Committee and National Action.

These issues are complicated because, though there is already a duty on the higher education sector to secure free speech within the law, universities have other legal duties that can come into conflict with their duty to secure free speech. In particular, they must have 'due regard to the need to prevent people from being drawn into terrorism' under the Prevent strategy – part of the government's counter-terror laws. They also have a duty of care to students and staff.

We believe that the government was wrong to have included universities in the Counter-Terrorism and Security Act 2015 because of the danger that interpretation of that legislation can seriously inhibit freedom of speech in universities. Among others, Baroness Manningham-Buller, the former Head of MI5, opposed this aspect of the legislation.

Arising from these concerns, guidance[18] on these matters was produced in February 2019 by the Equality and Human Rights Commission, with input from the National Union of Students, Universities UK, Charity Commission for England and Wales, Office for Students, Independent HE, Guild HE, Commission for Countering Extremism and Home Office. The guidance is designed to set out the legal rights and obligations to help protect lawful free speech on campuses. Both the outcome and the process by which it was agreed seem to us the right way to approach this difficult issue and make it clear that universities can and should robustly protect freedom of speech on their campuses. This has to be a high university priority and there should be no weaknesses in conceding to the threats of those who want to close down open discussion and debate.

In a similar way, it is very important for universities to be robust about ensuring open academic debate about history, including in areas that are rightly bound to be controversial, such as the history and ethics of the British Empire or of slavery. There are, of course, difficult areas such as the historic funding of universities and physical representations of their past. In our opinion, they are best addressed by open discussion of the history and practical commitment to a present and future which fully respects all human rights and values, rather than conceding to those who effectively want to suggest that the history never happened.

We have addressed these issues in a UK context but believe they also need consideration in all countries. As we say above, there are significant different challenges in different countries where the history and culture vary substantially.

Teaching

The quality of teaching and pastoral care is central to success in the fields that we have addressed in this chapter. We have emphasised the responsibility of universities to work actively to prepare their students for the changing world. This applies both in the narrow economic sense and in the broader sense of providing an education in which teaching, pastoral guidance and welfare are exceptionally important.

This is why, in Chapter 4, we emphasise the teaching role of universities and argue that this needs to be given real priority, which we do not consider to be the case in all universities. It is obviously the case that the teaching challenges vary very significantly between students of different kinds, where social and educational background, intellectual capacity, learning location, aspiration and experience, and language may often be very different and require very different teaching approaches.

Along with the higher level of commitment that is required, more research is needed into the best forms of teaching for different students in different circumstances, which then needs to be applied.

We support the pressure that governments are applying to get universities to focus upon their teaching quality, though we acknowledge that a great deal of work is still needed to find the kinds of metric and feedback that will genuinely raise standards. We address some of these issues in Chapter 4 and it is sufficient here to argue that the Teaching Excellence and Student Outcomes Framework (TEF) needs continued development and improvement, but not resistance.

Even more than the cost of university education, we think that students are looking for the highest quality support in their learning journey at university, so that they maximise the benefit they get from their course. And their success in that respect is also the best outcome for society as a whole.

Conclusion

This chapter has been more descriptive of the circumstances in which universities find themselves than a series of policy recommendations. However:

Governments should commit to continuing to expand university education opportunities, particularly to those from the lower socio-economic groups, and continue to review the steps that would enable better access to university from all sections of society, including student grants for some groups, better university–school relationships and strong access programmes. These programmes should be particularly targeted at the lowest socio-economic groups.

Universities should strengthen the quality of their teaching and pastoral care for all students.

They should develop strong university/FE college/school relationships with substantial exchange of people.

They should develop access and pre-university courses of a variety of types to encourage successful applications from a wide range of society and develop admissions policies and financial programmes to incentivise access from the poorest communities.

They should examine their admissions criteria with a view to encouraging applications at a variety of points in life, for example from mature students. These could include more deferred entry arrangements so that students develop wider post-school experience before going to university.

They should be vigorous in defending their democratic and rights culture and they should extend and develop their international relationships with universities around the world.

Chapter 7

Education is for life

Why education for life matters

Charles first came across lifelong learning when visiting an Open University summer school in 1974. Its vitality and exuberance illustrated the importance and potential of education for people later in life. Shortly before that, he had taught a couple of Workers Education courses and then maths on a Fresh Horizons course at the City Literary Institute in London, to help enable people who hadn't done well at school to get university opportunities.

With responsibility for education technology as a junior Education Minister in 1998, he then saw the development of MOOCs as emerging educational options, although they had some issues with regard to assessment and business models.

After 2010, he worked with the Open University both on its development of the Future Learn partnerships with a range of UK universities and on its plans to sell OU courses internationally. And he saw a little of the efforts of the Royal College of General Practitioners to develop an e-GP online continuous professional development resource for GPs, available throughout their working lives, and also internationally.

More recently, he has seen the inspirational programmes being developed by Arizona State University to create online degree-level education transforming the life opportunities of people from a wide variety of educational backgrounds.

Some of the most exhilarating moments in his educational life have come from meeting people who have fulfilled educational achievements by using their application and creativity for different purposes.

Those lifelong learning opportunities matter immensely in improving people's lives.

Introduction

One constant in the long history of universities in both East and West has been that their primary role has been the advanced education of young people which, as we discussed in Chapter 2, is even more enduring and consistent than their role in research.

We are certain that universities will continue to have this key role of educating school leavers and preparing them for the next stage of their life. In some ways, it is the raison d'être for having universities at all. It is their core business and principal source of funding.

It is also a role that universities understand how to perform well. As we describe elsewhere, there are of course strengths and weaknesses and the research commitment in some universities is a constant magnet, attracting academic staff away from their teaching mission to some degree or another. But, fundamentally, universities do a good job.

In future decades, universities will continue to hold the responsibility of educating young people well at the start of their adult lives. But, in the next few years, universities are going to need to provide a significant parallel education that will become almost as important as their purpose of educating school leavers. That is to offer opportunities of lifelong learning for hundreds of millions of people. This is, of course, an absolutely enormous challenge, but one that we believe will be very difficult for universities to side-step.

There is a plethora of issues, opportunities and challenges in this sphere. This chapter discusses these, as well as the ways in which they could transform how universities work and the arguments that universities face in being able to meet these challenges.

We begin with the fundamental reasons why the challenges of lifelong learning cannot be evaded, then describe the different types of learning that people may be looking for, the ways in which that education might become available and the sorts of courses that will be available. We finish by looking at what will be a highly contested marketplace, at whether universities will be flexible and adaptable enough to offer what is wanted, at the ways in which technological change will constrain options and at the diverse educational provision that will emerge.

Getting older in a time of rapid change

To start at the beginning, life expectancy is undoubtedly the key driver. In the Middle Ages when universities began, you were quite lucky to live to the age of 40. Mastery of one trade was all that could be hoped for and, in any case, universities then were devoted, in the main, to theology. Otto Von Bismarck, the iron Chancellor, is remembered by history as the creator of modern Germany. It is often forgotten that education was one of the key priorities and social policy strengths of the German Reich, which he built in the last quarter of the 19th century, drawing from the Prussian tradition. His model was very envied at the time and since. We have already discussed the birth of the modern research university in Berlin. There is a story, almost certainly apocryphal, where the Chancellor is reported as having seen large numbers of disabled veterans on the streets of Berlin. He wanted to do something more for them and asked an assistant to make enquiries of the eminent medical people of the day as to how long someone might reasonably be expected to live if they avoided infectious disease and the like. The answer that came back was 65 and so Bismarck set the retirement age in Germany at 65 and a small state pension followed. Many other countries followed that lead, with, if anything, a tendency to bring the age down a little with increasing national affluence. What answer might Chancellor Bismarck have been given today?

Life expectancy varies a little from country to country but, in affluent economies, it is in the high 70s for men and around 80 years for women. If one excludes individuals who die as a result of trauma, incurable cancer or other causes at a younger age and look at people who've reached the age of 60 in good health, the likelihood is that the great majority will live well into their 80s. If one looks at young people today with improvements in medical technology, average life expectancy is in the 90s. This increased longevity alone will, naturally, considerably increase the percentage of older individuals in a country.

In demographic terms, there is an additional factor, whose significance varies from country to country. It has long been known that with increased affluence comes a strong tendency to have fewer children. The drivers for this are well understood and are related in part to the economic costs of rearing children in affluent societies, the tendency to have two working parents, and the desire for women to pursue their own careers. Add to this the baby boomer demographic bulge working through many countries and we have the top-heavy age distribution well recognised in countries such as France and Japan and, at one time, the UK. Some countries have responded to this by more open immigration policies. The UK and others such as Japan have tried to restrict the entry of young people from other nationalities which has, of course, exacerbated the ageing demographic. In China, this is more marked than almost anywhere because of the one child policy which was enforced vigorously until very recent times. The population sums in China illustrate this point very strongly in that in a family group one has four grandparents, two parents and just one child. The consequences in terms of a progressive trend to having a higher percentage of older people in the community are obvious. In pure economic terms, it becomes increasingly difficult for the smaller subset of the population who are working to support an increasingly large non-working and ageing demographic.

In these circumstances, it can be seen that what applied in Bismarck's Germany, and has held true for over 130 years since, is no longer sustainable. In purely economic terms, almost uniform retirement in the mid-60s or even earlier (as in France, for example) is unsustainable.

Let's turn to personal preference. It is true that many people look forward to retirement and to some decades of reduced responsibility in a work sense. Many others do not: they are still vigorous and performing well at the normal retirement age and would like to continue working. In response to this, national retirement ages started to rise in countries such as the UK and Australia. Even in France, where the retirement age was lower, it is likely to start to rise again, though of course this is strongly contested. Those involved in private enterprise, especially those who run their own businesses or work in the professions, are likely to work for a longer period often well into their 70s.

An ageing demographic, with an economic need for more elderly people to participate in the workforce for longer periods and an increasing number of healthy individuals in their 60s who wish to continue working, has big implications for education and for universities in particular.

In the simplest formulation, a young person leaving tertiary education in their early 20s is likely to live into their 90s, may not retire until well into their 70s, so will have a working life of 50 or more years. Many will have two or three careers and it is likely that universities will play a key role in re-educating them at these transitional points. In that education for new challenges they will not require the co-curricular or extracurricular activities so important in an on-campus undergraduate education today and for family and financial reasons they are likely to need to continue to participate in the workforce while undertaking further education.

At the same time as these important demographic changes, fundamental transformations in the basic skills needed for both work and leisure are taking place with increasing rapidity. Whatever the ultimate impact of artificial intelligence upon the overall work/leisure balance in society as a whole, and at different ages, there is absolutely no doubt that, as we discuss in Chapter 3 in particular, people will need to acquire the skills and broader understanding to be able to live their lives to the full and take advantage of increasing opportunities of many different types.

This helps us to understand the nature of the education that people will increasingly look for at various stages throughout their life. This education will be undertaken for a number of reasons, of which the most important will probably be:

- **continuous professional development**, to improve individual knowledge and skills in a professional environment that continues to change rapidly;
- **education to change career** to a new life path altogether;
- **personal educational interest and self-development**, to enable individuals to follow their interests.

And there are a number of fairly obvious features of the types of education that will develop to meet these needs:

- It will mostly be part-time rather than full-time.
- It will need to be accessed at a number of points in the chronological year, possible at any time, not simply in the conventional academic model.
- It will be far more effective if students can transfer previously acquired modules to become a building block for a new course, which requires universities to work together on issues of recognition.
- It will need to be available very flexibly to take account of working patterns.
- It may have a residential component, but may not.
- It will be offered in a variety of forms, such as online education, and it will become an increasingly prevalent part of university portfolios.
- It will use a range of learning platforms such as computers, and phones, just as the Open University originally did with television.

We now move on to discuss these various forms of lifelong learning, and what part, if any, universities will play in offering the education that will be taking place.

In this chapter, we do not discuss the various funding issues that arise for all these forms of education through life. We address these in Chapter 8, along with other issues of student finance.

Continuous professional development

Lifelong professional development is already quite common within several different occupations. It has been said that 10,000 hours of dedicated work after initial training are needed to completely master a complex profession. The opportunities to repeat that even in a long working life are few. Most people who change direction will move into an area where the skills and knowledge they have already acquired are very useful to them.

The earliest stage of these educational and professional challenges often comes directly after graduation with postgraduate master's and doctoral studies. These can be either full-time or part-time and very often have a significant residential component at a university.

Postgraduate master's qualifications are becoming increasingly important for a number of reasons. We have already mentioned the US model, which is robust and well developed, though more costly both in terms of students' time and financial cost.

The one-year master's offered in the UK by most universities, often immediately following undergraduate years, is the equivalent of an honours year in Scotland and in countries such as Australia and New Zealand and, in educational terms, can reasonably be regarded as an extended and deeper undergraduate degree. However, too often it is seen as the first year of a PhD qualification rather than as an independent one-year qualification in its own right, though of course it does provide an entrée to doctoral programmes for those who want to pursue this path.

Master's degrees taken after a period in the workforce typically represent a professional career repositioning rather than entry to an academic pathway.

The coursework master's, whether taken over one or two years, offers an opportunity to acquire real depth in a professional field or in the sub-specialty fields where the student already has a primary professional degree at undergraduate level.

This type of master's, whether delivered physically in person or remotely through e-education, will become increasingly important as it is taken at various times throughout a professional career. It is an important means of professional development and will become more common.

The PhD has been around for over a century and has been increasingly prevalent since the Second World War as the major route to academic life. It is no longer the case that the only real reason for doing a PhD is a desire to pursue an academic or research career. Many individuals undertaking doctoral studies do so because of the desire to acquire much deeper specialised knowledge or analytical skills in an area without an intention to pursue a long-term university career.

An increasing number wish to take the knowledge and personal skills they acquire in the course of their doctoral studies into the wider business world. It is interesting to look at the much higher percentage of university students undertaking doctoral studies in Germany when compared to the UK. In Germany, there is a much larger proportion of leaders in industry and in business with doctoral qualifications than in most other European countries. This may just be a merely cultural phenomenon but the overall success of the German economy in the past 25 years has been second to none when related to the size and natural resources of the country. Their approach may have much to commend it.

Beyond the early years after graduation there is a variety of approaches towards CPD.

In the life-long learning educational agenda, some types of knowledge have currency forever such as many aspects of human anatomy. Other aspects that were thought to be equally certain have been revised from time to time. In the 1860s, Lord Kelvin famously commented that Maxwell's equations brought conclusion to the knowledge journey of modern physics. Within a few years, quantum mechanics and relativity told a different story! Less dramatic examples of knowledge improvement and extension now abound in every discipline. In practical terms, this means that the currency of the knowledge base a student has when they graduate from university has a validity limited to just a few years and of course as time progresses this worsens.

It is common sense in medicine, for example, that a graduate who continued to practise without any regular refresher training would rapidly find their knowledge was out of date. In all occupations, but notably the professions, there are professional structures that regularly refresh knowledge. It is increasingly a formal requirement for registration that a practitioner meets update requirements. In the UK, in medicine, this is particularly well developed with the need for periodic reaccreditation of a very vigorous nature. The same is the case with lawyers, for example. But this is by no means true for all professions. Teachers, for example, whether at school or university level, are encouraged to develop their skills, but it is not a requirement, for example for promotion. Practice varies across all the professions, but we think that one thing that can be said with confidence is that the requirement for validated continuous professional development will become far greater over time, and will indeed extend to these professions internationally.

The involvement of universities in this important aspect of lifelong learning is very patchy but, if properly addressed as we think it should be, it is likely that this will increase – often in partnership with the professional bodies with whom universities normally already have good relations. This is an area again that lends itself to technology-enhanced learning approaches and we will continue to see new approaches in delivery particularly as technological change gathers pace.

Formal retraining of this type will become increasingly important at more than one point in life's journey.

Changes of career and 'late' entry into university-level education

For the reasons stated earlier – faster changes in the nature of work and longer lives – it will be increasingly common for individuals to want to change their career more frequently. Some of these changes may only be fairly marginal in comparison to their past lives but a lot will be very substantial.

So, for example, increased numbers are choosing to go into teaching or social care at a fairly late point in their lives after a career in something entirely different, perhaps after earning well for 25 years.

And there have always been 'mature students' seeking university degrees later in life than most as a result of some aspect of their own life experience. Great universities – notably Birkbeck College, London and the Open University – were founded with the needs of those who wanted a 'University of the Second Chance' very much in mind. In the US, a large number of universities offer a wide variety of online courses. They often recruit specially among those communities which, for reasons of socio-economic status or ethnicity, have little experience of university education, Over time, there will be still more demand for such 'Second Chances', and from students around the world.

The university system as a whole will undoubtedly continue to develop educational and professional training programmes that support and target career change later in life. More mature students do not necessarily need (or always appreciate!) the personal contact at a social level that comes from university engagement in the post-school years. An e-education approach is ideally suited to many mature students who are changing career. There is already a really major need for high-level university master's degrees, especially in the business space for people who seek to improve their job prospects after a reasonably long period in the workforce. In the past, and to some extent currently, these are students in their mid-30s, typically studying an MBA. An increasingly wide range of more specialised postgraduate offerings are now available for this demographic and for older people.

Further opportunities to develop new types of educational offerings to support work or career change at even later stages of life will undoubtedly develop. There are many current examples of this. We mention just two: firstly, there is a shortage of skilled maths teachers in many Western countries. Many individuals who have had careers in industry with engineering expertise have a high-level mathematical capacity. In some areas, programmes exist to train people with a high-level engineering background in secondary school teaching with a maths emphasis. And, secondly, nursing shortages exist in many Western countries. Accelerated nursing training for mature students who wish to move from another career is well developed in Australia and has led to a new cohort of nurses entering the profession in their 50s. There will be many more examples of this type in the years ahead.

For all of these cases, and many more with applications across the whole range of work and skills, and at different ages, education and training will be needed, usually with accredited qualifications, particularly if the individuals concerned want to work in those fields.

Personal educational interest and self-development

There is a third domain to lifelong learning where the UK has long been a leader. There is a strong demand across society for educational offerings in adult life that are not all work-related but relate to improvement in knowledge in areas of individual interest. This may range from learning a new language to historical or philosophical studies to almost any area of human knowledge. For those who wish to tackle and explore an area in real depth, the Open University in the UK, founded just over 50 years ago, has for many years been a seminal example to the world as to how well this can be done. It continues to thrive and similar models have been adopted in other countries across the world. Wikipedia lists over 60 'Open Universities' around the world, some of which have well-established relations with the UK's original version.

Undoubtedly, one key role is to offer university education to those who were not able to pursue it at a younger age for a variety of reasons, as discussed above. An equally valid role has been to offer new educational opportunities to adults who wish to strengthen their knowledge in a given area and are prepared to put in the hours of study necessary to obtain a university degree. This undoubtedly overlaps with the re-education of an ageing population referred to earlier in this chapter but recognises the validity of a university experience for life enhancement as well as for career development.

Sometimes, 'adult education' can be disparaged as 'flower-arranging' or 'basket-weaving' and, over the years, it has gradually seen its resourcing reduced as governments have focused upon using limited resources to support more vocationally focused education and training. The often difficult arguments around funding these activities illustrate the need for clear thinking about the costs and benefits of different forms of adult education provision, particularly at university level.

Of course a major distinguishing aspect of this personal education, in contrast to further learning for professional or career change reasons, is that the formal qualification may be less important. And one result of this is that educational resources in this area can overlap with other forms of learning.

For example, many people use MOOCs of a variety of kinds to educate themselves, for example through Future Learn,[1] a partnership between the Open University and a range of UK universities to provide free online courses. And many US universities similarly provide online courses, some of which are free. These are all obviously available throughout the world and cover an enormous range of subjects.

And to even larger audiences, TV programmes like David Attenborough's *Blue Planet*[2] and Brian Cox's *The Planets* are produced in co-operation with, and with the involvement of, academics from the Open University. And they include education elements that viewers can follow up on to develop their knowledge if they've been excited by the programme. TV dramas like *Victoria* or *The Crown*, also viewed by millions, give rise to controversies about their historical accuracy and raise questions about 'fake history' and 'fake news'. For viewers, these pose real dilemmas to which broader access to education may well provide an important answer.

And of course there is a wide range of commercial learning materials, covering a wide range of subjects from language learning to practical skills, which clearly meet an educational need.

It is not at all straightforward for universities to determine what their role is in this marketplace, to which we now return.

Requirements of a lifelong learning agenda

Taken together, these three areas – lifelong learning in a professional sense, education for several careers, and the development of new areas of knowledge for personal interest – form the core of a lifelong learning framework highly relevant to universities.

As society realigns itself and continues to move remorselessly from a model where learning – whether at school or at university – is done in the younger years, and knowledge acquisition and learning becomes manifestly a lifelong process, this area will grow enormously in importance over future decades.

To some extent, this has always been the case but we consider that this fundamental though gradual shift has not been reflected clearly in individual or societal thinking and this will change dramatically within the next 20 years. Universities already need to change dramatically their attitudes to lifelong education and the need for this will intensify sharply in the coming years.

So we now move to some general issues that are likely to be important in the lifelong learning world in the years ahead.

Perhaps the major change agent in this whole area will be the nature of knowledge itself. Or, more precisely, how knowledge is stored and accessed. It is already clear that, in most disciplines, the core university undergraduate education teaches core principles and an ability to access and explore a vast and constantly changing knowledge base.

It is interesting to look back at how knowledge has been accessed historically at different stages of university development and to speculate on where this may go in the future.

In medieval times, the limited knowledge that existed was transcribed by monks onto vellum and was available to a handful of individuals who either lived in monasteries or had to travel considerable distances to access it. Prior to the information age, the discovery of the printing press was the seminal event in knowledge transmission. William Caxton and colleagues printed books that spread rapidly throughout Europe and across the globe. The accelerating effect that this had on human intellectual development, including on the rise of the High Enlightenment, cannot be underestimated.

But in recent years there has, of course, been a development in knowledge transmission which considerably exceeds that brought by the printing press and this is accelerating. The internet and all the things that go around it have fundamentally altered the nature of how knowledge is stored, accessed and used. We are in the midst of this process and its magnitude is not yet necessarily apparent but, when one steps back and looks at the potential of the technologies, the implications are vast.

The relationship between the educator, the lifelong learner and the massive electronic knowledge base that is constantly growing ever more accessible through the internet or its successors will define how lifelong learning evolves in the decades to come in ways that are difficult to predict.

Knowledge as content has already become more accessible and less memory-based than it was because it is so easy to look something up on one's smart phone, tablet or laptop. New advances in technology are likely to bring this even closer to individuals with transmission of knowledge through auditory devices or optical attachments which with increasing computing power should provide rapid access to almost any aspect of content knowledge the individual wishes to access at a given point in time. The university and the university educator will become increasingly important in a world of this type in providing clear signposts – context and guidance – rather than knowledge itself. The role of educators becomes to shape the analytical skillset and creative mindset needed to readily utilise knowledge in a knowledge-rich world.

Advances in technology contribute to new pedagogy but do not in themselves underpin new educational paradigms. Intellectual context and guidance will continue to be as important as it ever has been in a lifelong learning paradigm. New technologies will enhance and enrich this rather than replace it.

We pose some questions looking very much to the future. If most of us think back to our youth, there was a time when school and learning was a little like taking castor oil! It was something one did that was at times a little unpleasant to ensure a bright future. The majority of students acquire increasing self-satisfaction in the acquisition of new skills and knowledge quite early in the school years. Some very lucky people have it from the beginning. The type of family they grow up in clearly has something to do with this. Those who succeed academically certainly both take pride in and enjoy their studies. This mindset carries most through the first degree, the bachelor's years, if they progress to university education.

After that, it becomes more complicated. For some, further study, usually at a university, may be a life option, though there is always something of a tradeoff between work and study, especially when this can imply considerable personal expense in the form of tuition fees. The emotional boost that comes with further self-development may be enough to lead an adult student into graduate studies. For many, a desire for self-betterment is manifest more realistically through improved career options and it is this that drives their postgraduate study. Self-development and employment benefits have to be balanced against opportunity costs both in income and in other opportunities.

Ideally, lifelong learning occurs in an environment where it is part and parcel of everyday life in terms of both intense and lengthy periods of study that may occur only a few times in an individual's life and a daily exposure to new knowledge as part of the life journey. As our world becomes more and more knowledge-based and as knowledge becomes richer and ever easier to access, this is an almost inevitable part of the human journey.

Delivering lifelong learning

The methodologies that support lifelong learning have already been alluded to but let's delve into them a little more deeply. Already, we can see two contrasting approaches for those who wish to pursue taught master's studies at a mature age. The first involves in person physical attendance at the university where courses will be run with the term/semester structure not so different from the undergraduate experience. Points will be accumulated from a range of modules that lead to the award of a master's diploma. Students will attend, with a cohort of other students, lectures and tutorials and submit assignments in a rigid temporal framework.

In some countries, including the US, Australia and most of continental Europe as well as China, taught master's of this type will almost always involve two years of full-time study. In English universities, a tradition evolved long ago of a one-year master's offering.[3] Typically, this follows immediately after a three-year undergraduate degree and represents what would be regarded in Australia and Scotland as an honours year, seen as an opportunity to deepen studies in a particular subject and often as a lead-in to doctoral studies. The one-year master's model has also been widely implemented in England as the structure for master's programmes offered to more mature students. In MBA programmes across a range of countries, the one-year model is prevalent although the great American universities still adhere to a two-year model, even for MBAs.

It is self-evident that there are a number of issues in taking long periods of time out of the workforce for taught master's programmes, especially the two-year programmes, that may limit access even for students who are very attracted to the idea of postgraduate study. In the business education world, this has been long recognised and new approaches developed. Many business schools offer executive MBA programmes that can be taken through a number of much shorter periods of study, typically with very intense study of around a month in three or four blocks spread over two years. INSEAD,[4] just outside Paris, is an exemplar with its senior executive MBA programmes where modules can be taken on a number of physical sites in different countries. Such programmes are, of course, extremely expensive for the university to deliver and student fees are high.

The alternative to the one- or two-year highly structured course is offered through online education courses. Some university courses, developed through distance learning, are offered in a broadly similar structure to those where students attend the campuses in person. That is, students are taken through in a cohort in a fixed term structure, an academic model that is much easier for academic and professional staff to service.

Most universities that do this will have more entry points, typically at least four a year rather than one that pertains for their undergraduate operations. These approaches, however, lend themselves to a much greater degree of flexibility where students can enroll at any time and with considerable flexibility as to the rate of progression with progress based on completion of assessed work and acquired skills rather than a rigid term structure. The advantages of this for mature students are self-evident.

The preferred delivery structures for the two other key domains of lifelong learning – learning for personal development and interest and learning to maintain professional effectiveness and accreditation – have rather different drivers for the form of delivering learning. More flexibility is clearly desirable for the majority of potential students in this setting and for lifelong learning, and various forms of open university course structure can work very well.

For professional refreshment and reaccreditation, short courses with physical attendance are very useful and give the opportunity for peer interactions, which are an important part of a professional rejuvenation. The bulk of activity in this area is best delivered in a way where the professional student can undertake activities at the time that suits them best and accrue credit over a long period. Typically, this type of professional ongoing education takes part in blocks and covers some years and includes a range of activities: completion of short courses, journal reading, conference attendance among them. In both these domains of lifelong learning, flexibility is a crucial advantage.

Future choices

We now look to the future and pose four questions, the answers to which may determine the extent to which the university sector is a key player in the lifelong learning world going ahead.

1 What will the marketplace be?

How will the lifelong learning marketplace evolve over the next two decades? In Marketing 101 studies or MBA studies, the student is taught very early in the marketing module about the concept of market segment and of competing activities. The lifelong learning area can be considered as a series of very separate activities, each of which will be dominated by players of a different type. In this mindset, formal master's programmes may be the preserve of universities and other aspects of lifelong learning could be covered by other players. The market segmentation for a burger chain revolves around issues like, who are the competitors? The next question then might expand competition outside the fast-food space to include supermarkets that increasingly specialise in ready meals. The lecturer's point is always to encourage the student to think broadly, at least in initial formulation of business plans.

As we have discussed above, it is clear that there is a considerable overlap in the technologies and approaches in delivering lifelong learning for all consumer segments, and that skills learnt in interacting with one market segment will be relevant to others. It is even more clear that flexibility in delivery options provides a crucial advantage in the marketplace. The academic prestige and brand of the delivering organisation has long given the university sector big advantages. Branding matters at least as much in education as in any other field. There is no reason why different operators offering high quality, flexible options that meet market demand effectively cannot become extremely well regarded in the future, particularly if their offering is built on the quality of the teaching model, as opposed to the reputation for high quality research.

We've seen the beginnings of this approach through private university providers in the main in recent years. Increasingly flexible, technology-enabled and high quality approaches are almost inevitable in the years ahead as this market of global lifelong learning continues to grow. If one looks at how flexible educational offerings and approaches have become increasingly prominent in this space over the past 10 years, the future direction seems clear. In start-up businesses exploring new space, some failures are inevitable. Some of the early ventures into this space have not gone well but others are thriving. Entrepreneurial individuals who are thinking laterally about building businesses in the lifelong learning domain abound at the moment and we would expect them to thrive.

2 How adaptable will universities be?

Will the university sector have the adaptability to be the major player in the lifelong learning space? It is clear that many types of organisation will contribute to this massive arena. Professional bodies such as Royal Colleges have a major role in overseeing maintenance of professional standards and periodic reaccreditation. E-education generally has seen a number of new entrants over the past 10 years. Some of these aspire to and have become private universities such as the University of Phoenix (which has had mixed fortunes). Others, such as the Laureate group in the US which has been a pioneer in e-education covering a number of community needs, are built on a private university model which has more flexibility and more ingrained entrepreneurial strengthen in its DNA than any public institution. Major private corporations such as Kaplan are increasingly active in this space. It remains to be seen whether there will be calls for more regulation of these private providers beyond the usual consumer protection legislation.

In short, already there is no shortage of competition for established universities and no doubt this will increase. The increased flexibility that non-traditional providers bring to an arena where flexibility of delivery is perhaps the single most important market advantage between high quality offerings may be very important. Major well-established universities have started to form partnerships with commercial educational entities. Such joint ventures theoretically bring the huge academic firepower of a large academic community together with commercial activities that are business savvy in developing and growing markets in the lifelong learning space. Pearson, the massive international education business and publisher, has developed a large business in this space in recent years and is partnering with a number of universities including Arizona State University, King's College London and Monash University in Australia among others. This type of joint venture is already showing considerable success in attracting and graduating high quality students.

Whether the traditional giants in the university sector will have enough entrepreneurial spirit and inherent flexibility to compete effectively in this growing market is still an open question, as is their desire to do so. Undoubtedly, universities will have a major role in taught master's for mature students in the years ahead. Their academic firepower and brand ensure that. It is likely that private provision supported by new pedagogy may increasingly challenge university domination in this space unless universities can find a way to become more flexible and market-attuned than they are at the moment.

In Harvard Business School terms, universities are par excellence institutions of supply rather than institutions of demand. Put simply, they offer a product and it is there for potential students to take it or leave it. They have not traditionally been terribly adept at understanding their markets and developing specific products to meet market need. This is starting to change, especially in institutions that have traditionally been universities of recruitment (that is they have to proactively seek out students in the marketplace), rather than universities of selection (institutions that are fortunate enough to have many potential students apply for each available space) but there is a long way to go in a conservative sector where the rules have been set by institutions rather than the marketplace, though business schools have already been doing this for a long time.

It is relevant to note here that the market for lifelong learning courses varies in different countries, even where they speak the same language. And so a university that desires to market its courses internationally has to decide whether it is ready to invest to offer courses that vary slightly, but significantly, in different countries even in subjects where the fundamental core of knowledge is pretty internationally similar.

One major and relatively underused asset that universities possess is their alumni networks. These have been better developed, principally for fundraising purposes, in the US but other universities across the world are using these increasingly effectively for the same reason and to try to build their own endowments. However, these are also the natural market for lifelong learning opportunities, whether segmented into the particular professional disciplines or more generally. This would also provide universities with a genuine income stream for a particular product of benefit to their former students.

This approach would also transform the university–alumnus relationship from being simply one of fundraising and philanthropy to one in which universities see themselves as supporting their alumni, educationally speaking, throughout their professional and personal lives. They would obviously charge for this service but the identification that many alumni have with their alma mater could well be a very positive relationship.

3 How rapidly will technological development challenge current delivery models?

This is a moot question and has been touched on a little in earlier chapters. It has several aspects. We have already mentioned the question as to whether university campuses will survive in a physical sense. This depends quite a lot on how the information world develops but it is likely that the physical campus is here to stay, especially for undergraduate students. Where a university is based physically is but a small part of the technological question. Probably more important is how the personal interface of not only students but the community at large develops with the information world.

We're not that far away from the situation where auditory information can be transmitted directly to an ear device and an LED screen incorporated in a glasses frame can access visual information, both inputs being connected to the internet and to a verbal command interface. Within a few years, any of us will be able to ask our own computational infrastructure connected to internet-facilitated mega computing facilities in the cloud almost anything we like at any time. This could include real-time language translation, for example. This type of technology is already available and, as light follows dark, will be widely marketed and implemented over the next few years.

Just look back at what has happened over the past 20 years. Mobile phones only came in in the 1990s. They've been followed by MP3 players and tablets supported by increasingly sophisticated software. There is more intellectual effort devoted to this area than almost any other. Countless thousands of start-ups are concentrating in this technology space. Sophisticated software is being written related to almost every aspect of improvement in communications, including increased facilitation of access by relatively unsophisticated users. It is inevitable that this will impact profoundly on how education is delivered and knowledge is accessed in the decades ahead.

It is certainly difficult to see the large lecture with 500 undergraduate students in one room surviving this technological tsunami but one could envisage hundreds of students engaged simultaneously in one module on campus at the same time. Some might be sitting in a coffee shop, others might be sitting on the grass enjoying the sunshine, and still others might be at home enjoying a morning coffee or spending some time with relatives on the other side of the world. They could all be accessing the same material at the same time and have the ability to ask questions and interact intellectually with the lecturer.

This is just one example of many technological and pedagogical changes that will affect the university world in the years ahead and that will have relevance to lifelong learning as well as to current undergraduate experiences. As each advance occurs, the opportunity for new competitors to challenge the university sector's traditional preeminence will increase.

4 How diverse will education provision be for the lifelong market?

This is, perhaps, the $64,000 question. If the market is allowed to develop in an unrestrained way, the range and type of providers in the lifelong learning space will continue to rise exponentially. The volume of the business will grow in all of its aspects as discussed earlier in this chapter. Success will favour the innovator and those who bring high quality offerings to market in a flexible and user-friendly way. The university sector is replete with high quality teachers but has done relatively poorly in terms of flexibility and market responsiveness in improving its pedagogy in a way that meets potential mature student demands and that takes full advantage of technological advances.

Joint ventures between established universities and full commercial partners will help keep universities in this space mainly because of the academic credibility of university qualifications. A willingness by universities to become more entrepreneurial around their educational models is inevitable and is already under way. So much of the capacity for educational delivery in the lifelong learning space is held by universities with their incredibly rich academic bodies and with professional staff who understand how education is supported and delivered.

It is very likely that the moves towards increasing flexibility in delivery and core structure, already seen in many universities, will accelerate and keep universities reasonably competitive in the postgraduate-taught master's degree space. This, of course, involves ensuring that an offering in this form meets market demand when real alternatives are likely to materialise soon. In other aspects of lifelong learning, most universities have been peripheral players. Professional reaccreditation has largely been neglected by the university world.

Other than the Open University and very limited access to individual university modules by mature students, universities have largely neglected the lifelong learning for personal development equation for the population at large in the UK. In other countries, they tend to have done even less.

If one goes back to the old marketeer's stance, the concern, if the university world loses both of these markets comprehensively, is that the players who come to dominate them will start to eat into universities' traditional domination of other areas of postgraduate education. Increased richness of provision is probably an ideal outcome for society at large and, undoubtedly, universities will adapt and continue to be one of the major players in a very rich lifelong learning milieu.

Conclusion

Universities, as major custodians, creators and transmitters of knowledge, have the opportunity to be at the heart of the innovation and human capital development of the knowledge economy. In the field of lifelong education they therefore have the choice to be either the central player or one of a number of key players. But they may also be entirely peripheral if they fail to understand the process of change and the opportunities that it offers them. The coming years will reveal how well they have taken the opportunity and so strengthened society. This all comes back to the four pillars[5] that are pivotal to universities' raison d'être in the modern world and in particular the third, *Educating and training to high quality the specialist workers*, and fourth, *Creating a general intellectually engaging climate and culture across societies*.

In the evolving world of the 21st century, these pillars are going to become ever bigger in a purely business sense. Already, the world's biggest companies are tech companies concerned with communication. Their journey to engagement in all aspects of the knowledge world has already begun. Universities will have to rapidly adapt. We also believe that effective partnerships have a real role to play in maximising the human resources of society and so:

Governments should work with universities to develop a national framework within which lifelong learning can be promoted. This will include new approaches to funding lifelong learning, engagement with the professional educational organisations and frameworks of recognition of modules and qualifications from other universities in order to stimulate further study on the basis of prior qualifications.

Universities should work with employers and professional organisations to promote postgraduate courses, qualifications and degrees that can be taken up throughout life post-university. They should consider how they could provide flexible courses to assist those considering career changes and they should consider what lifelong education services they could provide for their alumni and for their local communities.

Chapter 8

Who pays for it all?

Why does it matter who pays for it all?

Both Charles and Ed have grappled with this issue, from different perspectives, Charles as the Secretary of State who put in place the UK's new system in 2003 and Ed as President of two large universities which recognised the potential inequities arising from unduly low government contributions but with an overriding concern for the financial security of the universities. Many find themselves in this position and so face such dilemmas.

Any university leader is bound to be focused on the viability of their institution and, as we discuss in Chapter 9, one important quality for any Vice-Chancellor or President is to place their university onto the strong and sustainable financial footing which truly allows universities, and all associated with them, to fulfil their potential. And in the political arena the subject arouses strong passions.

In 2003, during the discussions about tuition fees, Charles was challenged by one student leader in a debate, to widespread applause, 'If you were a true socialist you wouldn't ask students to pay tuition fees. To which Charles responded, 'If I were a true socialist I'd be putting all the government's education money into nursery and primary schools, since that's where investment has the greatest chance of transforming the lives and opportunities of the poorest in society.'

It was Aneurin Bevan who said in 1949 that 'The language of priorities is the religion of socialism'. That truth runs right through the core of the debate about who should pay for high quality universities that are doing their job well. And explains why people get so fired up about the subject and why it matters in so many different ways.

Introduction

The subject of university finance is both highly politically controversial and very complex. Everyone has a view, and many are purist in their view.

This debate is fundamentally about the proportion of university spending that should be paid for by the state, by students themselves (or their parents on their behalf), or by employers, and in what proportions.

The final outcome, which varies surprisingly widely between countries, determines the vitality of university finances and so the quality of universities' work and their ability to fulfil their responsibilities well. It determines important issues about the affordability of university education for individuals and influences the key issues of independence and control which are at the heart of university life.

This chapter will look at these issues from the angle of each of the three potential university funders. We will focus upon undergraduate teaching and learning, and comment upon funding for lifelong learning. The rather different series of questions raised by funding for research is addressed in Chapter 4.

In any country, the society itself, individual students and employers are all, in different ways, the beneficiaries of a high quality system of higher education. A good case can be made for each of these beneficiaries to make a contribution to the costs of a higher education system which needs adequate and resilient finances if a vicious circle of declining standards leading to declining admissions is to be avoided.

In many countries in the world, including the UK until 1998, there is no charge for students to go to university. The costs are met entirely by the state, sometimes through local government and sometimes national. In other countries, notably the US and Korea, student fees cover the lion's share of university expenditure.

This is a matter of national psyche and culture and isn't just a technocratic decision. It is still the case that university education in continental Europe is either free or incurs minimal fees for EU students and some countries extend that to international students. This reflects the overall view of society that free education should extend into the tertiary sphere and this has considerable moral attractiveness but sadly often leaves institutions rather underfunded!

Data from the OECD[1] summarised the position in 2013, comparing the contribution from public sources and those from 'households', students and their families.[2]

Country	Public (%)	Household (%)
Korea	32.5	43.9
Chile	34.6	51.9
Japan	35.2	51.0
US	36.3	46.5
Australia	42.5	42.2
Israel	50.3	32.9
New Zealand	51.9	33.0
UK	57.0	19.5
Portugal	58.1	32.2
Russia	64.9	23.1
Italy	67.2	26.3
Latvia	67.8	30.6
Mexico	67.8	31.9
Spain	69.3	27.4
Netherlands	70.3	15.9
Lithuania	75.3	18.9
Slovak Republic	75.5	13.0
Czech Republic	77.0	9.4
Ireland	77.7	19.2
France	78.9	10.8
Poland	80.4	17.6
Estonia	81.6	17.8
Slovenia	87.1	10.5
Turkey	87.3	12.8
Belgium	89.3	5.0

Country	Public (%)	Household (%)
Sweden	89.5	0.5
Iceland	91.2	8.2
Denmark	94.0	0.0
Austria	94.6	2.6
Norway	96.0	3.4
Finland	96.1	0.0
OECD average	70.5	21.4

This table demonstrates both the high variability between different national systems and the fact that both households and the state do, in practice, contribute. There is no fixed and accepted idea about what is right and the individual history and culture of each country have led to differing outcomes.

We will argue in this chapter that a balanced system of contributions is the best way and that any system of student contribution has to be set up in a way that is fair and at least does not discourage those from poorer backgrounds from applying to university. It is also crucial that universities are adequately funded for the mission their stakeholders, including nations and governments, need them to do. We argue elsewhere in this book for more diversity of mission than has typically been the case in England and Australia and we would expect that to be reflected in funding arrangements.

It is often argued in England, where since 2011 domestic student fees have perhaps been the highest outside the US, that all the evidence is that the loan pool concept (with students repaying their loan through tax after they graduate) has been efficient in eliminating barriers to student demand. However, especially for people in poorly paid professions, such as nursing, there may well be an upper limit of payments that can be charged without generating unforeseen consequences. The move away from nursing bursaries is evidence of that, like the availability of teaching bursaries in England and Australia.

In the cases of nursing and teaching, the government is, directly or indirectly, the employer and these moves point towards forms of employer contribution, whether through bursaries, national insurance or other means.

There are also issues of intergenerational equity between graduates of different generations. We are both graduates from a time when, either de novo or through generous scholarships, university education was essentially free for us and our peers. We appreciate the issues and concerns raised in the debates about student debt.

We will make the case that employers of graduates should contribute more than they currently do towards the financing of universities and that the systems of finance that are established should incentivise universities to offer a wider range of courses and qualifications that better enable universities to support students seeking to enter and work within the modern world of work, which we have addressed in Chapters 3 and 7.

It is crucial that funding systems facilitate rather than restrict flexibility and course design. We are entering a more bespoke world and funding should reward rather than disincentivise this kind of development.

In this context, it is important to appreciate that the relationship between universities and their students is not a straightforward commercial one. You can't buy a degree. Universities cannot and should not offer first class degrees to people who want to pay for them. They can only offer an environment in which people have the best opportunity to fulfil their capacity. Of course student satisfaction may well be related to degree outcomes but universities cannot lower the standards according to which they classify degrees.

Indeed, the reputation of any university underpins the value of its degrees and any debasement by lowering of standards adversely impacts all of its graduates, past, present and to come! That is why one of the UK Office for Students' (OfS) conditions of functioning as a university is that 'qualifications awarded to students hold their value at the point of qualification and over time'. If a university is found to be in breach of this requirement, it may be fined, suspended from the register or deregistered altogether.

Universities seek to maintain their standards by supporting the professional development of academic staff and external examiners, by reviewing and publishing evidence on their degree outcomes, and by bringing more consistency and explanation into their calculations that turn marks into degree classifications. In December 2018, the OfS published a report[3] assessing concerns on this subject and we expect that universities will respond effectively.

There is always likely to be some level of competition between universities, some of which may not be healthy. But there is a case for developing a wider range of courses to meet different needs and some universities may modify the way in which they operate in those circumstances.

We now turn to the issues to be considered as university-level education expands and the potential contribution of each beneficiary is assessed. The discussion will mainly be based upon the situation in the UK, though the issues extend across all countries. And indeed the basic situation in Australia is rather similar.

The state

In most countries, the norm is that the state pays for universities. That is the established pattern in the same way that the state is principally responsible for school education.

The fundamental case for the state to support university education is that a strong and well-educated population is both a benefit in itself and also a strong driver for good economic performance. Governments need to ensure an appropriately balanced and skilled workforce in all domains and tertiary education is clearly crucial from this point of view.

As we argue in Chapter 6, it is also indisputably of great benefit to countries to have a populace who are educated citizens who contribute fully to national debate and mobilise lateral and critical thinkers who can bring social mobility and entrepreneurial thinking to the workforce. Modern countries need high-performing university systems.

It is also the case that the proportion of the population going to university is steadily increasing across all OECD countries. Again, the OECD data illustrates this clearly.[4]

	Age spans (showing percentage with tertiary education)				
Country	25-64	25-34	35-44	45-54	55-64
Australia	42	48	46	38	33
Austria	30	38	33	27	21
Belgium	37	44	42	34	26
Brazil	14	15	14	14	11
Canada	54	58	61	51	45
Chile	21	27	24	17	14
China	10	18	9	6	4
Colombia	22	28	23	18	16
Costa Rica	18	21	19	17	17
Czech Republic	22	30	21	20	15
Denmark	36	42	41	33	29

Country	Age spans (showing percentage with tertiary education)				
	25–64	25–34	35–44	45–54	55–64
Estonia	38	40	39	35	36
Finland	42	40	50	44	34
France	32	44	39	26	20
Germany	27	28	29	26	25
Greece	28	39	27	26	21
Hungary	23	32	25	20	17
Iceland	37	41	42	36	29
Indonesia	8	10	9	8	4
Ireland	41	51	49	34	24
Israel	49	46	53	48	47
Italy	17	24	19	13	12
Japan	48	59	53	47	35
Latvia	30	39	31	27	23
Lithuania	37	53	38	30	28
Luxembourg	46	53	56	40	32
Mexico	19	25	17	16	13
Netherlands	34	44	38	30	27
New Zealand	36	40	41	32	29
Norway	42	49	49	36	32
Poland	27	43	32	18	14
Portugal	22	31	26	17	13
Russia	54	58	55	53	50
Saudi Arabia	22	26	22	18	14
Slovakia	20	30	21	15	14
Slovenia	29	38	35	24	18

▶

	Age spans (showing percentage with tertiary education)				
Country	25–64	25–34	35–44	45–54	55–64
South Africa	7	5	7	8	7
South Korea	45	68	56	33	17
Spain	35	41	43	30	21
Sweden	39	46	46	32	30
Switzerland	40	46	45	38	31
Turkey	17	25	16	10	10
UK	42	49	46	38	35
US	44	46	47	43	41

The first column of this table demonstrates that in most developed countries 35–50% of the population have participated in tertiary education. The later columns show that the proportion has been steadily increasing in each younger age group.

Many analysts have suggested a close correlation between high standards of living and economic performance and this proportion of the population in tertiary education. Substantial research demonstrates this relationship and almost every government in the world accepts the importance of this.

Beyond such general correlations, universities make a very direct contribution to the wealth of a country.[5] For example, in 2014–15, universities across the UK generated more than £95 billion in gross output for the overall economy. Their contribution to UK GDP was estimated at £21.5 billion. Directly and indirectly UK universities supported more than 940,000 jobs in the UK.

This is a substantial economic contribution in its own right which persuades the state that universities are a national asset that should be supported by them.

However, this powerful argument for state support for universities, which is widely supported, faces a number of important qualifications.

Expansion of numbers

First and foremost, the steady expansion in the number of university students has forced countries to consider the extent to which they can afford it. The shift from under 10% of the population going to university in the 1970s to over 40% now is enormous and inevitably raises sharp questions of affordability.

In addition, for the past 30–40 years, most developed countries have accepted substantial political constraints upon the extent to which they can raise taxation to fund public expenditure, however desirable. Since the 2008 financial crash, an even sharper 'austerity' has been the order of the day.

The effect of this political and economic climate is that all areas of public spending have been challenged, even when their case is strong. Many parts of public services have faced financial stagnation or worse. If governments and universities wanted to avoid this fate for themselves other, supplementary, sources of income were needed. The Willets reforms in the UK, which transferred most of domestic undergraduate funding from the state to the student, were driven in part by a desire to protect universities from general fiscal tightening affecting public funding of universities.

This argument is acute when there is a public spending choice, as there always is, between spending on different levels of education, from nursery through primary and secondary to further and higher education. In such instances, it really is the case that more money spent on university students means that less is spent on primary school children. Faced with this choice, governments will also listen to the overwhelming research that suggests that education spending on younger generations, at nursery and primary levels, is far more likely to improve educational outcomes, particularly for students from poorer backgrounds, than money spent on university students.

That is why the UK Labour Government, from 1998 onwards, decided to focus on the younger age groups and introduce loans for tuition fees for university students. It is also why the Conservative-led Coalition Government, in 2010, decided to raise the fee cap to £9,000, then £9,250, though this time to cut basic state support to universities, as part of their regime of 'economic austerity', which had not happened under the Labour Government. In May 2019, the report of Philip Augar's review, set up by Theresa May following her 2017 election setback which some attributed to student tuition fees, recommended reducing the fee cap to £7,500[6] on condition that the Government should increase the teaching grant to universities to replace the lost tuition fee income.

The conditions within which higher fees are set are also important. Measures such as Education Maintenance Allowances[7] and Aim Higher[8] were important components of the Labour proposals that were subsequently abolished.

Possibly the most striking example of this was Julia Gillard's '20–40' policy when she was Education Secretary in Australia. This was a departure from educational tradition in Australia with the emphasis that 40% of the population should have at least an undergraduate degree and that 20% of university entrants should come from the lowest socio-economic levels. This was supported in Australia by removing the cap on student numbers and increased government funding.

Independence and sustainability of universities

In addition to this economic argument for widening the basis of university funding, there was an important ideological and institutional argument.

This emphasises the importance of guaranteeing and indeed enhancing the academic and financial independence of universities. There are important issues of university governance, which we deal with in Chapter 9, but the key point of independence is to allow universities to develop, for example in the ways that we highlight in this book, to meet modern challenges. That means being able to raise resources, including from students, to be able to fulfil those responsibilities, to set student numbers independently and to determine their own priorities. It may be no coincidence that many of the world's greatest universities have considerable funding independence from government.

There should be no doubt that the increased capitation fee per student and the increase in student numbers that came from the combination of removing capping and higher domestic fees has contributed considerably to the independence and strategic capacity for nation-building of the university sector in both Australia and the UK.

The fact is that it is very difficult for a financially starved university sector to flourish and deliver what a modern nation needs from it. However you look at it, universities are costly concerns to run, especially if they have substantive research and innovation missions.

In other countries, the independence of universities from the state is a more pressing issue than it is in the UK (though, as we discuss in Chapter 9, the establishment and role of the Office for Students is challenging this), Australia or US. However, in all cases, reducing the direct dependence of universities upon the exchequer is an important aspect of university freedom. In some continental European countries, significant underfunding, at least relative to the UK, has undoubtedly contributed to lesser positions in world league tables.

This sustainability was an important goal of the student finance reforms of 2004, but it was unfortunately significantly eroded by the changes of 2011 and subsequently, though some aspects of the Augar Review[9] in May 2019 recommend reversing some of these changes.

The financial sustainability of the student loan model depends upon minimising state support for the system. The lower the proportion of students who repay their loan in full, the more state financial support for the system is needed. A small-seeming change in 2012 was to increase the threshold for graduates to repay their loan from an income of £15,000 a year to £21,000 per year. This threshold is a figure to which the overall finances of higher education are very sensitive. The main reason for this short-sighted change was a response to the political embarrassment of the Liberal Democrats on this issue. This was done in the mistaken view that the increase in the threshold would reduce financial pressures on students and gain political kudos for the government parties. However, the impact was in fact to reduce significantly the proportion of students expected to repay their loan in full and therefore to render the whole student loan system less sustainable, since more state financial support had to go into the system in a way that undermined confidence in the whole system.

At the 2017 Conservative Party conference, Theresa May announced in response to her poor General Election result that this repayment threshold would, in April 2018, be increased again, to £25,000 (and then to £25,725), which made the situation still worse, raising the long-run cost to the taxpayer by a whopping 'over £2.3 billion a year'.[10] The Augar Review criticised this change[11] and recommended reducing the threshold to £23,000 which, if implemented, would improve the situation somewhat, though in our opinion not enough.

The 2012 changes, following the Government's decisions responding to the Browne review, meant that the UK Government ended up funding the high costs of the system through a major direct subsidy through writing off a huge proportion of the student loan pool, on the basis that loans would not be repaid. This had not been the original intention of the 2004 system and had led to greater state involvement in universities' strategic decisions, for example in relation to capping student numbers.

The Australian comparison is of government funding upfront from the tax base, so that households pay less and loans are paid off properly. Ed contrasted the Australian and UK funding systems in detail in evidence[12] to a House of Lords subcommittee.

The UK system should be modified accordingly as it remains vitally important to restore the system of student finance to full sustainability and strong university independence. As it is currently run, the very considerable state contribution is poorly understood and not deployed in any coherent, strategic way. Interest rates are too high and student debt on the current scale unfair.

The resulting balance

The outcome in the UK of the process described here is that the overall balance of funding of universities (though with enormous variation between universities) in 2017–18 was:[13]

Income	
Tuition fees and education contracts	£18.9 billion
Research grants and contracts	£6.2 billion
Funding body grants (teaching and research)	£5.1 billion
Other income	£7.2 billion
Endowment and investment income	£0.2 billion
Total income	£38.2 billion
This covered the total expenditure of	£37.2 billion

This shows the continuing substantial contribution by the state to funding UK universities, but the absolutely essential nature of the contributions made by student fees.

We conclude this section with just a brief mention of one possible solution to financing increased state funding of universities that is often canvassed. This is that governments should levy a 'graduate tax', essentially an extra income tax paid only by graduates, to pay for the costs of universities. This idea was actively canvassed in 2003 when the Labour Government was considering its student finance proposals. There was a political problem in that, at least during the 2001–5 Parliament, the then Chancellor of the Exchequer was not prepared to contemplate any tax increase except for the increase in National Insurance to pay for higher NHS funding. But, in addition to that, the implications of a graduate tax were controversial in terms of university independence, resilient income, even in bad economic times, possible emigration to avoid the tax and some other issues.

The students (and their parents)

The fundamental case for students to contribute towards the costs of university education is that they benefit directly, in contrast with those who do not get the opportunity to go to university.

This benefit is obvious anecdotally as the leaders in most walks of life now have a university education, with remuneration to match. Moreover, most employers require a university degree for appointment to their more senior roles.

It has also become customary across developed countries for children from better-off families to seek university education as an essential stepping stone for later life, as we discuss in Chapter 6. For these people, a three-year university course is the almost automatic concluding stage of their education at the beginning of adult life. The relatively recent requirement to pay tuition fees has not reduced this demand.

Indeed, there have been many academic studies to try to quantify the economic benefit an individual receives from their university degree. These have generally demonstrated that an economic benefit does exist which is, on average, greater than the fees that students have to pay.

For example, the Destination of Leavers from Higher Education Survey in England,[14] asked a sample of graduates who left higher education in 2012/13 what they were doing in November 2016:

- 87.5% of UK domiciled graduates were in employment, 5.8% were in further study only and 2.2% were assumed to be unemployed.
- Of those UK domiciled graduates in employment, 84.1% were in professional jobs.
- The median salary of UK domiciled leavers in full-time paid employment was £27,000 after three and a half years.
- 87.5% of graduates reported being satisfied with their career to date.
- 65.3% thought their course had been good value for money.

Similar surveys demonstrate similar results.

These are all powerful arguments for students making a contribution towards the costs of their university education.

In the UK, the first, pioneering, steps were taken in 1998 when David Blunkett announced the introduction of upfront undergraduate tuition fees set at £1,000 per year for full-time, first degree students entering higher education from 1998. Only students from wealthier households would pay the full amount and students from the poorest backgrounds did not have to pay fees at all. This enabled the government to put more desperately needed money into primary schools and pre-school.

So, for the first time in Britain, the idea that students should contribute to the costs of their university education was established. The political response led to the 2003 reforms, which meant that the loans would be paid back after graduation, through the tax system, rather than being paid upfront by the student or their parents.

The single biggest concern about requiring students to pay such fees (other than the naked self-interest of those paying) is that the fees might disincentivise university applications from students from poorer backgrounds.

In the UK, that has proved incorrect, both when fees of £3,000 per year were charged from 2004, and then £9,000, and upwards, a year from 2011.

That is because the higher fees have been accompanied by a set of measures (introduced in 2004) that work to mitigate any potential disincentives of this type. It remains to be seen what the impact will be on university entry from lower socio-economic classes of the government's decision after 2010 to remove important incentives such as the Education Maintenance Allowances and the Aim Higher programme.

Nevertheless, the most important aspect of the UK system is that a loan to pay these fees is available from the government, in the UK's case through the Student Loan Company. The money is paid back through the ordinary tax collection system, at a payment of 9% of your income annually above a threshold of £25,725 (initially £15,000, then £21,000, £25,000 and £25,725 now recommended to decrease to £23,000; see above).

The effect of this system is that the debt does not stand as a separate charge against the student, but simply means an extra payment is made from tax. It is not complicated to pay and is an automatic process.

While overall debt levels in Australia are lower because of more explicit upfront contribution from the government and the fact that more students live at home, the system has fundamental similarities with the English funding system and the loan pool system has had some success in both countries.

The second important aspect of the English system is that, if the debt is not paid back after 30 years,[15] the loan does not need to be repaid. In May 2019, the Augar Review recommended that this figure should be further increased to 40 years,[16] so that graduates would be more likely to pay off their total debt over their working life. The system means that individuals who have actually not earned well during their life, either through misfortune or through the choice to work in relatively low-paid jobs, do not need to repay and will not have any debt standing over them after that point.

These characteristics of the English and Australian systems avoid the problems of the US-style system which offers no means for people from poorer backgrounds easily to raise the money to pay their fees (though a number of US states do have systems to provide loans for students from poorer backgrounds).

But, in addition to these key aspects, there have been important further measures to mitigate any potential disincentive effect.

For example, the original interest rate, in 2004, for student loan borrowing was set at zero. A real rate of interest was imposed in 2011 and the rate of interest was increased to 6.1% in 2017, which is such a high rate that it may well disincentivise many. The Augar Review[17] recommends removing the interest during the period that a student is studying full-time, but retaining it through the rest of the graduate's repayment period, but with an overall cap of 1.2 times the initial loan amount in real terms.

Augar's recommendation goes closer to the Australian model in that it only starts after graduation, though the Australian interest rate is equated to the true inflation rate in the economy rather than the UK RPI +3%.

We continue to be of the view that the student contribution should only bear a zero real interest rate, rather than the RPI +3%.

An Education Maintenance Allowance had been introduced in 2001 in order to provide financial support to encourage 16–18 year olds to remain in full-time education. This proved very successful but was removed as part of the austerity package imposed by the incoming Coalition Government in 2010.

Similarly, in 2004, a system of student grants for the poorest families was rolled out. It had provided a real study incentive for students from poorer backgrounds. This was ended in 2015, but Theresa May acknowledged,[18] in parallel with the publication of the Augar Review, that this was a major mistake. Augar recommended[19] that 'the government should restore maintenance grants for socio-economically disadvantaged students to at least £3,000 a year and that the expected parental contribution should be made explicit in all official descriptions of the student maintenance support system'.

And in 2004 an effort was made to change the culture and galvanise the aspiration to enter higher education by establishing an 'Aim Higher' programme to explain the benefits of university education to communities that traditionally had not seen this as a possibility.

An Office of Fair Access (OFFA) was established to promote individual universities strategies, such as bursaries and a variety of access programmes. This system has now evolved into the Access and Participation Plans,[20] which the Office for Students requires a university to put in place.

This range of measures has had an impact and has succeeded in ensuring that the number of people applying to university from poorer backgrounds has continued to increase. So the strongest criticism of a student loan system has not been substantiated.

That said, more changes are still needed in the system. One thing that has emerged is that some universities have been innovative in developing new undergraduate pathways, but the societal impact of these has yet to be proven.

Linking the size of the fee to the university and course

In the UK, the new system in 2004 set a real terms £3,000 cap on fees. In 2011, this cap was raised to £9,000 and then in 2016 to £9,250 to reflect inflation. The Augar Review recommends a maximum of £7,500.

The £3,000 cap was deliberately chosen, albeit on a relatively arbitrary basis, to allow the principle of differential fees to be established, while not permitting the level of fee to go so high as to discourage potential university applicants.

However, even after the increase in the cap to £9,000, a system of differential fees has been established only in theory rather than in practice. That fact has been a surprise to most policy-makers, and to us.

Universities are not, and should not be, identical in their mission or purpose. Each has its own strengths and weaknesses both across these broad responsibilities and across subjects. Each teaches in different ways, with different approaches to educational technology, different mixes of students, different relationships to work and different pedagogical methods. Consequently, the qualifications from each HEI vary in their quality and relevance and so also in their economic value to the student who pays for them.

One of the purposes of the 2003 White Paper was to persuade the higher education world to recognise openly that these differences do exist in practice, that the sector is diverse, it is not a monolith, and that economic consequences flow from these differences, including the implication for student fees so that different fees would be charged for different courses at different HEIs, in accordance with their differing quality and value for future life.

However, in practice, the £3,000 cap turned out to be a level at which almost all universities felt that they could set their fees for all courses at the maximum level. That turned out also to be true after the fee cap had been trebled, to £9,000. The Open University and some others do charge lower fees than the annual £9,000 cap but this is very much a minority of universities. Price bunching around the £9,000 fee point became the norm in the sector, and those institutions that under-priced ran the risk of being accused of having low quality degree products, even though such an accusation would be patent nonsense with no economic or other rationale.

It is a myth that all university qualifications have the same value to the student but the myth remains in practice. The consequence is that many students may well be paying more for their degree course than its economic value would actually allow.

Other countries do this differently. For example, Australia differentiates student fees by field of study. The fee is based on three criteria: differences in underlying costs, the earnings potential of graduates from the field and the popularity of the course.

On this basis, courses are assigned to one of three bands for setting the fee: Band 1 (arts, humanities, social sciences, nursing and visual and performing arts) A$3,300, Band 2 (computing, sciences and engineering, business and economics) A$4,700 and Band 3 (medicine, dentistry, veterinary science and law) A$5,500.

The current operation of the system in the UK is unfair to those students studying on courses and at universities where the financial value to them of the qualification is likely to be significantly less than a degree at one of the UK's elite universities. It is doubtful whether this is sustainable and it would be desirable for a genuine range of fees to be established, though it is difficult to see how a government could impose this. It was expected that the market would drive this when the maximum fee was increased to £9,000 but the mandated fee band turned out to be too low to allow this to happen across the board.

Inadequate maintenance loan

In many cases, the maintenance loan is not enough for students reasonably to live on during their studies, as a range of evidence to the Augar Review recognised. This is particularly because of the very high rent levels that both universities and the private sector are charging. In addition, accommodation standards are sometimes very poor, even to the extent of discouraging study. This is especially the case in London where variable living conditions, dispersed campuses and high rents may contribute to London's poor performance in the National Student Survey.

The full maintenance loan has to be set at a level sufficient to cover genuine student living costs. If it is not, and in the absence of a supporting system of grants, students will need support from elsewhere to be able to cover their costs and those from poorer backgrounds may well be unable to manage.

Undergraduate students' time at university should be among the happiest and most fulfilling of their lives and it is a shame if an inappropriate financial situation or working long hours prevents this.

It is worth observing that the less sustainable the whole student loan system is, for reasons described elsewhere in this chapter, the more governments will resist increasing the maintenance loan to an appropriate level, which is an additional argument for improving the sustainability of the overall loan system.

Independence at the age of 18 and the responsibilities of parents

One consequence of the introduction of tuition fees in England was to shift the system of student finance towards full independence and choice for students at the age of 18. The changes made significant moves in this direction, though there is still some distance to go to achieve this in full. This shift is socially desirable in many ways and should be completed.

The means-tested maintenance loan remains a problem in that some parents do not, or cannot, pay their share and the students concerned then can face real financial difficulties. Moreover, the increased number of family breakups has led to more complicated family financial relationships which mean that the current means-testing rules are not always just.

Our basic view is that young people should be independent at 18 and should be treated as such. Every student should receive the full maintenance loan and means-testing should be removed. This would have the additional advantage of significantly reducing the administrative costs of the student loan scheme and removing the cause of many of the bureaucratic problems that are experienced.

This is a controversial view that provokes strong reactions from those who argue that it is socially unjust to treat the children of wealthy families in the same way as the children of poorer families and that the wealthier parents should be required to contribute to their children's educational costs after they are 18.

However, we believe that the way to deal with the social injustices that obviously exist is through incentives for the children of poorer families, such as re-establishing maintenance grants and re-introducing Education Maintenance Allowances for 16–18 year olds. In addition, if so desired, wealthy parents should pay more to the state through the tax system rather than through their children.

Extend the loan system to other courses, and lifelong learning

We discussed in Chapter 7 the case for developing a more coherent and effective support for lifelong learning. Of course, financial support is an essential element of that, through extending the system of student loans to include groups of students, and courses, not currently covered.

It is therefore excellent news that the Augar Review has made strong recommendations[21] in this field which move in the right direction. From its analysis of the decline in Level 4 (eg Higher National Certificate) and Level 5 (eg Foundation Degree, Higher National Diploma, Diploma in Higher Education) qualifications in comparison with Level 6 (Degree), it rightly recommends the establishment of a flexible single lifelong learning loan allowance for tuition fee loans at Levels 4, 5 and 6 for those over 18 who have not previously been publicly funded; similarly they recommend that learners should be able to access such support for modules of these qualifications.

Both Australia and New Zealand have, for some time, operated successfully with a flexible lifetime loan entitlement for tertiary study and Singapore also offers all adult citizens a 'skills account'.

Augar also recommends simplifying the fees charged for Level 4 and 5 courses and strengthening the capacity of the national network of Further Education Colleges to ensure that access to these courses exists across all parts of the country.

And at lower levels of qualification it recommends making a first full Level 3 (eg 'A' Level, BTEC) course available free to all learners and funding the first 'full' Level 2 (eg GCSEs Grades A–C) qualification for those who are 24 and over and who are employed.

These are important recommendations which, if implemented, would represent significant steps towards the kind of financial support that would permit the type of structure of lifelong learning that the country needs. They would also remove many of the barriers to social mobility which remain within post-school education. Moreover, this kind of support would help widen access to professions such as law which are currently socially exclusive.

For the government, a key issue in agreeing to implement such recommendations would be confidence that the loans would be repaid, since the students doing those courses would be likely to find employment. This approach would also incentivise universities and colleges to begin to deliver the range of courses suggested in Chapters 3 and 7.

There is a strong case for taking these steps in the right direction still further. The case for a 'National Learning Entitlement' was argued in a paper[22] by Tom Schuller, Alan Tuckett and Tom Wilson from University College London in February 2018. They proposed that up to £10,000, offset by other education financial support which had been received, be available for anyone to be spent on a university, college or training place of their choice to pursue further education, apprenticeships or other accredited routes.

An important, and particular, element of such support is for postgraduate master's and doctoral courses. Following announcements in 2014, non-means tested loans of up to £10,000 were introduced for postgraduate students taking master's courses at higher education institutions in the UK. By 2016–17, students starting courses in 2019–20 could receive loans of up to £10,906 and in 2018–19 non-means tested loans of up to £25,000 for doctoral students were also introduced. These are important developments that we strongly support.

And, finally, in response to the changes in the international labour market, it would be entirely appropriate that British students could be granted some loan scheme provision for helping support the cost of courses studied abroad. This would be a progressive step for the country in the spirit of 'Global Britain'.

Employers

The third main beneficiaries of university teaching are those public and private sector organisations that employ university graduates, both those who have studied the more vocational courses and those who have had a more 'academic' education. In general, their more highly educated workforce leads them to be more productive and effective.

Employers, however, have no formal part to play in the actual financing of universities though they do support teaching at universities in a number of ways, for example through work placements, sandwich courses, other work-oriented degrees such as foundation degrees and funding support for particular individual students, as we discuss in Chapter 3.

In 2015, the government established new 'degree apprenticeships' as a flagship policy and provided seed funding for universities to develop these degrees. And, since 2017, about 2% of all employers, those with a turnover of over £3 million, have been required to pay a levy of 0.5% of their payroll to fund training for their employees, some of which goes towards the 'degree apprenticeships'. There have been similar systems before this was introduced in 2017.

Thus far, these new approaches have not really got going and the Augar Review made a number of criticisms about the way that they are developing. One of the problems really is that the traditional apprenticeship is an outdated concept, even an outdated word, in today's rapidly changing world of work.

There have been other efforts to encourage employers, through voluntary means, to pay for training for their employees, up to and including at university level. However, these have, in general, not been successful and some statutory requirement really is necessary.

We believe, however, that there is a good case for employers of graduates to contribute to meeting the costs of high quality university teaching. This could probably best be done through the employers' National Insurance part of the tax system, with a higher rate for graduates.

This could be implemented through a fairly simple change to the tax declaration, whereby graduates would state their undergraduate qualification and the university at which they had studied. It is true that Her Majesty's Revenue & Customs, and other tax authorities, would resist this as they constantly press, for good reasons, to simplify the tax system.

Others have suggested similar approaches. The idea of a graduate levy was suggested by Johnny Rich in a paper published by the Higher Education Policy Institute in November 2018[23] and by Ryan Shorthouse, the Director of the 'Bright Blue' think tank, in an article for the *THES*[24] in January 2019.

And a different approach to raising resources from employers might be a small addition to corporation tax (a 1% increase would raise about £3 billion), hypothecated to post-school education spending. This would, of course, mean that the only employers to contribute would be those liable for corporation tax but it would acknowledge some of the benefit received from universities and post-school education.

There are various ways in which employer contributions could be achieved and the positive benefits of such a contribution from employers are great.

Firstly, it would bring a further income stream to universities. If desired, and we would recommend this, those resources could go directly to those universities that had educated the taxpayer.

Secondly, it would give employers a greater stake in increasing the quality of university education and its relevance to their employment needs in the modern workforce.

Thirdly, it would give universities an incentive to improve their graduates' employability if the levy were paid to the higher education institution where the graduate studied.

Fourthly, it would create a framework though which all graduates, including those who never had to receive a student loan, would contribute to university finances, and so create greater intergenerational equity between different generations of student.

The biggest disadvantage of such a scheme, which is a real one, is that it might lead to employers preferring to employ non-graduates who would cost them less as no National Insurance payment would be made. However, we think that in practice this would be unlikely to be a significant response.

Other possibilities, as mentioned above, are structured schemes of student bursaries for specific subjects and courses. This may be of particular value in the public for professions such as teaching, nursing and the armed services.

We are well aware that the suggestion that employers contribute more to university spending will be controversial, and that there are, in general, difficult issues about corporate taxation that are matters of public discussion. However, we believe that this issue should be given consideration given the highly interlinked interests of employers of all types and a vital university sector.

Conclusion

The complexities and political challenges of university finance are clear. It will always seem easier to maintain the status quo than to undergo a controversial and difficult reform process.

However, the danger of 'no change' is that universities can stagnate to such an extent that the most dynamic sections of the community look for more high quality, more internationally respected, alternatives. That has happened in a large number of countries and it is not a good way forward in even the medium term, let alone the long term. We understand the concerns of many in the sector who are afraid to change things too much because of concerns that the complexity of the current model may not be appreciated and universities may be left with funding gaps, but we don't think that their judgment is right.

Moreover, the kind of dynamic universities that we promote in this book, addressing our four pillars to help the world deal with the challenges of a rapidly changing world, require funding mechanisms, along the lines set out in this chapter, that can sustain that necessary range of activity. Effective universities do cost money and the question of where those resources come from has to be confronted openly and honestly. That is one reason why we welcome the decision in December 2018 of the Office of National Statistics to reclassify the way in which student loans are recorded in the public finances, which will help ensure that the costs of tuition fees to the government can be seen clearly and properly understood.

Universities sometimes think governments feel they are rolling in money whereas, in fact, institutions that lack large endowments have fine margins, though of course there is always room for more efficiency, which we address in Chapter 9. That is, we think that:

Governments should create a sustainable system with clarity about the purpose of the funding system in a way that reduces university dependence on the state. We believe that serious consideration should be given to requiring employers to contribute to the higher education costs of those graduates they employ, and we hope that the government will extend the loan system to other courses, and lifelong learning, along the lines recommended by the Augar Review.

As far as the current system is concerned, the £25,725 student loan repayment threshold should be reduced and the interest rate be cut to align with the Consumer Price Index, to reflect only real price changes.

The maintenance loan should fully cover actual student living costs and maintenance grants should be re-established for those from the poorest family backgrounds. Students should be treated as fully independent at the age of 18 and early repayment of student loans should be incentivised, to help the public finances.

Universities should strengthen philanthropic support for their universities, and develop their endowments aggressively and develop education services for their alumni.

Chapter 9

University governance, leadership and the state

Why university governance, leadership and the state matter

Ed says that the university world abounds in humorous anecdotes about recognition of the need for change but resistance to anything beyond talk. One very eminent Vice-Chancellor said: 'Much more is said in our world than is done. It is our responsibility in our time of leadership to make sure something is done.' Incremental improvement around a clear vision usually works but must not be too slow. With intrinsically conservative workforces, vacillation and blocking of progress by a few negative voices effectively shifts the balance from incremental positive action to passivity. It can be seen as solving a problem (or not solving it) to create another committee or constrained and logically irrational structures.

Probably the two most important things a university leader can do are to work very hard to get the vision and direction right and then ensure they have a great team who can at least start to deliver it.

Military lessons in leadership sometimes stand out for their clarity. Hannibal of Carthage, like Napoleon and Robert E Lee, was the greatest tactician of his age. All three won battle after battle but essentially lost their wars. Robert E Lee's superior generalship kept a war going for years that should have been over in months and supported the side that approved of human slavery – brilliant leadership but a dreadful cause. Leadership in the wrong direction, however charismatic or powerful, does a lot more harm than good. Where the direction is right, even suboptimal leadership can achieve significant advances.

For years, Ed felt universities did best when left alone by government. Give them enough autonomy and enough resource and they would thrive! But the societal responsibilities that fall to universities are vast and will not always be met if left to purely voluntary alignment. Look at Oxbridge's dismal performance around equity and failure to abandon relentless promotion of privilege in spite of words to the contrary. Look at the increasingly demanding civic and service responsibilities that universities bear and the patchy institutional response. Ed has therefore become a firm believer in the role of both top-down and bottom-up inputs both within institutions and in the interactions between universities and government.

That's why university governance and leadership matter.

Introduction – the tension of leadership styles

Leadership matters. In today's world, the critical question that comes up for any organisation is the quality of leadership. Whether this is a large corporation meeting shareholder expectations, a government ministry or an NGO, who leads the organisation, how the leader is selected, who oversees the leader, what is the overall governance structure and, most importantly, how the leader performs are open to wide scrutiny. This of course is exactly as it should be. Leadership is more important than ever in times of challenge and change, which of course is exactly where universities find themselves today.

So the first part of this chapter looks at the nature and challenges of leadership within an individual university institution, with the related issues of governance. At the end of the day, its overall quality is the underlying strength, or weakness, of the whole university system. In the second part, we turn to the related question of national 'system-level' leadership: the way in which a government or state governs its universities.

The two parts are, of course, closely interrelated since effective university governance and administration has to take place within the national strategy for universities and the frameworks that have been established for university governance, not least the financial arrangements. These vary very widely from country to country but in this chapter we mostly discuss leadership within the frameworks that have been established in the UK, Australia and the US. As we discuss later, a vital and engaged university sector should itself contribute to the national strategy.

Jo Ritzen,[1] the Dutch Minister of Education from 1989 to 1998 and then President of Maastricht University, makes the point that great universities have three attributes: autonomy, great academic leadership at multiple levels and high levels of funding per student (irrespective of where the cash comes from). We look at these questions from that standpoint and believe that generally the US, UK and Australian systems have done particularly well on these measures.

University governance and leadership

At the institutional level, there needs to be effective strategic leadership through a university President and their team but with clear and transparent processes and strong voices for students and the academic community and with oversight by a broadly based University Council. This structure, when it works well, both justifies and supports the traditional model of university autonomy that has led directly to the emergence of almost all the great universities in the West and is increasingly prevalent on other continents. But, unfortunately, it does not always work well.

Universities must recognise that this institutional autonomy is only a birthright in a small number of historic cases. For most, at least in the modern era, it was something bestowed upon them by government and the populace to help them meet national needs. Ministers and governments should hold universities accountable but recognise that the university part of the knowledge economy works best with a reasonable degree of autonomy.

The model of leadership is also influenced by who appoints the leader. The European Rector is often elected by the university's academic staff. This contrasts sharply with a UK Vice-Chancellor who is appointed by the University Council after a recommendation from a small committee (often the business people on Council). The powers of the VC/Rector/President vary a great deal, even *within* a country let alone *between* countries. A university's establishing Royal Charter provides legal guidelines and can enable the distribution of power within the university. Delegation can drive the scale and speed of decision-making.

Within universities, the concept of leadership is itself a great deal more contentious than most outside the university sector would expect. Any serious attempt at strategic leadership is often labelled as 'managerialism' and criticised, often strongly, by many academics.

Those who promote this catch-all concept of 'managerialism' often argue that universities need very light leadership indeed. They feel that academic communities are essentially self-governing, and that the key to success is to let 1,000 flowers bloom and just leave people to get on with it. This approach has something to commend it, at least in some universities. It has certainly been the predominant philosophy at Oxbridge and at the Ivy Leagues and these universities have flourished and inspired great research and academic insight. In these very great institutions, it is argued that the academic community very actively monitors and maintains quality around academic issues, notably research (though there is room for scepticism about how true this actually is). However, it should be noted that, throughout the world, there are only a handful of these great institutions where light touch leadership is the norm.

Even here, however, there are plenty of examples of reforming Vice-Chancellors, Presidents or Heads of Colleges who have come up against very conservative academic bodies, almost opposed in principle to any change, who have got rid of the reforming leaders. The decision-taking processes described (of Cambridge) in *Microcosmographica Academica*[2] in 1908 sometimes seem alive and well. And certainly the need for clearer leadership has been acknowledged, for example in the decision of Cambridge to appoint, from 1989 onwards, full-time Vice-Chancellors, each for a seven-year term, to replace the part-time, almost honorary, one- or two-year appointments that had existed for the previous 575 years. Often, general discussions of overall strategy and transformation in these universities are complicated by their collegiate structure which can create a culture of 'too many cooks' and an absence of overall responsibility.

The concept of 'academic tenure' overlaps with these considerations. Established to protect the intellectual freedom of university academics, it can often become a serious barrier to a university's ability to define its future mission and purpose. Such 'tenure' was abolished in the UK in 1988 but still remains in the US, though some states have considered legislating to abolish it, and in parts of Europe, and it creates very real leadership challenges, not least in promoting younger academics to the top level.

But with the extraordinarily high academic research reputation that these universities possess across the world, any criticism of their governance arrangements can seem gratuitous, even though there are serious issues about how well these great universities are themselves placed to face the challenges of the future.

But however much their great success at world level mitigates any criticisms of governance of this small number of universities, the argument is far less applicable to the overwhelming majority of universities across the world, whether they are planning their own growth journey or seeking to expand and to improve across the board. Those who criticise too much 'managerialism' are not always thinking, perhaps, of the whole range of universities where there is a very strong argument that some strategy to promote performance improvement is essential.

Hans Peter Hertig from Lausanne, Switzerland, has examined this in his book *Universities, Rankings and the Dynamics of Global Higher Education: Perspectives from Asia, Europe and North America*,[3] which looks at some universities that have faltered in recent decades and others that have thrived. He illustrates this with a number of detailed case studies and sets out very clearly the attitudes, directions and ambitions of the university leadership. Hertig is emphatic in his conclusion that the quality of leadership is the single most important differentiator of success. His conclusion that leadership is important is difficult to refute and indeed is exactly what could be expected if we look at all kinds of social and economic institutions across the world.

This tension between 'managerial' leadership and the traditional concept of universities as 'communities of scholars' underlies what is an unresolved controversy about the nature of modern university leadership and governance which needs to be addressed openly.

Consideration of a series of issues such as the appropriate role of University Councils, expectations of university teaching and research staff, student representation and Vice-Chancellors' pay can only be dealt with on the basis of a clear, and ideally shared, understanding of the way in which modern universities should be led and governed. This understanding does not generally exist at the moment.

University leadership often falls between the devil and the deep blue sea. Too much direction from the top with inadequate consultation even if strategically sensible looks a bit like managerialism in the true sense. It may not be all bad in intention but will not be terribly effective at the end of the day. Too much anarchy with strategy coming from thousands of voices is also not likely to be at all effective in meeting the very tough challenges that universities have to address, particularly if they are to move in the directions, and take on the responsibilities, that we urge in this book.

Universities, and institutions more generally, do best where consultation is open, when knowledge flows openly and people know how decisions are made. People know that their voice will be listened to but also understand that individuals are appointed, often but not always from the academic body, who have responsibility for making those decisions that are endorsed or approved by a University Council. This, of course, must always be within the framework of national legislation and align with national requirements.

In almost all cases, it is possible to find an equilibrium where staff are respected and listened to, where the student voices are heard yet there is sufficient trust in the leadership in terms of transparency for a sensible strategic direction to be adopted.

In the UK, in recent years, this has all come under stress with a general lessening of confidence of university communities in their leadership. At the end of the day, this should be considered a good thing because we have moved to an era where people are justifiably challenged about decisions and where discussions are much more open. But this requires high quality leadership, and articulacy, at all levels of the institution. The leadership should persuade people rather than simply relying on autocratic decisions.

The qualities of a modern university leader

It is worth examining the qualities that a modern university leader requires. Obviously, for any university, a lot depends upon the historic and contemporary context of the university itself, its own identified mission and purposes, and the national framework within which the university exists. These contexts all differ substantially for every university. And whatever the formal legal arrangements for universities, each university also carries a reputation, whether deserved or undeserved, that strongly colours the view of the community around it, its alumni and current staff and students, and national opinion-formers.

These varied perspectives all create the first challenge for any university leader – to give the university a sense of its own place, its own ambition for itself, its own sense of mission and direction. The university leader has to establish a clear mission and set of goals for the university.

This first leadership challenge isn't at all easy. In any university, the right balance between research, teaching and knowledge transfer – particularly with the local economy and society – can be difficult to find. For example, as we argue in Chapter 4, the spectrum of research quality, just in the UK, is immense, ranging from world-leading to not much contribution. An individual university has to find its own place in that spectrum either seeking massively to improve its research standing – and in which disciplines? – or accepting that research won't be a major part of its mission. These are diametrically opposed responses and leadership has to help find the right one.

Equally challenging choices are posed as an individual university tries to find its best relationship with the world of work which, as we argue in Chapter 3, raises a series of important questions about subjects studied, modes of study and examinations and qualifications.

And the perpetual context is the need to attract revenue, whether in the form of undergraduate students, postgraduate study, research support or endowment. There is no getting away from the fact that universities are expensive concerns to run and it is no surprise that university leaders find that a large proportion of their time is spent on fundraising in a variety of forms.

Individual university leaders need strong self-confidence, self-awareness, integrity and clear vision and analysis as they face up to this leadership challenge.

It is extremely difficult to find the correct balance between the potential place, mission and roles of the university. The overall culture in which universities exist does not make it easy to address these challenges. There is a university world 'groupthink' which likes to imply that all universities are much the same, at least formally, whereas in fact there are sharp distinctions between universities and their capacities. Ideas like 'academic drift' have arisen because, for example at the time when polytechnics were given university status, there was (and still is) usually a strong desire in universities to favour high-level research rather than teaching, strong relations with the world of work or other university functions.

So, even in the best of times, it is difficult for individual university leaders to get right their fundamental university leadership challenge. But it is even more difficult now when the higher education world, across the planet, is more challenged and changing faster than has ever been the case in history. And that is why the quality of leadership features is an exceptionally important determinant in the success of any university, as identified in Peter Hertig's study mentioned above.

But of course the answers to these questions of a university's 'place', ambition, mission and direction cannot simply be provided by the university leader themselves. They have to be determined by the whole university, its staff, students, wider community and funding supporters.

This is particularly important since fears about change can easily prevent a university leader properly addressing this fundamental first leadership challenge. Many within a university may well see the prospect of even a clear definition, and certainly possible changes, as threatening to their own roles and even careers.

Good governance and effective collegiate leadership

That is why the second university leadership challenge is for an individual university leader to behave in a collegiate way which effectively engages the university as a whole. It means respecting the interests, goals and ambitions of the main stakeholders in the university such as staff and students and financial supporters. It means respecting the rights of a wide range of minorities.

The concept of 'academic autonomy' has established itself for good reason and is important. Universities are institutions whose formal staff structure, especially on the academic side, is very flat. University Presidents typically effect change by influence rather than direct control. Effective university Presidents need to be a voice for the university community, especially the academic community, in developing a vision that people empathise with and buy into and that aligns with ever improving quality and impact in both education and research. Effective leadership also acknowledges the importance of the civic role, of broad engagement in communities and equity and diversity as essential underpinnings of a modern university. In all of these areas, collegiate leadership is important.

Autonomous universities by definition have a governing body which is the University Council. A rather similar model has evolved in the UK and Australia which is mirrored, to some extent, in the US and more fully in Canada. Council composition may vary but almost always includes some students and staff members and a reasonable proportion of independent Council members. One of the big student campaigns of the 1970s[4] was to get reasonable student representation on these decision-taking bodies. This had not existed before and some leftists described it as 'repressive tolerance',[5] a strategy by university establishments to take the edge off protest!

In some countries, such as Australia, many Council members are directly appointed by government. In others, such as the UK, the Council is essentially self-nominating. In the US, there is considerable variation depending upon the nature of the institution but with very heavy state government engagement in the institutions which come under state government control. However established, University Councils generally operate with a reasonable degree of autonomy from government. They oversee all aspects of university function and the university President (or Vice-Chancellor) operates both as the Chief Executive and as the senior academic. Traditionally, Council oversight has been relatively light but, over the past decade, in part driven by the increasing financial complexity and increasing financial size of universities, it has strengthened and in many ways is not too dissimilar to the oversight given to a private company by its governing board.

University Councils typically have the type of subcommittees that large companies do such as the finance committee, the risk and audit committee and a remuneration committee.

They differ from corporations in having an academic Senate or academic board, usually chaired either by the university President or by an independent chairperson. This will either be the major subcommittee of the Council, or will act independently within the university statutes. This group comprises appointed and elected academics and almost always includes some students. Academic Senate/board underpins the academic quality of the university and is the cornerstone of institutional autonomy.

In essence, institutional autonomy means that institutions are academically self-regulating. This gives them considerable freedom in setting their own academic direction. It is a huge privilege for a university sector when a nation accords it this degree of freedom and should be acknowledged through close alignment and commitment to national needs. In the UK, as in Canada and Australia, academic boards or senates have traditionally sat alongside University Councils but over the past decade, it has become increasingly acknowledged that the academic Senate is responsible to Council for accrediting and overseeing academic quality in the institution.

Academic board/Senate is clearly a very important place for both the academic and student voice to be fully expressed and, when it works well, it does not merely accredit courses and oversee examinations and academic outcomes but is a vital voice in all of the important issues affecting the institution. The most interesting and contentious debates in successful universities often occur in academic Senate and it is crucial that the academic Senate or board has a significant voice into the University Council.

This formal structure is fundamental to the operation of the university and an important part of the leadership challenge is successfully to handle these structures as well as the teaching and research staff (and possibly their trade unions), and the student body. But, beyond the formalities, it is still more important for the leader to listen and to engage throughout, and outside, the university. Everyone in the university needs genuinely to feel that their own contribution has at least been understood and appreciated. An autocratic or heavily directive and hierarchical style of decision-taking is unlikely to succeed on a long-term basis as support from the rest of the university steadily erodes.

Many academics in universities start with a fairly simple mission – that they personally wish to teach and do research well. Often, their principal concerns are their own research and the students whom they teach. They do not necessarily see institutional ambitions as a high personal priority.

Therefore, identification of, and getting people behind, the more strategic vision that we have discussed earlier is immensely hard work and requires a number of very concentrated and aligned individuals working together in a team as part of the university leadership. Any significant change cannot be achieved by diktat but involves wide consultation and buy-in, certainly of deans, certainly of key opinion leaders and, ultimately, of the majority of staff. The student voice is also becoming increasingly strong and is often aligned with the staff voice, though there are many occasions when there is real conflict, for example on some issues relating to teaching and learning and the broader student experience.

As staff and students at the end of the day are the university, woe betide any university leadership team that does not understand and listen to that voice when it speaks strongly. A university is not simply an institution, it is a living, breathing, thinking community.

There are occasional examples of charismatic leaders who transform an institution and take it to a new level, such as John Sexton at New York University and Michael Crow at Arizona State University. But almost always effective change leadership requires Margaret Mead's group of committed citizens[6] to work together. Fortunately, the university world abounds with individuals who have both this mindset and this potential.

A critical success factor in a leader's engagement with the rest of the university is a commitment to transparency about the way in which the leadership team operates and the way that decisions are formulated. This transparency is of course an essential component of modern leadership everywhere and is by no means limited to universities. But transparency makes autocratic leadership even more difficult to conduct successfully. It makes genuine engagement of a leader with their 'followers' even more important. The leader must have integrity and be trusted.

Some university leaders have spectacularly fallen from grace, at least in part, because of their failure to carry with them the rest of the university they lead and a failure to get this relationship right. Lord Acton's famous Victorian dictum that 'Power corrupts and absolute power corrupts absolutely'[7] certainly holds true in universities. A proper system of checks and balances is essential in any university. Failure to operate such a system is one of the causes of the issues around Vice-Chancellors' pay, which we discuss below, and extends to a wide range of other aspects of conduct.

The personal skills required for success in this second university leadership challenge, behaving in a collegiate way, include the ability to articulate clearly both the overall purposes of the university and key decisions in all aspects of university life and to communicate vision, clarity of direction and a readiness to innovate with a charisma that engages attention.

This is not a common range of skills and there are certainly many current university leaders who do not have them. It is very difficult to be an effective Vice-Chancellor in today's world, as Ed knows from experience leading two great institutions. One is constantly caught between the Scylla of aligning with popular opinion (everyone wants to be liked) and the Charybdis of top-down strategic leadership that does not take people with it. The key skill of a successful university leader is to negotiate this divide. Failure to do so leads to non-alignment with either community or Council, or both, and an early exit.

Building a leadership team and engaging publicly

The third university leadership challenge is to build a leadership team across the university that can unleash the innovative and entrepreneurial potential and energy that effective change requires.

This means effective delegation of power from the Vice-Chancellor or President and the development and sustenance of informal networks of leadership and support across the institutions, combined with effective monitoring of performance. 'Leadership' very much needs to be seen as not about one individual, but about the development of a culture of engagement and leadership across the university.

Especially in countries where universities in the main are not directly funded by the state and where much of their income must be derived through direct self-generated activities, it is important that university leadership supports an entrepreneurial attitude among staff. This is especially important in all three countries we are discussing here where all universities, whether private or public in their governance, have a need to raise significant funds especially to support complex research missions. A university President who leads an academically strong but financially chaotic or perpetually financially precarious institution has not been doing their job very well! Effective university leadership therefore involves not only academic leadership but also leadership around equity and around financial issues. This will involve convincing the university community that resources are being used well.

An important component of this approach is to build a structure that identifies and hones future potential leaders of the university to try to sustain the mission and direction of the institution. Many universities are not successful at achieving this sustainability which is very important.

Our fourth university leadership challenge is to articulate and then facilitate the university's contribution to solving the social and economic challenges facing its local and national communities. We address some of the issues around locality in Chapter 5 but, as we express from the very start of this book, high quality universities are a key contributor to addressing and overcoming the challenges facing our world.

A very important university leadership challenge is to ensure that this is true for the individual university – and that the work being done by the university does in fact contribute to society. This requires building a wide range of partnerships and opening out a large degree of silo thinking. It is necessary to articulate this contribution in a wide range of fora and to put it into practice. Fundamentally, any individual university will succeed in the longer term only if it can make a widely understood and appreciated contribution to the wider society. The university leader has a greater responsibility than anyone else to ensure that this actually happens and to help challenge comfort zones that exist in the academic community that serve as barriers to such a civic role.

These four university leadership challenges that we have identified are important for leadership, and therefore university, success.

At an anecdotal level, it is clear to us that the actual quality of university leadership, set against these challenges, is highly variable. We are not aware of any serious effort to measure leadership quality on these criteria – and of course it would be difficult to do so on the basis of any serious and objective metric. However, we do not conclude that the quality of leadership does not matter because we cannot measure it very well.

Overall, we urge that there should be far more focus upon the quality of university leadership, as there is upon professional leadership in many other spheres of the public and private sector world. In the UK, Advance HE[8] plays a role in this respect but we believe that there would be great benefit from strengthening the focus on this aspect of university life and the focus on professional development of leadership capability at multiple levels of universities.

Diversity and respect

Universities committed to helping the world deal with change should, in their own practice, embody that change themselves in the ways they work. They should organise their institutions in a way that mobilises the full capacity of all those who embody that change.

But many universities don't do that and so change has to mean facing up to the deep problems of gender and race inequality which still damage many universities, particularly the most research-intensive.

At the moment, universities are a long way behind where they need to be. Just 34 of the top 200 universities in the 2018 ranking have a female leader, according to an analysis[9] of Times Higher Education World University Rankings data.

Sweden has the highest proportion of female university leaders: 4 of the 6 Swedish institutions in the world top 200. The US has 11 female Presidents (including Harvard, Cornell and Berkeley) and 7 of the 34 female leaders are based in the UK (including Oxford, Imperial College London and LSE).

Only 18% of elite US universities are headed by women, while UK universities outperform the global average, with 23% of their top universities having a female leader.

Of the 27 countries that feature in the top 200 universities, 17 have no female university leaders at all.

According to data[10] from the Higher Education Statistics Agency in 2016/17, 26% of professors in UK universities were women, an increase from 22% in 2012/13. And 22.5% of female academics, compared to 35.6% of male academics, earned over £50,000 a year.[11]

In March 2019, a BBC analysis[12] of the pay data reported by employers to the Government Equalities Office identified a big university gender pay gap. British universities report a higher median pay gap, 13.7% on average, than the national average gap of 9.1% in 2018.

Ninety per cent of British universities had reported that they pay their average male employee more than they pay their average female employee, contrasting with 78% of companies and 63% of local councils (and about 25% of local councils on average pay women more than men).

In April 2019, the THE also produced an unusual league table[13] of universities' approach to gender equality. Their methodology included measures of the proportion of senior female academics, the proportion of a university's total research output that is authored by women, the proportion of first-generation female students, the extent to which there is research on the study of gender, their policies on gender equality and their commitment to recruiting and promoting women.

Of the top 10 universities in this table, 2 are from the UK (Worcester and King's College London), 2 from Australia, 2 from New Zealand and 1 each from Sweden, the Netherlands, Italy and Spain.

In addition to these shocking statistics, which demonstrate that, on gender, universities lag well behind other major national institutions, there are also issues about the effectiveness with which universities address issues of sexual harassment by staff of students. Research in 2019 by the Brook charity and the Dig In database[14] demonstrated unacceptable levels of harassment in UK universities and *Silencing Students*,[15] published in 2018, identified shortcomings in complaints and disciplinary processes. The 2017 report of the Australian Human Rights Commission, 'Change the Course',[16] describes unacceptable levels of harassment on Australian campuses. And, in the US, a series of reports, including from the National Academies,[17] have identified the existence of serious problems and there have been a number of high-profile dismissals of university leaders because of their failure to address these issues properly – particularly in response to the #Me Too movement.

At an anecdotal level, there are too many accounts of misogynistic behaviour at universities and too many examples of insufficient determination to root out unacceptable practices.

Similar comments apply in relation to racism and the treatment of black and minority ethnic (BME) groups.

A September 2018 survey from Advance HE[18] showed that in 2016/17 there were 25 black women and 90 black men among 19,000 professors in UK universities. BME staff remained more likely than their white peers to be in junior positions, to be less well paid and to be employed on fixed-term rather than permanent contracts.

A December 2018 BBC survey[19] of BME pay by Russell Group universities showed average salaries of £52,000 for white academics, £38,000 for black academics and £37,000 for academics from an Arab background, so that, on average, black and Arab academics at these universities earn 26% less than their white colleagues.

Eighty-six per cent of academic staff at Russell Group universities are white, 6% are Indian and South Asian, 6% Chinese and East Asian, 1% black and 0.4% Arab, suggesting that BME academics are less likely than white men or women to be promoted to better paid, senior positions. They also tend to be in lower pay bands.

The gender pay gap is more pronounced for ethnic minority women at Russell Group universities where white male staff are on average salaries of £55,000. On average, white women earn 15% less than white men, Asian women 22% less and black women 39% less.

The only silver lining behind this cloud describing an appalling state of affairs is that this data should act as some sort of corrective to the kind of complacent liberal academic mindset that tends to see universities as some kind of progressive island, separate from and better than the rest of the world.

In the private words of one senior female professor, 'Far from being liberal and progressive, universities have become the last large bastions of the worst sort of chauvinism, racism and snobbery. How that advances the cause of science, or illustrates its worth, I have no idea.'

It is obvious that this is a completely unacceptable state of affairs that universities themselves need to continue to address urgently in order to ensure that they are institutions that give proper respect to the contribution of women and BME people at all levels and that they are places where the culture promotes fairness and respect.

This state of affairs exists at the same time as in recent decades most universities in many Western countries including the US (in part), the UK and Australia have increasingly diverse student populations. For example, King's College London now takes 51% of its commencing undergraduate students from a BME background. Over many decades, the proportion of women and male students has equilibrated in all three countries, reflecting population demographics. Of course students broadly expect, quite reasonably, that the composition of the academic workforce will increasingly resemble the make-up of the student body.

Similar expectations arise in relation to the curriculum, which they expect will become more internationalised so that the traditional European perspective will be improved and broadened by incorporation of knowledge and teachings from other civilisations. This is one area where success in improving the equality and diversity of the student body has not been fully matched by changes in workforce.

With regard to gender, the proportion of women academics in the lower academic grades in most universities is similar to that of men but a very marked male predominance emerges on the progression towards full professorship. The issues behind this are complex but it is very likely that bias – whether conscious or unconscious – is operating to maintain this disequilibrium. The situation is even worse when one looks at the position of BME people in UK universities where there is a very poor representation even in the lower academic ranks and very, very few BME people progressing to full Professor status.

In the UK, the Athena SWAN (Scientific Women's Academic Network) Charter was established in 2005 to recognise and celebrate good practice in higher education and research institutions towards the advancement of gender equality.

In summary, the Charter embraces a set of values and aspirations that:

- agree that academia needs to benefit from the talents of all if it is to reach its full potential;
- understand the commitment required from all levels of the organisation to advance gender equality – particularly in the form of proactive leadership from those in senior roles;
- make a commitment to the advancement of gender equality in academia, with a particular emphasis on the lack of women in more senior roles and the loss of women across the career pipeline;
- acknowledge that a commitment is needed to address the unequal gender balance across all disciplines, professional roles and support functions, and to recognise disciplinary differences such as:
  - the underrepresentation of women in the more senior roles in the arts, humanities, social sciences, business and law disciplines;
  - the unusually high loss rate of women in science, technology, engineering, mathematics and medical discplines;
- endeavour to remove the obstacles women face, especially at turning points of career development and progression – this includes the transition from PhD to a long-term academic career;
- a promise to address the consequences of short-term contracts for retaining and progressing staff in academia, especially women;
- a commitment to overcoming the gender pay gap.

This Charter, and associated action to promote its values, has forced institutions to concentrate on remedying gender balance as failure to have proactive programmes underway resulted in ineligibility for several of the major government scientific grounding programmes. Dame Sally Davies, a key leader in this area, drove these reforms through and they have been broadly embraced. So most UK universities have detailed programmes underway to increase the representation of women in senior leadership roles including across academia, though of course there's still a very long way to go.

Advance HE is developing a version of this Charter for the Canadian higher education and research sector.

Progress in the BME community is desperately needed, as the statistics above demonstrate. Many gifted BME students are starting to graduate across the board with strong doctoral theses and the task will be to ensure that they have open access to entirely satisfactory academic careers with good prospects of promotion.

The development of a workforce that mirrors, to some extent, the population in which a university is embedded and, to some extent, its student intake is essential. Great universities will always have a significant international component to their workforce and indeed a measure of their success is their ability to recruit talent from around the world.

In an increasingly internationalised world with increasing academic standards in most regions, internationalisation should aid diversity in the workforce rather than restrict it. However, that has not been the case in previous decades as much of the mobile workforce has come from Europe and North America.

The same factors that apply to senior university leadership should also apply to University Councils which should reflect an appropriate gender and ethnic mix with role models on Council that both staff and students can identify with.

The importance of role models in this regard cannot be underestimated. For example, a recent King's College London exercise to show the strength of women academic mentors across the University established a 'wall of fame', showing the pictures of 100 outstanding women professors with a summary of their academic achievements. Unfortunately, this contained few BME professors, which students of course noticed and commented upon. The University took steps to remedy this and the students developed an alternative display of outstanding BME women. Events like this can lead to a serious sense of disenfranchisement for a significant part of the student body and this and other instances led the University to gear up markedly its determination to achieve BME equity within a reasonable timeframe.

The US, Australia and the UK all continue to have major challenges in this area, though of course there are historic and cultural differences between the three countries.

We simply want to emphasise the immense importance of all universities becoming diverse and respectful communities if they are to achieve the positive respect that they need in order to address the challenges of change that we describe in this book. We acknowledge the difficulties but they cannot and must not be ducked. These are exactly the kinds of areas where universities should lead good practice, not lag behind, and where governments will, at the end of day, intervene, over-ruling university autonomy, if sufficient progress is not made.

A note on Vice-Chancellors' pay in the UK

The questions of leadership quality that we discuss in this chapter clearly overlap with the controversies about university leaders' pay which have been a feature of public debate in the UK as in Australia in recent years.

A number of former education ministers[20] have made criticisms of the levels of some Vice-Chancellors' pay and, wrongly in our view, linked this to the level of student tuition fees. We address, in Chapter 8, the complex issues around student fees but it is absolutely clear that there is no relationship between student fees and Vice-Chancellors' remuneration, which forms a miniscule proportion of any university's income from student fees. The level of university leaders' pay has been used simply as a political device, in a very damaging way, to focus public debate on student finance – a perennially controversial subject.

Moreover, university remuneration cannot be compared with top-level public sector pay, another field of politically charged and ill-informed debate. Universities are self-governing institutions that generally and rightly should govern themselves in a transparent and accountable way. There is no strong case for any government institution to regulate the pay levels of university leaders. And, in addition, the traditional comparisons with the pay of the Prime Minister suffer from the traditional defects of that comparison, that it doesn't factor in a range of other benefits from houses to retirement packages.

We consider it highly unfortunate that, under public pressure from former ministers, government and the lecturers' trade union, the UK's Office for Students plans to publish full details of VCs' pay in an annual report starting in 2019, including basic salary, performance-related pay, pension contributions and other taxable and non-taxable benefits. Apparently, the OfS also wants to look at the ratio between the head of institution's pay and that of all other staff, as well as the number of senior staff paid more than £100,000, and their requirement to provide justification for a VC's salary must include a 'detailed' explanation of the value they have delivered to the institution and the process by which their performance was judged. There is also a suggestion that Vice-Chancellor's pay should be linked to the nature of the institution on a basis that is unlikely to be satisfactory.

Full transparency in Vice-Chancellors' salary arrangements is essential. They are appropriately found in annual university accounts where they can be readily accessed. For some time, this information has been referred to in tables in the press. In autonomous institutions, these salaries should be set and monitored by governing councils guided by their renumeration committees. The value of additional input from government either directly by ministerial comment or through regulatory bodies such as the UK Office for Students is at best questionable and at worst signals a loss of institutional autonomy that may be regretted in the future.

None of this is to say that universities have, in general, got the process of setting pay right. Too many universities have allowed Vice-Chancellors to be direct participants in the pay-setting arrangements, for example as members of the University Council's remuneration committee, in a way that should never be the case. Moreover, the level of remuneration for some Vice-Chancellors does seem difficult to justify on any obvious performance basis, and has certainly been inflammatory at a time of substantial and difficult reform of university lecturers' pension arrangements.

The approach ought to have been for universities to proclaim their independent status but to acknowledge that there are issues that raise genuine public concern, most notably the independence of the pay-setting processes, and the measurement of performance in setting pay. They should have led in putting in place the necessary reforms that would have followed, for example through the University Councils, establishing basic advice on the best way to do this. It should not be necessary for the OfS to do this. It is desirable to be transparent and to publish salaries, pensions and conditions, but it should be done by the universities themselves. This is where university individual and collective leadership is required.

The whole effect of this ill-conceived controversy (and possibly the intent of some in the UK's difficult political climate) has been to weaken universities' voices in public debate about their future. We know of many examples where universities' communications or PR offices have advised their

Vice-Chancellors not to do interviews on any matter, for fear that the first question will be about their pay. This is a disastrous state of affairs where universities' advocacy is more than ever needed in public debate.

But overall the first order challenge for universities is to get high quality leaders. Though reform is certainly needed, their pay is a second, or even third, order problem.

Effective national and governmental university leadership

A central proposition of this book is that universities should take direct responsibility for running themselves well and contributing in the right way to addressing the challenges of national economic and social life. We consider that this is both right in principle and will also lead to the most effective university contribution to society, from a government's point of view.

This autonomous model has been the strong basis for universities' success in the past and should be developed to deal with current and future challenges. However, of course we note that our approach contrasts with some countries in the world where national governments play a much more direct role in running universities.

The autonomous university model means that national leadership should concern itself mainly with the major strategic issues related to the sector. Sector expertise is also important and this applies to universities as much as anywhere else so that national university bodies, major academic figures and individual institutions would be expected to make a full contribution to the national debate as to the type of university sector a country wants.

This is very much the case in the UK, Australia and the US. For many decades, the prevailing voice has been to ensure as much autonomy as is practical within a framework that ensures core standards are met and, as part of this, to encourage diversity. This undoubtedly has contributed to a strong university sector in all of the three countries on which we are concentrating our discussion in this book.

We consider that the three issues of strategic importance that clearly need government oversight, responsibility and leadership are:

- the overall nature and structure of the university system;
- the funding basis for universities, including research; and
- the quality of university performance.

These are all sufficiently important to be included in electoral manifestos, for example, and to be regarded as part of the political process to be tested – in the UK, for example, in Parliament. We address these three issues.

Nature and structure of the university system

Firstly, even allowing for institutional autonomy, the basic shape of the university system is very much a national issue. There is of course considerable national divergence in this area. The US has probably the most diverse university sector in the world. Incredibly, vigorous private institutions sit side-by-side with state land grant universities of the highest eminence. Education-focused private providers abound. E-education is very prominent, especially in the private world. Enrolment rates are reasonably high but completion rates, compared to many other countries, are very poor. Other than the private sector, the responsibility for most universities sits with state government.

It may be fair to assert that the US has both the best university system in the world and one of the worst of any advanced economy. The elite providers have few equals whether Ivy League or land grant. The lower-level private providers, especially those that have concentrated on e-education in massive numbers, are rather weak. Overall, however, there is both a great diversity and a huge availability of university places. The 'let 1,000 flowers bloom' philosophy seems to have worked, at least in part.

In the UK, the basic shape of the university sector has both risen organically and been guided by a series of very strong government initiatives. Organic growth has led to Oxbridge and the great civic universities. The move to turn Colleges of Advanced Technology, polytechnics, colleges of education and technical colleges into full universities was very much government-led at various points in history. At around 150, the number of institutions is relatively small compared to some countries, but institutions in general offer a reasonably good education, though with, as mentioned in Chapter 4, very variable research output.

In Australia, the development of universities, sponsored by provincial governments, very much followed that in Scotland and England. A relatively small number of universities existed until the mid-years of the 20th century. Both provincial and central government then worked together to expand the university sector with an increase in the number of institutions and, in more recent years, actively promoted massive expansion of enrolment. These decisions – both to increase the number of institutions and to greatly increase the number of students – were very much government-led. The universities supported this and adapted to it but did not lead.

Another major initiative in Australia and the UK, and which is gathering momentum in the US, was the development of an international student market. In all countries, this involves maintenance of admission standards but attraction of students from other countries who in general pay high fees. The high fee is justified morally by the argument that local students and their families have contributed indirectly to university infrastructure by the tax base often over generations. Not everyone will accept this and it is not the view in continental Europe where international fees are a relatively minor contribution.

The decision to open these markets was very much government-driven, especially in Australia. There, a Labour Government identified international education as a major potential service industry for the country. Favourable visa conditions were developed and institutions were actively encouraged to develop this. Having said this, the university sector adopted this opportunity more readily than most would have thought likely. Governments control the international student market both in terms of the regulatory environment institutions work in (which in all three countries is very open to international enrolment) and in terms of the visa conditions offered to students both for study and for post-study work. This is clearly very much the preserve of government as to the extent to which an individual country wishes to develop an international student market. It should be the preserve of individual institutions as to how far they want to move in the available regulatory environment.

University funding and performance

The second strategic issue, where government takes the lead and there is great public interest and concern, is how the university system should be funded. For a university, the key issue is that it is funded at an adequate level. However, universities are not themselves the driver as to where the funds come from, especially in public institutions. For completely private universities such as the Ivy League it is a different matter. The private university system is extremely well developed in the US but very modest in its extent in the UK and Australia.

Traditionally, in Australia and the US, universities were funded at their beginnings by benevolence supplemented by some direct student contribution. With the rise of the welfare state, most state institutions eventually became fully funded through the tax base. In more recent years, difficulty in fully supporting great universities from the public purse has been increasingly recognised. In both Australia and the UK, this has led to a very significant student/family self-contribution funded through a loan pool which is repaid when the student salary passes a certain threshold. We have discussed this in detail in Chapter 8. We simply state here that the key sources of national public and private funding for universities is very much the preserve of government, to be tested in election manifestos and through the ballot box. Many in universities will have a view on this but the internal university view should not be the major driver.

The quality of university performance

The third major strategic responsibility of national government is to ensure that the country's universities perform at a reasonable level. Of course this applies to the quality of education and the student experience but increasingly takes in issues such as diversity and equity. It is entirely within governments' preserve to insist on high standards across-the-board, though we believe that there is a good case for universities themselves taking on the challenge of high standards of performance in all fields, so that government does not need to get involved. This is an area where poor performance by a relatively small number of universities can force government intervention which significantly affects the ways that all universities are governed.

Government direct intervention is not the best way to secure good university performance in relation to what we have described as the four pillars of university impact in the modern world:

- *understanding and interpreting the process of change;*
- *offering approaches to harness the process of change for general benefit;*
- *educating and training to high quality specialist workers;*
- *creating a general intellectually engaging climate and culture.*

In each of these areas of vital significance, a combination of excellent university governance and leadership with skilful national policy-making, including incentives and alignment with other government strategies, is the combination that will be most effective.

Government structures and ministers

At the end of the day, national responsibility for all of these issues lies with the government of the day. In the UK, ministerial responsibility for higher education has alternated between the Department for Education (and Skills) and the Department of Trade (and Industry). Sometimes, responsibility for science and research has been separated from responsibility for universities.

This is not coherent or consistent but is a consequence of the very fluid governmental system that operates in the UK. There are competing pulls between responsibilities for science and research, which relate to industrial and trade success, on the one hand, and the need for coherence between secondary and tertiary education, on the other. These issues are apparent in a large number of other countries where ministerial responsibility and regulatory and funding agency functions are also divided in ways that are not necessarily consistent and this can create a distorted approach.

In the UK and Australia, in the current public/civil service climate, there is a tendency to wish to, in a sense, rein universities in. Their degree of autonomy may be resented or felt to be inappropriate given the degree of public funding. This has been acute in the UK since 2010 and can place ministers in a conflicted position. Moreover, this desire is at odds with a steady hollowing out and weakening of public service capacity in these fields, which needs to be redressed.

Paradoxically, the UK Government's reforms in 2012 to student finance in England, which meant that a lower proportion of fees were repaid and so placed a greater financial burden on the state than the previous arrangements, have led to much greater direct governmental intervention in university governance. A further factor was the political need to justify the major rise in direct student fees to young voters and their families.

This has reached spectacular levels in the UK with a series of targeted interventions that have dramatically reduced university autonomy (eg the increasing role of the Office for Students, including the Teaching Excellence Framework). Interestingly, these interventions came from a Conservative Government in the UK while there have been similar developments in Australia from the left of politics, though with much lesser degrees of intervention. The UK has yet to follow the Australian regulatory experience with TEQSA.[21] This came in in 2011 with great powers that were reduced as government appreciated the deleterious effect on important university autonomy. The UK Higher Education and Research Act 2017 mentions the importance of autonomy in the preamble but empowers the OfS as a hands-on and potentially intrusive regulator. There is every evidence that the OfS intends to use these powers, and time alone will tell whether this further strengthens an already very strong sector or has the opposite effect. The outcome of the OfS experiment in the UK will depend, in large part, on the skill of those appointed to governance and executive roles. Fortunately, at both a governance and leadership level, people have been appointed with a deep understanding of the sector.

In the US, where government interference is less well tolerated in most things, university autonomy is high in most states, although direct state involvement is increasing and government appointment of trustees and indeed of university Presidents or system presidents is commoner. This can lead to spectacular firing of well-regarded leaders. The most memorable, some decades ago, was the firing of the greatest US university leader since the Second World War, Clark Kerr at Berkeley, by Ronald Reagan when Governor of California.

In these varied circumstances, it is fair to ask what type of university Minister or Secretary of State is therefore optimal. Universities need a relatively stable ministerial role for an individual who is consultative in character with good links with the sector and who is sensitive to international trends in both education and research. There are significant dangers in an interventionist minister who becomes too hands-on with too sharp an ideological agenda. Attempts to redesign the university system through the introduction of new national drivers such as the development of the Teaching Excellence Framework in the UK have to be handled extremely carefully. In our view, establishment of appropriate academic standards, reasonable financial performance and high diversity and equity standards are certainly within the preserve of government. Very occasionally, major reform is needed to update the whole sector as has happened on a number of occasions both in Australia and the UK in recent decades. For the most part, however, government ministers should remain well removed from the academic engine of the university as attempts to tinker in depth risk interfering overmuch with institutional autonomy.

Conclusion

University leadership is a complicated and difficult matter and we do not claim to have dealt with the subject comprehensively in this chapter.

But the central point, which we hope that readers will draw from this account, is the need for both individual universities and governments to pay proper attention to the nature and quality of leadership, both of individual universities and of the university system as a whole.

We contend that the contribution of universities to our future is important, but it will be maximised only if the system is well led at all levels. Government policy ought to be to encourage, but universities have to put leadership quality at the top of their agendas.

Governments should establish a stronger and collaborative government structure for developing leadership of the sector.

Together with universities they should support well-recognised and strong higher education leadership training institutions and work with universities to develop clear indices of successful university leadership.

They should reduce the regulatory role of the Office for Students and encourage universities to take on their own leadership responsibilities.

And they should reform the funding system to promote more independent universities.

Universities should establish better and clearer processes for recruiting and firing university leaders and review their governance structures to enable them to face up better to the challenges of the future.

They should create transparent regimes for Vice-Chancellors' pay and conditions and review academics' career patterns from the point of view of promoting institutional leadership quality at all levels.

And they should take very active steps to promote diverse and respectful university communities in the ways that we have described in this chapter.

Chapter 10

Ten questions about the future of universities

The first challenge that Charles faced upon appointment as UK Secretary of State for Education and Skills, on 24 October 2002, was what to do about student finance. This was a very controversial area but one where the government needed to act, including legislation, before the next General Election, expected in 2005. After intense and rapid work, he published the White Paper with his proposals on 22 January 2003, which was then implemented, though not without plenty of ups and downs.

This was not a good method of making policy and is not to be recommended, though this process is not atypical of many political decisions in controversial areas.

This chapter identifies 10 questions about the future of universities over the next couple of decades. The questions are fairly easy to set out, the answers much more difficult to predict and they depend upon what universities do during that time.

And universities have to decide who they want to answer these questions: mainly the universities themselves or mainly governments imposing their views, which might be excellent or might be terrible.

And of course the questions are about the future. The past, in this case the chronicle of the university sector, may be misinterpreted through the eyes of the present but is at least based on some historical bedrock. The future is a different matter especially when society is changing at such a dramatic pace.

The great Harvard business scholar Clayton Christensen, who has pioneered concepts of disruptive change[1] in the business world, believes that the current university model is broken and that the combination of societal change with new needs and solutions made possible by the evolving information revolution will render the current university model obsolete even for the greatest institutions (and Christensen comes from Harvard!) within a generation. Michael Barber's book *An Avalanche is Coming* predicted that technological change in teaching, and even research, is so rapid and existing universities so unprepared that the current structure of universities will be entirely swept away within a generation.

Others, possibly with their heads in the sand, take a diametrically opposed view. They feel that academic truths are almost unchanging and that universities will continue through the rest of the century more or less as they did in the last.

Who is right? Certainly not the second group who are behaving like dodos. But probably not the prophets of total disruption either. The picture will be nuanced and that is why it is worth posing some key questions about the future, to which we then try to offer some answers.

These questions both align and overlap with earlier chapters and seek to draw out key themes around the future of universities in this rapidly changing world to which they need to be able to contribute so much.

We hope that one response to these questions is that:

Governments should ensure that the country faces up to the problems and challenges set out in good time to address them and that these issues are debated openly in Parliament and elsewhere.

They should consider what these challenges mean for the accepted national framework and culture of universities.

Universities should continually make the case for the utility and value of university education for the society as a whole and on that basis continually re-examine their missions.

Ten questions

1. Will the research-led university, which has been the key model for a century and a half, persist into the future or has it had its day?
2. Will the multi-faculty university survive?
3. How many universities will be there be, and what size?
4. Will the proportion of international students increase or decrease?
5. How many students will be studying courses by different modes?
6. Will technology take over and eliminate current approaches to teaching? With increasing e-education, what will happen to the current geographic institutions with large campuses?
7. What will happen to the quality of university degrees and 'grade inflation'?
8. Will freedom of speech be maintained in universities?
9. Will academia continue to be an attractive and sustainable career?
10. How much will thriving economies devote to the university sector in GDP terms?

Question 1

Will the research-led university, which has been the key model for a century and a half, persist into the future or has it had its day?

We have discussed the background to this existential question at some length, particularly in Chapters 2 and 4, and we do not really believe that it has a 'Yes or No' answer.

This model – where research and teaching are combined and where teaching is, in principle, informed by research – works well for staff and most would say reasonably well (though this proposition has been challenged, for example in the teaching rankings) for today's students. Many great people are attracted to university life by a desire to contribute new knowledge in an important field, that is the entirely honourable research motivation.

For staff, it provides a career structure where new knowledge creation is combined with teaching others. That is an extremely satisfactory emotional position for most academics. There are important issues around tenure (and permanent contracts) that may last decades beyond an individual's creative research contribution or teaching capacity. Particularly in some disciplines, great research often takes place relatively early in an academic's career. Tenure, which lasts for life in countries where it exists, is, however, very highly valued for the good reason that it maintains the academic independence of the individual researcher and prevents investigative and challenging thought being compromised by seeking advancement for venal reasons.

However, one important consequence of long-term tenure is that it makes it more difficult to give younger people the academic security they need to be able to conduct their research. There is an echo of this dilemma in current controversies about the appropriate retirement age for academics in an era where discrimination on the grounds of age is illegal. The lack of an established retiring age for senior academics undoubtedly leads to significant cross-generational inequities.

There are parallel dilemmas around the university complacency that this can create and that makes it extremely difficult to reform traditional academic staff and university structures, sometimes despite very obvious needs for change, such as the arrival of new modes of teaching, or the need for more flexible forms of learning.

However, it's likely that academic life, at least in the vast majority of universities, will have to come much closer to work expectations in the rest of society, in that ongoing employment will be linked to performance.

It also defines, at one level, the traditional difference between a university teacher and a secondary school teacher, the fact that the academic creates as well as imparts knowledge. This is at the core of much of the prestige and most of the appeal associated with academic life. The very close alignment between teaching and research still pertains in most universities for most academics. However, even top research institutions now often have teaching-focused parallel promotion schemes that recognise the crucial value of the non-research-active dedicated educator.

For students, the benefits of research-led teaching are less immediately visible. It makes empirical sense that the teacher who is at the forefront of knowledge creation could well be able to inspire students with the excitement of the new and lead many of them to research interests themselves in a way that someone who has never been research-active may well find more difficult.

It is also probable that the intellectual environment in an institution where new research ground is being broken is more vibrant than in a purely teaching institution. On the other hand, in spite of some efforts, there has been a tendency in the great research universities for research to dominate career structures and promotion prospects and for teaching to take second place. This has been recognised in the UK with the introduction of a Teaching Excellence and Student Outcomes Framework (TEF) to balance the well-established research excellence framework. This is clearly an attempt to rebalance university priorities in a way that will probably also rebalance academic careers.

It is also undeniable that an excellent university education can be provided by institutions that are not research-active in a major way. The private Laureate group is a more complete example. It runs excellent universities, especially in the Spanish-speaking world where research is carried out as needed to meet registration criteria and not part of their core mission.

These institutions teach well and have first-rate professional schools. What do they miss that research-active institutions can offer? Certainly, stimulation of students to probe new frontiers themselves and perhaps (though this is highly questionable) a vitality of intellectual excitement at the highest level. Does this matter to most students? Possibly not. Most wish to get an education that fits them for a career in the wider world. Only a small proportion will choose to pursue a direct academic or research career and, if they do, their first degree in a teaching-only institution, they are always able to develop research interests through postgraduate experience and qualifications at many points in their life.

The reductionist national policy analysts note that teaching-only institutions are more efficient, they are more focused on the educational outcomes (again this can be disputed) and they are perhaps less turbulent! In short, going to such an institution may not be so different from the senior years of secondary or high school.

Of course, those who argue for teaching-only universities as the predominant model may miss the 'ghost in the machine' – that co-existence between research and teaching that has served universities so well over the past 150 years.

Universities that are set up in this way tend to be the most productive in brilliant graduates and, for obvious reasons, attract the most outstanding research staff. It is their existence that marks academia as an exciting career profile and helps draw brilliant people into it.

Research and education can, of course, be separated. To some extent, this happens in Germany where the Fraunhofer and Max Planck Institutes co-exist with a vibrant university sector. It works in Germany because tight alliances are developed with PhD opportunities being offered through universities in affiliated institutes. Perhaps if the great scientists in the Max Planck institutions were more engaged in teaching roles, German universities would be stronger again!

None of the above reflections answers the question as to whether the research-led education university model will survive as the general model over the next 50 years. For the reasons set out above, biased academics who have spent careers in this system often think its merits should prevail but it is far from sure that they will.

Reductionist thinking from governments and others may fail to see or value that special spark that makes the research university shine. It could be legislated out of existence. The way that the current UK Government has developed the TEF has the potential to unravel and do great harm to very strong institutions that are still doing great things for the country and more widely.

If university teaching were simply to be offered in the most cost-effective way, then the current research-led model may find itself under fatal pressures as it faces competition from both public and private universities using a variety of modes of learning.

That would be a great shame for the reasons set out at the beginning of this book – that for universities as a whole to contribute to addressing the rapid process of change in the world, we need universities that operate well in all of the four pillars that we identify:

- *understanding and interpreting change in the world;*
- *offering approaches to harness the process of change for general benefit;*

- *educating and training the specialists whose skills are necessary to address change;*
- *creating an intellectually engaging climate and culture across societies.*

Teaching, vital though it is, is just one of those key university roles and we need universities that can play the wider role that we have identified.

We are clear that neither the 'resist almost all change' dodos, nor the 'avalanche of change' advocates offer a helpful way forward. One of the key things that frighten all education reformers is that what looks like sensible reform may be overly simplistic and damage the valuable heritage of universities that has contributed so much to our society.

The golden key to this process of change is to find an organic development that blends the positive opportunities that technology and other forms of change can bring and the strong university values that are so important.

In this book we try to offer suggestions as to how this organic development could be fostered through better relationships between research and teaching, more fluid networks of institutions, more positive and dynamic interaction between workplaces and universities, less rigid mechanisms of teaching and learning, better international relationships and more promotion of university-level learning through life to enable people to address accelerating change in their lives ever more effectively.

Our conviction is that a positive attitude to this process of change will not happen at the behest of governments but has to be embraced by universities themselves and their leaders.

In each of the areas that we describe there have been a few initiatives and projects in the places where change is needed. Some have been extremely positive and encouraging. But there are very few, if any, examples of the kinds of systemic transformation in any of these areas that would give confidence in the capacity of the university system to transform itself to meet modern needs.

Government cannot impose a process of change that meets these needs, but it can encourage it, including by creating a legal and sustainable funding framework within which change can flourish.

The question that we pose does not have a clear 'Yes or No' answer. The key to successful transformation towards universities of the future will depend upon high quality leadership and thought, both in individual universities and in governments and that has to be fostered.

Question 2

Will the multi-faculty university survive?

It is interesting that most of the world's really great universities are now multi-faculty, another way of saying that they encompass the sciences and the humanities broadly. In Chapter 4 we mention Paul Wellings' demonstration of this.

The humanities interpreted in this way include law and business schools as well as the social sciences and the arts and humanities. The sciences include the applied sciences of engineering and medicine, information technology and the natural sciences of physics, chemistry and mathematics. Traditionally, these came together because it has proved more efficient to maintain academic structures that relate to a number of faculties and have a critical mass. This co-existence has been significantly reinforced over the past decade by the rise of interdisciplinarity in both education and research.

The intellectual power that can be brought to bear around the challenges of the age, both large and small, is significantly enhanced when individuals from different disciplines who look at the problem from different perspectives can be brought together. Universities are just starting to educate the next generation of students in a way that puts interdisciplinarity at the core of their thinking processes. This is already proving immensely valuable.

At its high point, one can see examples such as the Earth Institute at Columbia University, probably the leading environmental institute in the world, but examples abound in every university. Much of the most exciting work going on in the university world at the moment brings different disciplines together to attack important problems. This is increasingly recognised through research funding bodies, notably the research councils in the UK. That is not to say that disciplinary depth does not continue to be crucial. Of course, it does.

One cannot build a house on bricks of straw. But institutions that crack the interdisciplinary problem in their structures will thrive more than those that do not.

In some countries, single discipline universities have been the standard model. This is reflected to varying extents in a number of European countries. In the US, some of the greatest institutions specialise in a small number of disciplines. MIT is one example but it is noteworthy that expertise has been built up in a wide range of disciplines over the years and that wide collaborations with other institutions have filled the gaps.

Imperial College in London, a great engineering and natural sciences university, has now acquired a first-rate medical school and spawned a leading-edge business school.

Other institutions continue to thrive in a narrow space and do extraordinarily well. Researcher for researcher, Caltech may well be the strongest scientific institution in the world in university terms. It is very small but it is outstandingly strong. UCSF and the Karolinska in Stockholm are outstanding medical universities not closely affiliated with other disciplines. The London School of Economics provides superb training in the social sciences. All of these exceptions to the rule do not disprove the key point. Each of them has overcome disciplinary isolation in novel ways. It may be by a focus on those areas that are attackable through single disciplinary approaches and they are many, or it may be through appropriate alliances with neighbouring institutions.

Their success does not negate the proposition that a multidisciplinary approach is a massive asset in today's university world. The grand challenges, as defined by international authorities, all require a multidisciplinary approach to effect solution whether it be healthy ageing or a sustainable economy and a sustainable planet. It is likely that the multidisciplinary institution is here to stay, at least for a while longer!

These arguments for multi- and cross-disciplinary study, which apply very strongly in many fields of research, pertain perhaps even more strongly in undergraduate teaching. Despite recent developments in permitting single discipline universities in the UK, such as the University of Law, there is little doubt that both individual and the wider society benefit from education across the range of knowledge. The 'Two Cultures',[2] about which CP Snow wrote 60 years ago and which so alarmed policy-makers at the time, remains a pressing policy concern both in the purely educational arena and in the cultural politics of what makes an educated and civilised society.

As we argue elsewhere in this book, one of the central functions of universities is to educate, in the widest sense, citizens of society to deal with the complexity and range of challenges that arise increasingly rapidly across the world. That is better done in a multi-faculty context and for us will remain a convincing argument for the dominant role of multi-faculty university, at least in the early stages of university student life.

We suspect that the demand from researchers to work in a cross-disciplinary way, and for potential undergraduates to learn in a multi-faculty context, will be powerful agents to encourage multi-faculty universities to go from strength to strength, perhaps enhanced by a stronger international dimension.

However, monotechnic university teaching will increase its challenge to multi-faculty universities for reasons of cost and also quality, even if perhaps narrowly defined.

Universities need to work harder to create internal structures that promote interdisciplinary research and teaching and build strong partnerships with other universities. This may well mean breaking down the walls of some silos that exist.

And governments need to keep under close review the decision to allow monotechnic institutions to use the title 'university', a decision that, in the UK, happened only recently.

Question 3

How many universities will be there be, and what size?

What is the right number of universities for a city like London?

The current 40+ is the result of organic change over centuries, but has no particular rationality. It includes a collection of entirely different types of institution, some great research centres, other strong teaching institutions, some multi-faculty and some just researching or teaching one discipline.

A large number go back well over a century, though many have only relatively recently been called 'universities'. This pattern of universities in one city may or may not well reflect the needs of the future, either in research or teaching. And the same could be said of other cities both in the UK and the rest of the world.

Since 1945, many Western economies have moved to about two universities per one million citizens. This ratio may well turn out to be quite durable, even with the advent of new technology. It would mean a significant reduction in the number of universities in the UK.

In most other worlds, such as business or government, there would have been a process of 'rationalisation', either through government diktat, or through a process of 'mergers and acquisitions' influenced predominantly by market factors.

In the university world, the way forward has been much less clear. Mergers certainly happened in the past, notably when the polytechnics were created and before they became universities. And they are happening in the present, for example when recently the Institute of Education, a world-leading research institution, joined University College London in 2014. And the major university merger between the Victoria University of Manchester and the University of Manchester, Institute of Science and Technology, created the current University of Manchester in 2004. This was intended to add competitive research strength in the North West of England, well away from London and the South East of England where England's strongest research universities are concentrated.

Other proposed mergers, such as that between Liverpool and Lancaster universities, have crashed in flames when exposed to academic opinion. A planned major Australian merger that attracted a lot of international attention, that between the Universities of Adelaide and of South Australia, has recently collapsed because of cultural mismatch.

There is a series of different types of motive for 'mergers and acquisitions' in the university world. They include merging to maximise research strength and cross-fertilisation; merging to develop a better student experience, including a wider range of modes of learning and more efficient use of teaching facilities of all kinds; and merging to create a range of business and functional economies, both of scale and for other reasons.

It might additionally be the case that where universities are facing financial difficulties, as some are at the moment, it might well be better for them to merge, or to be 'acquired', to create institutions with the strong financial base needed to develop their teaching and/or research.

Many communities across the country desire to build university capacity in their own city, a motive that reflects the civic approach to the foundation of many of the oldest universities, as we discuss in Chapter 2. And, as we discuss in Chapter 5, this desire to have a university in their locality is usually justified by the experience that the presence of a local university can provide an additional economic boost to the locality, in a variety of ways. This certainly includes teaching and the provision of courses, particularly when there is an increasing proportion of home-based undergraduate students. But it often also includes applied research which can contribute directly to the local economy.

Following the 2003/4 legislation, the establishment of universities was deeply welcomed in counties like Cheshire, Cornwall, Cumbria, Derbyshire, Dorset, Gloucestershire, Lincolnshire, Northamptonshire, Suffolk and Worcestershire, which had previously had no universities at all. Visits to some of those places now, 15 years on, show clearly the major positive local impact that those universities have created for their communities.

And one important side-effect of this reform is that many of the higher education institutions that became universities at that time changed from being mono-faculty institutions, for example in teacher training or art, to multi-faculty. This happened, and continues to happen, in many creative ways.

The issue of size is less clear. It used to be the case that, in the UK, the size of individual universities was essentially determined by the government, through its control of funding mechanisms. However, the decisions in 2012 (Australia) and 2015 (England) to end the 'capping' of university numbers has enabled more of a free-for-all to emerge and remains a subject of political controversy including at the 2019 Australian General Election.

Competition between universities now takes place in a more aggressive way, primarily around brand and perception, and the current state of affairs is rapidly evolving.

The competition based on fee level in England, which was anticipated from the 2004 reforms onwards, and strongly expected after the increase in maximum fee from £3,000 per year to £9,000 per year in 2010, has simply not taken place.

It would be difficult to maintain, on educational grounds, that any particular university, or even faculty, size is optimal though some note that the great Ivy League universities in the US in general enrol rather fewer students than many of the successful research universities in the UK. However, as online learning becomes more prevalent, there will probably be a reducing correlation between success and size.

As a result, we do not expect any 'preferred' size of university to dominate, but university size will simply be a residual arising from the process of mergers and acquisitions that otherwise takes place. It will be right for some universities to increase student numbers, like UT in Canada or UCL in London, while others' strategic ambitions may cause them to contract in student size and many of the very best universities are small in student numbers.

So how will this pattern of universities develop in the future? When new legislation was being considered in 2003/4, Charles was urged by some regulators to give powers to the Secretary of State to require universities to merge if this was in the national interest, for example for reasons of raising research quality or increasing local choices of courses or increasing economic impact.

Obviously, such a power, while seemingly attractive, was potentially threatening to university autonomy and these suggestions were not followed through for reasons of both principle and politics.

However, it was fully expected that, even without such a governmental power, there would be a natural and organic shift towards fewer universities and more co-operations and collaborations between them than has in fact been the case over the succeeding decades.

This is not because the current distribution of universities is optimal but is more a credit to the fundamentally conservative nature of universities that are very cautious about change of any kind, least of all one that leads to the disappearance of a university.

However, it should be noted that one impact of the increased competition between universities, which follows the uncapping of student numbers, may well be one or more university closures or bankruptcies, which many anticipate. One solution to such a crisis is likely to be an 'acquisition' by another university, local or not.

There may also be more positive motives, for example to establish universities in parts of the country that currently don't have one, for example in the way that the University of East Anglia and the University of Essex combined to create what ultimately became the University of Suffolk in 2016.

We are very doubtful whether the current pattern of universities can last as it is for long, given the massive changes, particularly in modes of learning and technology, to which we refer throughout this book.

We hope that university leaders will face up to these challenges themselves. It would be far better for universities themselves to consider, together with their local communities, what might be the best way forward, possibly with new international connections. The alternative is that government – at least in the UK – will come under increasing pressure to take the powers that were not taken in 2003/4 and themselves create a more 'rational' pattern of universities. This is not the best way to make this type of change happen.

So, we would suggest that universities in particular cities should give active consideration to the most rational pattern of university research and teaching in that locality and consider what steps should be taken to enable that to happen. And governments should consider what incentives they can offer to encourage a more rational pattern of universities across the country.

Question 4

Will the proportion of international students increase or decrease?

We discuss in Chapter 4 the place of international students and researchers in universities. World student numbers are projected to double in the next 20 years. Will they come to the UK or will the UK have to go to them?

In addition to their educational benefits in improving the university culture and quality, international students have played a vital financial role. They provide the fee income which is absolutely essential for many UK and Australian universities. This is less important for most universities in the US and continental Europe.

The question is whether these numbers of students, and so this income, will continue in the future.

We think that there is a general complacency about the prospects. The fact is that the number of tertiary level students around the world is expanding rapidly and all the projections are for this number to continue increasing. For all the reasons we set out in this book, we think that these projections are in the right direction. The number of tertiary students will continue to increase.

Moreover, English (including the Australian and North American versions) will continue to be the dominant world language. English fluency will continue to be highly desirable, if not an absolute requirement, for those seeking to work in major economic and social sectors around the world.

The only effective linguistic challenge comes from China but we do not believe that even the growing importance of China will threaten the dominant role of the English language in global higher education.

Indeed, it is notable that, in China as well as many other countries in Asia, Europe and Latin America, English is continuing to expand as the language of higher education in many countries where English is not the language of the country concerned.

But the reason for this expansion is a key to understanding why the dominant position of the UK and Australia may be threatened. The world market for international students is now so large and opportunity-rich that universities in many countries around the world see benefits for themselves in offering high quality undergraduate courses, through the teaching medium of English, to attract those international students.

Universities making that decision to pursue internationalisation of course offer a measure of competition for the universities that have traditionally been the natural home for international students. But there are three even more serious threats to British and Australian global market share and standing.

The first is the US where there have been relatively far fewer opportunities for international students. In absolute terms, there are many university places for international students in the US, though it is a relatively small proportion of the total number of students in US universities. This is changing as more and more US universities are attracting international students. Universities like the University of Southern California in Los Angeles are able to attract very large numbers of students from countries on the Pacific Rim and more widely, who are ready to pay substantial fees. We believe that this trend will intensify, even if the Trump administration leads to long-term tighter immigration control and a trade war with China. Even in those circumstances, we expect that the US will become a more and more realistic option for students from around the world seeking undergraduate qualifications to enable them to work in the upper levels of the world economy.

The second is the massive expansion of high quality university education, including in English, which is taking place in the main countries of origin themselves, such as China, India, Japan and many others. These universities are themselves becoming increasingly enmeshed in the world economy so that English-speaking graduates of those universities can realistically look to work in world companies on the basis of good qualifications from their home countries, which is for them a far less expensive option than seeking university abroad in very expensive countries.

The third threat is the growing strength of online university-level qualifications. This of course means that students are increasingly able to study for their university qualifications from their own countries, perhaps with only a relatively small number of visits to their university campuses.

So the complacent view that international students, with their funds, will keep coming to UK and Australian universities for their undergraduate and master's qualifications is one that will become increasingly stressed in coming years. It will be an increasingly competitive world within which current destination universities really will have to look to their laurels.

This is of course why the UK Government's self-harming focus on erecting visa barriers to international students coming to the UK is so deeply damaging in a number of ways. This is not the place for a discussion about the policy illusions that have preoccupied the government's decisions, not to mention the whole Brexit psychodrama, except to say that now is absolutely not the time to be building additional hurdles for international students wanting to come to the UK to study.

But it goes beyond that idiocy. In the increasingly competitive marketplace that we predict, universities need to be very sure that they are both welcoming international students properly and providing education at a high level of quality for all students who come to study. There are issues that need to be addressed here and future success will depend upon how well that is done.

Whether the proportion of international students increases or decreases will depend upon the way in which the various factors that we have identified here play out. On balance, we would expect the proportion to decline over the next two decades, but strong university performance could well swing that expectation in a more optimistic direction. But that requires university leadership and government encouragement, if it is to happen.

Question 5

How many students will be studying courses by different modes?

There have been many efforts to increase the number of modes of acquiring an undergraduate degree.

The three-year course traditional in the UK and similar systems has gradually become the norm that other university systems have moved towards, not least through the European 'Bologna process'.

The British approach was seen as far more efficient than the type of extended university life, up to six or seven years, which had been conventional, for example in German universities.

In parallel, there have been regular efforts to offer different approaches from studying for three academic years in two or three terms or semesters that provide, say, 32–36 weeks' study a year (or about 100 weeks' study over three years) with consequent under-utilisation of equipment, teaching and learning facilities and staff time.

In 1968, the then universities minister, Shirley Williams, proposed two-year degrees. Her proposal has been followed by a whole series of models, including Diplomas in Higher Education (DipHEs), foundation degrees, sandwich degrees, with full-time work interspersed with study, and now degree apprenticeships. Most recently, we have seen 'accelerated' and 'fast-track' degrees.

All of these, and similar models across the world, have their merits and are designed to meet certain types of educational need, often valuably relating study more closely to work opportunities. Changes towards a more significant 'work' component in a university degree could well lead to a renaissance of 'sandwich-style' study.

A different form of variety was stimulated by the Open University in the UK, now with many imitators across the world – many of which are extraordinarily successful. Online education has developed rapidly, though perhaps not yet as rapidly as many people expected, with entirely new types of university as well as an extension to this mode of learning from more traditional universities. This type of degree could well be supplemented by strong residential components with a price premium.

As these different approaches to degree qualifications swirl and eddy across universities in every continent, many of them opening up university possibilities to students who never had the chance before, the question arises how the patterns will develop in coming decades. With these challenges it is not at all certain that the conventional three-year degree will continue to be the absolutely dominant mode as other forms of getting a degree become increasingly commonplace.

The new modes of learning may even come to dominate the number of degrees that are awarded so that most students get their degrees online, with the ability to study at the times and in the environments that seem most convenient to their own circumstances.

The only prediction that we feel able to make with any confidence is that, over the next couple of decades, there will be a declining proportion of students getting their undergraduate degrees through the traditional route of a residential three-year degree away from home.

We do not predict this because the absolute number of students following such a course will decline, but because there will be an expansion in the number of students getting their degrees by other, more diverse, routes.

In fact, we think that it is unlikely that there will be a great deal of change for university study from 19 to 22 after leaving school. There is little doubt that, students, their families and potential employers will continue to see this residential degree as valuable if it can be afforded. Whatever its educational merits it has become a rite of passage for a very large proportion of the children of middle-class families across the developed world, and an increasingly large proportion of the children of working-class families. Changes will be more likely to enhance this experience, for example through a more substantial international component, than to reduce it.

The decision to take a break between school and university may become more common, which both enhances the quality of students' choices about their courses and improves their capacity to work at university. But it will not reduce significantly the number of students choosing the traditional university course mode of study.

So, our conclusion is that a wider range of course modes of study will be developed, which will have the effect of increasing access to university qualifications, and so the proportion studying by the conventional route will decline. But the conventional option will remain popular and desired. And we expect a larger number of students to take qualifications later in life for the reasons we discuss in Chapter 7, and that almost all of these will be through online education with limited residential elements.

The universities that will achieve most success will be those that can best improve the quality of student education on that basis and so improve the overall student experience.

And governments will need to find funding systems that encourage diverse forms of learning.

Question 6

Will technology take over and eliminate current approaches to teaching? With increasing e-education, what will happen to the current geographic institutions with large campuses?

We have discussed in our answer to question 5 the development of online learning which we think will open far wider opportunities and enable more people to study, but will not close down traditional residential education.

Many people have observed with great interest the chess battles between the best players of the day. In the world of chess, Garry Kasparov held his own against Deep Blue but Watson in the end proved unbeatable. There is no doubt that new computer-based learning paradigms will have the capacity to take some of the strain at the early stages of undergraduate education in the years ahead. It is just conceivable that by mid-century this will have replaced the human component and it could be seen as an extension of the technology-enhanced learning methodologies currently coming into practice. In science fiction, it is uniform to have computer assistance in managing complex databases.

This has not found its way into everyday life at the moment but it is reasonably clear that eventually it will and it will be a small step from scanning a database of information to asking one's computer to do more analysis and more of the intellectual groundwork. We look forward immensely to the day when that comes to pass but I'm sure that academics and other teachers will still be talking to students and assisting with their development many decades into the future.

Joseph Aoun's book,[3] to which we referred in Chapter 3, discusses this in detail.

The technology will, however, significantly change the way in which much teaching is delivered. This process of change will have a big impact on current university buildings and infrastructure. This is already happening.

If conventional on-campus education is transformed by the irresistible onward march of e-education, then of course current massive campuses used for undergraduate educational purposes for a relatively modest proportion of each year will no longer be needed and will be converted into apartments, townhouses and whatever else will generate money for developers!

Whatever the level of technological change in learning methods, significant changes will occur. Increased inroads from technology-enhanced learning into highly traditional schools are both appropriate and unstoppable. The large lecture, typically to first-year students, where 500 or more students may sit in a room and listen to a lecture little different from information they could read in any standard textbook with no opportunity for questioning or dialogue, has almost certainly had its day. Most academics enjoy the lecture process and many great universities are wedded to it so change will be slow. Even modest steps like lecture capture on video meet resistance.

Technology-enhanced learning re-badged as large group learning, where a single tutor oversees and contributes to a large number of students working in smaller groups, probably is viable.

More and more educators' time will be spent in direct dialogue with small numbers of students using new technologies to lighten the teaching load. This means, at the very least, that the plethora of large lecture theatres currently seen on most university campuses will be a thing of the past. More and more learning is likely to be done in informal surroundings which may well continue to be on university campuses but may also be in people's homes, community centres or even their other workplaces.

This also means that individual students will get more personalised teaching attention, really focusing on their own individual learning needs, and this is likely to be beneficial, though of course is potentially very time-consuming and expensive, possibly prohibitively so.

Research needs in terms of laboratories and workshops are likely to continue more or less as they are at the moment.

Whatever the level of e-communication between students and teachers, a physical hub where personal communication takes place is still likely to be both educationally desirable, and desired.

The end result is that university campuses may be a little smaller and on-campus student numbers may even be reduced a little. But the university as a significant campus entity is likely to continue even in the age of e-education.

But the way that will work requires a good deal of thinking and preparation.

Question 7

What will happen to the quality of university degrees and 'grade inflation'?

'Standards aren't what they were in my day' is a refrain that echoes down the ages at all stages of education, very much including in modern universities.

The views of such critics, often broadcast widely in the media, give rise to a genuine no-win situation for universities: if universities get better at teaching and learning, as we should wish, the likely outcome is that a higher proportion of students will get first class or other good honours degrees and a lower proportion will get low grades. That should be seen as a sign of university success, and not of insufficiently rigorous attention to standards.

If the proportion of 'good' degrees goes down, then universities are seen not to be doing their job properly. Students paying large fees may also expect high grades and some have even taken legal action to try to guarantee the return in their investment!

And, if universities decide to give first class degrees to a specific percentage of students, do they end up giving degrees to individuals who in previous years would not have got a first class degree in order to fulfill the quota; or, conversely, are they not giving certain people the first class degrees that they deserve because that would mean too many first class degrees? Either way, there are significant issues of equity between generations.

Equity between institutions is also problematic. We do not believe that all first class mathematics or law degrees from any university in the country demonstrate equal levels of achievement. And certainly public perception values similar degrees from different universities very differently. Whether fairly or unfairly, degrees from some universities, mainly the most research-intensive, are given greater status by employers and sometimes universities when considering people for doctoral studies than others.

It is very difficult to test the fairness of such perceptions, which can have significant consequences for the students concerned.

Moreover, there are challenges around incentivisation. As the world of university entrance becomes more competitive, there is a contest for students (and their fees) which can lead to more 'unconditional' university offers[4] and the controversy that invites. At the same time, universities, not unreasonably, want to be able to assure applying students that they have a good chance of a 'good' degree if they come to their university.

These issues of course affect schools as well as universities, and they mostly reflect educational and political fashion rather than issues of substance.

But they do pose challenges to universities and will continue to do so.

It is very important to ensure that the quality of qualifications is protected against cheating, plagiarism and other such problems and rigour is needed in that respect.

And it is even more important to put in place systems of assessment that help students to learn and to develop themselves so that they emerge from university with the highest possible capacity to fulfill themselves and to meet the challenges that they face.

We suspect that the issues in this area will continue to flurry, without the imposition of a national system of awarding degrees which removes this right from individual universities.

It is yet another matter to which universities will need to continue to give focused attention if they are not to find themselves unduly criticised.

Question 8

Will freedom of speech be maintained in universities?

Given the history of universities, this question really should be quite unnecessary. Freedom of speech has been central to the development of universities as we know them. But as we have discussed in Chapter 6, there are a number of important issues of conduct and controversy that universities need to address.

In recent years, it has inescapably become true that there are increasingly frequent challenges, in a variety of ways, to freedom of speech. Forty-five years ago, the controversies swirled around 'no platform' for racists and fascists, with all kinds of definitions of those words and, as always, the conflicts in the Middle East were a significant part of the disputes, notably around the proposition adopted by the United Nations between 1975 and 1991 that 'Zionism is Racism'.

Today, the same arguments continue in universities, with additional reference to terrorism and a wide range of other concerns, such as transgender identification. In historic institutions, there have been campaigns to remove statues of individuals such as Cecil Rhodes who are deemed to have played an unacceptable role in establishing the British Empire or a repressive role more generally in history.

In the UK, the government created significant difficulties for universities by including them, mistakenly in our view, in the 2015 Counter-Terrorism and Security Act, which gave UK universities a statutory duty to have 'due regard to the need to prevent individuals from being drawn into terrorism'.

And, over the years, the legal situation has moved on as the statute now seeks to prevent 'incitement to hatred' on grounds of race and religious belief.

It should be no surprise that universities are places where the boundaries of good practice, and the law, are tested most sharply.

But it seems to us exceptionally important that universities, as the homes of controversy and critical thinking and challengers of conformist thinking, should not, in general, accept the position of those who believe that they have the right to prevent others speaking their views, however offensive and provocative.

In fact, we would go further and maintain that it is the duty of universities to go further and take whatever steps are necessary to protect the ability of such people to express their views.

This is often difficult because of potential public order issues, which do need to be dealt with sensitively – often easier to write about than actually to do.

That said, the principles should be clear:

1. Universities should act within the law of the land, and it is the responsibility of the police and security services to uphold that law.
2. Within that constraint, universities have a duty to uphold freedom of speech under the law, and to sustain a university culture that gives priority to a true and rounded intellectual and cultural history that deals with history as it is and not how it might or should have been.

This is, of course, not easy but we remain convinced that universities without genuine freedom of speech are ultimately unable to fulfill their responsibilities for preparing for the future.

Question 9

Will academia continue to be an attractive and sustainable career?

This is a very difficult question because, at one level, academia has never been more attractive as a career option than it is at the moment. Why do we say that? Because the pathway to academic life is still a PhD and there are now more students doing PhDs at universities around the world than was ever the case in the past. Granted, many of them will end up working outside universities in productive roles in industry and business but others will be the great academics of the future. This all sounds rosy but of course there is a downside.

The jobs for life, which tenure used to imply, are not the norm in wider society. And here academics need to be a little careful. It sometimes seems as if their work expectations in terms of issues such as tenure, workload and pensions don't align fully with what's going on in the rest of society.

In today's world, lifelong tenure is unusual and pensions based on final salary are going out both because of the financial implications of dramatically increased longevity and because of intergenerational fairness.

Workloads where the educational component is centred on less than half of the calendar with very high degrees of personal freedom aren't the norm.

These very well-established characteristics of academic life are bound to change in the coming years. The movement may well be significant.

The majority of individuals who do a PhD and who succeed in getting a postdoctoral position (the first step in an academic career) will find it very difficult to progress to the next level and get a lecturer's position ('Assistant Professor' in the US) in their university or another simply because there are a lot more postdoctoral students than lecturer positions and even fewer new lecturer positions become open each year because of retirement or new creation. The result is a lot of young researchers struggling to establish research careers.

Many of these will leave with a degree of disenchantment. Others will persevere and of course outstanding individuals will always find a way through. This does lead to a degree of cynicism which at times can be palpable when careers are discussed with young researchers and aspiring academics. The key thing that draws most academics to an academic career is the opportunity to do research and to teach. Most individuals who become academics do so because of an attraction of this rather unique mix. If the research component is diminished or eliminated in the future, academic careers are likely to be significantly less attractive.

If one looks at the march of history, however, more and more human endeavour is now devoted to new knowledge generation than ever before. This is likely to continue to grow, possibly exponentially, and academic life will be at the heart of this activity. Given a little good fortune, therefore, academic careers will be even more attractive in the future than they are now.

Some would regard this is as an optimistic view and any number of missteps could result in a very different picture. At the end of the day, university work and academic work is a real privilege and exposes people to the most vibrant of intellectual atmospheres. While there are many pressures now in academic life, it could be argued that they are less than in the commercial world with a lot more freedom to pursue one's interests.

But the fact is that high quality university leadership will need to work hard to create academic career structures which both reflect more modern scenarios of working life and ensure that academics are fully equipped to play the very important roles which society is seeking from them. If that is done successfully, they will retain the confidence of the rest of society which, at the end of the day, pays for it all. But it's a massive challenge.

Question 10

How much will thriving economies devote to the university sector in GDP terms?

As with most areas of national life, resources matter for the quality of university life. Whether the resources come from the individual 'consumer' (as in student fees) or the state, through taxation of some form or another, scrutiny of the way that money is spent is both inevitable and, we would argue, desirable. An example of this scrutiny is the increasing scepticism about the financial value of a university degree and the suggestion that relatively more public money should be focused upon 'technical' or 'apprenticeship' qualifications.

And the arguments about resources bring one inevitably into the fields of politics, both partisan and not. Through the political process, choices are made in the way that money is raised and spent. In the past 35 to 40 years it has been extremely difficult to win arguments that citizens should pay more taxes for the services that they receive. In our view, this state of affairs is unlikely to change significantly, though it is the case that the more attractive services are to ordinary citizens the easier it is to raise money. That is why money has consistently been allocated to raising standards of health care.

And this similarly explains the dramatic reductions in spending on defence the further that we move away from 1945, the constant focus upon welfare reform to ensure that welfare resources go to those who really need them, and the rise of alternative means of funding public investment.

This is the context within which education spending, and university spending in particular, has to fit. There is strong popular support for spending on pre-5 education and schools, and indeed significant research demonstrates that money invested at earlier ages is more effectively spent in reducing educational and class divisions.

It is the case that research and university investment is, as it should be, a high priority for promoting economic growth and knowledge about our world. But this truth should not permit the university world to escape the kinds of discussions in Chapter 4 about where research is located and how it contributes to our national life.

These are all very relevant points as governments consider what proportion of GDP should be spent upon universities. The share varies quite a lot at the moment. If one takes private investment and public investment together, approximately 1.5% of GDP is devoted to the university sector in most countries in the old West. In the UK, it is of that order, in the US a little more and most parts of continental Europe somewhere between the two. China, as it grows its university sector at an exponential rate, is currently investing a much higher percentage of GDP but it is likely that that will fall as the Chinese university sector matures and the major capital investments made in recent times flow through.

It is unlikely for the reasons set out in earlier chapters that the contributions universities make to life will become less important in the years ahead than they are at the moment. Increasing participation rates among young people, major increases in university engagement at later stages in life, the importance of university research outputs, especially interdisciplinary outputs and the increasing focus on education and knowledge as the information revolution continues to evolve exponentially, all make it likely that the place of universities in national and community life will strengthen rather than weaken in the decades ahead.

All of these factors make it more likely that there will be a good case for increasing the percentage of GDP invested in higher education over the next two or three decades. But this outcome is by no means pre-ordained. In a hugely competitive field for public resources, there is absolutely no room for complacency about the future resourcing of universities. There can be no sense of the entitlement that can sometimes raise its head in the university world. The case for resources, and for the public value of universities, has continually to be made and justified.

That is why in this book we have focused on what we think are the four pillars of universities:

- *understanding and interpreting the process of change;*
- *offering approaches that would harness the process of change for general benefit;*
- *educating and training to high quality the specialist workers whose skills are necessary to address change properly;*
- *creating a general intellectually engaging climate and culture across societies that promotes the virtues of understanding and science.*

Each of these are difficult in principle and even more difficult to sustain. Each of them requires focused and committed university action. And each of them makes an enormous contribution to the capacity and strength of our societies and economies, which more than justifies the relatively small proportion of GDP that is needed to fund the work of our universities.

Universities need to commit in practice to these ambitions, face up to the challenges of reform that this would mean, and explain and justify how they are achieving these goals and so deserving the public support that they need.

Chapter 11
Conclusion

The centrepiece of this book is the conviction that high quality universities are the best way to help our world deal with the enormous challenges of accelerating change. We have set out the four ways in which we think this should be done. But we also think that universities have to change a great deal in order to do this as well as they need to. In this chapter, we summarise the conclusions that we have come to in each chapter, firstly for universities themselves and secondly for governments. These observations are written around a UK setting but also apply in principle to the other countries, we have focused on.

In practical terms, the most important message of this book is that universities can and should determine their destiny and the vital contribution that they are able to make; and that governments should set up frameworks and systems that support that contribution. Our arguments are set out below.

For universities

Mission and strategy

Universities should place, at the centre of their own missions, addressing the challenges of a rapidly changing world. They should identify clearly the ways in which their work:

- *understands and interprets change in the world;*
- *offers approaches to harness the process of change for general benefit;*
- *educates and trains the specialists whose skills are necessary to address change;*
- *creates an intellectually engaging climate and culture across societies.*

They should clearly explain their strategy to achieve their mission and these aspirations. They should base this upon a narrative of the contribution that the university has made over its history to the local, national and international community, including the roles that they play most strongly and effectively, and present a clear transformation approach for the university. They should extend and develop the future international activity of the university, including provision for international students.

A clear component of their strategy should be the development of their interrelationship with their local communities including with local business, industry and civic leaders. This should include discussions with these partners and other universities in the locality about the best future form of university research and teaching provision in that area and consider what steps should be taken to enable that to happen.

Universities need to commit in practice to these ambitions, face up to the challenges of reform that this would mean, and explain and justify how they are achieving these goals and so deserve the public support that they need. On that basis, they should continually make the case for the utility and value of universities to society as a whole.

Governance and leadership

Universities should establish better and clearer processes for recruiting and firing university leaders and review their governance structures to enable them to face up better to the challenges of the future.

They should review academics' career patterns from the point of view of promoting institutional leadership quality at all levels and creating academic career structures which both reflect more modern scenarios of working life and ensure that academics are fully equipped to play the very important roles that society is seeking from them, so that they retain the confidence of the rest of society.

Universities should create transparent regimes for Vice-Chancellors' pay and conditions. And they should take very active steps to promote diverse and respectful university communities.

Universities should work harder to create internal structures that promote interdisciplinary research and teaching and build strong partnerships with other universities. This may well mean breaking down the walls of some silos that exist.

They should take steps to separate clearly their research and teaching budgets, in order to increase transparency and develop confidence in their missions. They should also strengthen philanthropic support, develop their endowments aggressively and develop education services for their alumni.

Access

Universities should develop strong relationships with their local schools and colleges, develop various types of access and pre-university courses to encourage successful applications from a wide range of society and develop admissions policies and financial programmes to incentivise access from the poorest communities.

They should examine their admissions criteria with a view to encouraging applications at various points in life, for example from mature students. These could include more deferred entry arrangements so that students develop wider post-school experience before going to university.

Teaching and work

Universities should work hard to improve the quality of their teaching and pastoral care for all students. This includes developing stronger international components of their courses such as education in languages and cultures. They should continue to focus on maintaining academic standards, including taking steps to avoid the suggestion of 'grade inflation'.

Universities should form strong relationships with both local and national employers in their main fields of research and teaching strength. They should develop their courses with future employability and work in mind, including preparation for modern work and new modes of study, structure of courses and systems of delivering education throughout life with different entry points. They should offer a range of courses for continuous professional development and professional updating and a wide range of postgraduate degree opportunities, which could be taken at all stages from immediately after graduation to much later in life. These would be mainly part-time and online.

They should prepare for introducing new teaching technologies that may well have significant implications for the nature of their campuses.

And universities should be vigorous in defending their democratic and rights culture to ensure that they remain bastions of genuine freedom of speech.

Research

Universities should focus research on problem-solving, meeting grand challenges and developing the knowledge that illuminates how we address change, particularly in disciplines where evidence of this is weakest. They should develop stronger systemic international research partnerships across the world including in developing countries.

They should develop local research and 'knowledge transfer' to strengthen local economic development and proactively organise around themselves researcher networks to engage in the research work that is being done with teachers at other universities, further education colleges and local sixth forms.

For governments

Mission and strategy

Governments should regularly make a clear statement of the contribution which they hope that universities will make to developing the society and economy of the country and indicate the ways in which they will support and promote that. They should incentivise and reward universities that place the addressing of change at the centre of their work.

The statement should be based upon a clear narrative of the history and contribution of universities in their country and the ways in which they hope to develop this to meet the challenges of the future.

This strategy should include the establishment of a comprehensive framework of post-school education and training which covers the vital 14–19 years and also promotes lifelong learning for all. This requires a resilient and buoyant funding basis.

Governments should ensure that these issues are debated openly in Parliament and elsewhere so that the country faces up to the problems and challenges in good time to address them, including an appreciation of what these challenges mean for the accepted national framework and culture of universities. Governments should consider what incentives they can offer to encourage a more rational pattern of university provision across the country.

Local, regional and national governments should develop their strategies for encouraging universities to develop strong, productive and durable partnerships to support local university economic and social engagement.

And governments should promote systematic and constructive dialogue between employers (private and public) and universities and the wider education system about the ways in which they can support each other and meet each other's needs.

Governance and leadership

Governments should work with universities to establish a stronger, collaborative framework for developing leadership in the higher education sector. They should support well-recognised and strong leadership training institutions and work with universities to develop clear indices of successful university leadership.

They should reduce the regulatory role of the Office for Students and encourage universities to take on their own leadership responsibilities and they should reform the funding system to promote more independent universities.

And governments should keep under close review the decision to allow monotechnic institutions to use the title 'university', a decision that, in the UK, happened only recently.

Access and finance

Governments should commit to continuing to expand university education opportunities, particularly to those from the lower socio-economic groups, and continue to review the steps that would enable better access to university from all sections of society, including student grants for some groups, better university–school relationships and strong access programmes. These programmes should be particularly targeted at the lowest economic social groups.

They should work with universities to develop a national framework within which lifelong learning can be promoted. This will include new approaches to funding lifelong learning, engagement with the professional educational organisations and frameworks of recognition of modules and qualifications from other universities in order to stimulate further study on the basis of prior qualifications.

Funding systems should encourage diverse forms of learning. They should create a sustainable legal and funding framework that promotes flexibility and within which change can flourish. This framework should have clear goals including the aim of reducing university dependence on the state. Serious consideration should be given to requiring employers to contribute to the higher education costs of those graduates they employ. We hope that the government will extend the loan system to other courses, and lifelong learning, along the lines recommended by the Augar Review.

As far as the current system is concerned, the student loan repayment threshold should be reduced, the interest rate should be cut to reflect only real price changes in line with the Consumer Price Index, the maintenance loan should fully cover actual student living costs, maintenance grants should be re-introduced for those from the poorest family backgrounds, students should be treated as fully independent at the age of 18 and early repayment of student loans should be incentivised.

Research

Governments should directly target a greater share of research funding upon the strongest research universities (about a third of UK universities) and should promote these, for example by seeking to develop them in those parts of the country that have disproportionately low levels of research funding. This could be done by encouraging university mergers and partnerships. Barriers to their success, such as unnecessary immigration restrictions, should be removed. Their definition as 'research universities' should be encouraged and the Russell Group should be deprioritised in formal government policy on the basis that it does not comprise all of the most highly rated research universities in the UK.

The agreement between research funders and universities should recognise the importance of blue sky research in all disciplines as leading to the breakthroughs of tomorrow and great universities will always explore blue sky and applied domains. But we also recognise that research is funded as a means to inform and transform the world. Governments should continue to reward research that can demonstrate a strong societal impact and promote research on how impact can be improved on a discipline by discipline basis, in order to increase understanding of the ways in which research can more successfully bring about positive change.

Structured dialogue between researchers and practitioners should be encouraged in order to increase the impact of research, for example through the What Works Network, which should be strengthened and widened.

Notes

Introduction

1 https://guildhe.ac.uk

Chapter 1 Changing universities in changing times

1 https://www.officeforstudents.org.uk

2 https://www.amazon.co.uk/Robot-Proof-Higher-Education-Artificial-Intelligence/dp/0262037289

3 https://www.amazon.co.uk/Robot-Proof-Higher-Education-Artificial-Intelligence/dp/0262037289

4 Comments from Professor Linda Woodhead.

5 For example, *The Better Angels of our Nature*: https://www.amazon.co.uk/Better-Angels-Our-Nature-Violence/dp/0141034645/ref=sr_1_1?adgrpid=54093381795&gclid=EAIaIQobChMI3pnS7bSb4gIVSrftCh0UUwOHEAAYASAAEgKWgvD_BwE&hvadid=259115930807&hvdev=c&hvlocphy=1006598&hvnetw=g&hvpos=1t1&hvqmt=e&hvrand=8160392200995997872&hvtargid=kwd-299965536442&hydadcr=10809_1789874&keywords=steven+pinker+better+angels&qid=1557850373&s=gateway&sr=8-1

6 For example, *The Perils of Perception*: https://www.amazon.co.uk/Perils-Perception-Wrong-Nearly-Everything/dp/1786494566/ref=sr_1_1?keywords=bobby+duffy&qid=1557850486&s=gateway&sr=8-1

7 For example, *Factfulness*: https://www.amazon.co.uk/Factfulness-Reasons-Wrong-Things-Better/dp/1473637465/ref=sr_1_1?crid=1A1797Z2H6G13&keywords=hans+rosling&qid=1557850590&s=gateway&sprefix=Hans+Rosling%2Caps%2C168&sr=8-1

8 For example, *Sapiens*: https://www.amazon.co.uk/Sapiens-Humankind-Yuval-Noah-Harari/dp/0099590085/ref=sr_1_1?crid=391T3JBNMQLZ9&keywords=sapiens+a+brief+history+of+humankind&qid=1557850672&s=gateway&sprefix=sapiens%2Caps%2C174&sr=8-1

9 https://web.archive.org/web/20071002100441/http://www.hm-treasury.gov.uk/consultations_and_legislation/lambert/consult_lambert_index.cfm

10 https://en.wikipedia.org/wiki/Office_for_Fair_Access

11 https://assets.publishing.service.gov.uk/government/uploads/system/uploads/attachment_data/file/228984/0118404881.pdf

12 https://www.amazon.co.uk/End-Alchemy-Banking-Future-Economy/dp/0393247023

13 https://www.teqsa.gov.au

Chapter 2 Historical perspectives and international comparisons

1 David Willetts, *A University Education*: https://www.amazon.co.uk/University-Education-David-Willetts/dp/0198767269

2 For example, the London Polytechnic, which became Westminster University, and Woolwich Polytechnic, which became the University of Greenwich.

3 Jo Ritzen, *A Chance for European Universities*: https://www.amazon.com/Chance-European-Universities-Avoiding-University/dp/9089642293

4 For example, in the UK the Athena SWAN (Scientific Women's Academic Network) programme, designed to improve academic opportunities at all levels for women, is showing some success.

Chapter 3 Universities and work

1 https://www.weforum.org/agenda/2016/01/the-fourth-industrial-revolution-what-it-means-and-how-to-respond/

2 https://www.amazon.co.uk/Robot-Proof-Higher-Education-Artificial-Intelligence/dp/0262037289

3 http://s-f-walker.org.uk/pubsebooks/2cultures/Rede-lecture-2-cultures.pdf

4 https://www.amazon.co.uk/Robot-Proof-Higher-Education-Artificial-Intelligence/dp/0262037289

5 For example, https://www.thersa.org/action-and-research/creative-learning-and-development?id=62295

6 For example, https://www.cipd.co.uk/Images/cipd-submission-to-hoc-business-select-committee-on-automation-and-the-future-of-work_tcm18-51802.pdf

7 For example, https://www2.deloitte.com/content/dam/insights/us/articles/5136_HC-Trends-2019/DI_HC-Trends-2019.pdf

8 https://www.amazon.co.uk/Times-Good-University-Guide-2020/dp/0008325480/ref=dp_ob_title_bk

9 http://www.educationengland.org.uk/documents/robbins/robbins1963.html

10 https://www.timeshighereducation.com/student/best-universities/best-universities-graduate-jobs-global-university-employability-ranking

11 https://www.erasmusprogramme.com

12 EU member states plus North Macedonia, Serbia, Turkey, Norway, Iceland and Liechtenstein.

13 https://dfat.gov.au/people-to-people/new-colombo-plan/pages/new-colombo-plan.aspx

14 For example, *A Modern Utopia*, published in 1905: https://www.amazon.co.uk/Modern-Utopia-H-G-Wells/dp/1980778108/ref=sr_1_3?adgrpid=51943364783&gclid=EAIaIQobChMIr8aGsNGq4gIVSkPTCh0nXglIEAAYASAAEgL6D_D_BwE&hvadid=259036452375&hvdev=c&hvlocphy=1006598&hvnetw=g&hvpos=1t1&hvqmt=e&hvrand=4051229210467297894&hvtargid=kwd-364823565077&hydadcr=10776_1749359&keywords=a+modern+utopia&qid=1558373423&s=gateway&sr=8-3

15 https://www.amazon.co.uk/Player-Piano-Kurt-Vonnegut/dp/0385333781/ref=sr_1_1?keywords=player+piano+vonnegut&qid=1558365790&s=books&sr=1-1

Chapter 4 Research: understanding and transforming the world

1 https://www.ukri.org

2 *Universities, Rankings and the Dynamics of Global Higher Education*: https://www.amazon.co.uk/Universities-Rankings-Dynamics-Global-Education-ebook/dp/B01HT1F9WG/ref=sr_1_1?keywords=

Universities%2C+Rankings+and+the+Dynamics+of+Global+Higher+Education+Perspectives+from+Asia%2C+Europe+and+North+America&qid=1558795136&s=digital-text&sr=1-1-catcorr

3 https://www.timeshighereducation.com/rankings/impact/2019/overall#!/page/1/length/25/sort_by/rank/sort_order/asc/cols/undefined, which use this methodology: https://www.timeshighereducation.com/world-university-rankings/impact-rankings-2019-methodology-sustainable-cities-communities

4 This ranking includes data for 128 universities in the UK, not including University College, Birmingham; Trinity Saint David, University of Wales; and the University of Wolverhampton which did not release the necessary data.

5 Vice-Chancellor of Wollongong University, and previously Lancaster.

6 https://www.timeshighereducation.com/world-university-rankings/by-subject

7 Created by the Carnegie Commission on Higher Education in 1970 and most recently published in 2018.

8 For example, Russell Group, 'Jewels in the Crown': https://russellgroup.ac.uk/policy/publications/jewels-in-the-crown-the-importance-and-characteristics-of-the-uk-s-world-class-universities/

9 Each university was profiled as follows: 4* world-leading, 3* internationally excellent, 2* internationally recognised, 1* nationally recognised and unclassified. For funding in 2013–14, HEFCE weighted a 4* profile by a factor of 3, 3* by a factor of 1 and 2* and 1* by a factor of 0. The overall score is presented as a percentage of the possible maximum (ie 3, which would mean that all staff would be at 4* world-leading level). https://www.thetimes.co.uk/article/methodology-for-the-sunday-times-and-the-times-good-university-guide-2017-fl6r5vq0l

10 The universities asterisked in this table are members of the so-called 'Russell Group', a self-selected association of research universities.

11 The Universities of Buckingham, Highland and Islands, St Mark and St John and Suffolk were given no rating under Research Quality in these rankings.

12 The exact number of 'universities' depends upon the precise definition of 'university' or 'higher education institution'. The Higher Education Statistics Authority gives the number of 'higher education providers' as 167.

13 http://www.n8research.org.uk

14 In 2017/18, 59% of full-time undergraduates were studying in one of the 42 universities with a research quality ranking lower than 30%, as identified above (data from Higher Education Student Statistics: UK, 2017/18 SB 252).

15 HESA HE Staff Statistics, Figure 3: https://www.hesa.ac.uk/news/24-01-2019/sb253-higher-education-staff-statistics

16 In the *Times and Sunday Times Good University Guide 2017*.

17 Based on the 2014 Research Excellence Framework.

18 Based on HESA data on the proportion of students enrolling in 2014/15 projected to complete their degrees.

19 Based on HESA data on the proportion of students in professional jobs or in graduate levels study six months after graduation.

20 Based on responses to the 2016 National Student Survey.

21 'Where do student fees really go?': https://www.hepi.ac.uk/wp-content/uploads/2018/11/Following-the-pound-1.pdf

22 This paragraph owes a lot to Hertig's book, previously cited, *Universities, Rankings and the Dynamics of Global Higher Education*.

23 https://www.economist.com/china/2018/11/17/tsinghua-university-may-soon-top-the-world-league-in-science-research?cid1=cust/ddnew/email/n/n/20181119n/owned/n/n/ddnew/n/n/n/nUK/Daily_Dispatch/email&etear=dailydispatch&utm_source=newsletter&utm_medium=email&utm_campaign=Daily_Dispatch&utm_term=20181119

24 The Higher Education Funding Council for England, the Scottish Funding Council, the Higher Education Funding Council for Wales, and the Department for the Economy, Northern Ireland.

25 http://www.ref.ac.uk/about/whatref/

26 King's College London and Digital Science (2015) *The Nature, Scale and Beneficiaries of Research Impact: An Initial Analysis of Research Excellence Framework (REF) 2014 Impact Case Studies*. Bristol, UK: HEFCE. http://www.hefce.ac.uk/media/HEFCE,2014/Content/Pubs/Independentresearch/2015/Analysis,of,REF,impact/Analysis_of_REF_impact.pdf

27 http://www.hefce.ac.uk/pubs/rereports/year/2015/analysisREFimpact/

28 http://impact.ref.ac.uk/CaseStudies/

29 https://www.gov.uk/guidance/what-works-network#the-what-works-network

Chapter 5 The local economic and social impact of universities

1 http://www.statsguy.co.uk/brexit-voting-and-education/

2 https://www.brookings.edu/blog/fixgov/2016/11/18/educational-rift-in-2016-election/

3 https://www.amazon.co.uk/Smartest-Places-Earth-Rustbelts-Innovation-ebook/dp/B06XKY1CC7/ref=sr_1_3?keywords=The+Smartest+Places+on+Earth&qid=1557241098&s=digital-text&sr=1-3-catcorr

4 https://sunypoly.edu/research/albany-nanotech-complex.html

5 https://www.brookings.edu/blog/the-avenue/2017/12/19/tale-of-two-rust-belts-higher-education-is-driving-rust-belt-revival-but-risks-abound/

6 https://www.brookings.edu/blog/the-avenue/2017/12/05/a-tale-of-two-rust-belts-continued-can-the-midwests-smaller-communities-succeed/

7 https://www.amazon.co.uk/Our-Towns-000-Mile-Journey-America-ebook/dp/B074LRHLJ3/ref=sr_1_1?crid=34WAQPHN6AA36&keywords=our+towns&qid=1557241173&s=digital-text&sprefix=Our+Towns%2Cdigital-text%2C153&sr=1-1

8 https://www.pennconnects.upenn.edu

9 https://re.ukri.org/knowledge-exchange/the-higher-education-innovation-fund-heif/

10 https://re.ukri.org/knowledge-exchange/the-connecting-capability-fund-ccf/

11 https://re.ukri.org/knowledge-exchange/university-enterprise-zones/

12 http://www.rcuk.ac.uk/about/aboutrcs/research-funding-across-the-uk/

13 https://www.publicengagement.ac.uk/about-us

14 For example, https://edtrust.org/engines-of-inequality/

Chapter 6 Who benefits from a university education?

1 For example, Sathnam Sanghera: https://www.thetimes.co.uk/magazine/the-times-magazine/sathnam-sanghera-elitism-the-oxbridge-access-problem-and-why-i-never-felt-i-belonged-at-cambridge-8dtm77jvf

2 Sutton Trust, December 2018: https://www.suttontrust.com/wp-content/uploads/2018/12/AccesstoAdvantage-2018.pdf

3 The Sutton Trust's Leading People 2016 report: https://www.suttontrust.com/wp-content/uploads/2016/02/Leading-People_Feb16.pdf

4 President of Arizona State University.

5 For example, *Designing the New American University*: https://www.amazon.co.uk/Designing-American-University-Michael-Crow/dp/1421417235

6 http://data.uis.unesco.org

7 This issue is addressed in more detail in Chapter 7.

8 The Universities and Colleges Admissions Service.

9 https://www.ucas.com/file/225551/download?token=nGdxoNQn

10 UK Government, April 2019: https://www.gov.uk/government/news/universities-urged-to-review-unacceptable-admissions-practices

11 That is, an offer that did not depend on the student's school exam results.

12 The condition being that the student would be admitted if they made the university their first choice.

13 https://www.studyinternational.com/news/country-home-largest-international-student-population/

14 For example, the Migration Advisory Committee's Shortage Occupation List which in May 2019 identified shortages in fields like mining engineers, 3D computer animators, cyber security experts, emergency medicine and paediatric consultants.

15 https://publications.parliament.uk/pa/jt201719/jtselect/jtrights/589/58902.htm

16 https://www.bbc.co.uk/news/education-43544546

17 https://www.bbc.co.uk/news/education-45447938

18 https://www.gov.uk/government/news/free-speech-to-be-protected-at-university

Chapter 7 Education is for life

1 https://www.futurelearn.com

2 Fourteen million UK viewers in 2017, the most watched programme in the UK, and an estimated 80 million in China. This included more 16–34 year old viewers than *The X Factor*.

3 And even – at Oxbridge and Dublin – the utterly ridiculous *zero*-year master's degree which requires no study at all. Charles holds this MA from Cambridge, for which he had to do nothing at all! He has never used it.

4 https://www.insead.edu

5 As discussed in Chapter 1.

Chapter 8 Who pays for it all?

1 https://data.oecd.org/eduresource/spending-on-tertiary-education.htm, Figure 4.2: page 81.

2 Other contributors include private businesses, non-profit organisations, private companies on work-based training, together with spending on research and development by educational institutions.

3 https://www.officeforstudents.org.uk/news-blog-and-events/press-and-media/universities-must-get-to-grips-with-spiralling-grade-inflation/

4 http://stats.oecd.org/Index.aspx?DatasetCode=RGRADSTY; https://data.oecd.org/eduatt/population-with-tertiary-education.htm

5 https://www.universitiesuk.ac.uk/facts-and-stats/Pages/higher-education-data.aspx

6 https://assets.publishing.service.gov.uk/government/uploads/system/uploads/attachment_data/file/805127/Review_of_post_18_education_and_funding.pdf, Chapter 3.

7 Financial support to help students from poorer backgrounds to stay in school or college from 16 to 18.

8 A programme to help university students from 'non-traditional' backgrounds to go to university.

9 https://assets.publishing.service.gov.uk/government/uploads/system/uploads/attachment_data/file/805127/Review_of_post_18_education_and_funding.pdf

10 Institute for Fiscal Studies: https://www.ifs.org.uk/publications/9965

11 https://assets.publishing.service.gov.uk/government/uploads/system/uploads/attachment_data/file/805127/Review_of_post_18_education_and_funding.pdf, page 170.

12 http://data.parliament.uk/writtenevidence/committeeevidence.svc/evidencedocument/economic-affairs-committee/the-economics-of-higher-further-and-technical-education/written/70524.html

13 https://www.universitiesuk.ac.uk/facts-and-stats/Pages/higher-education-data.aspx

14 https://www.hesa.ac.uk/news/19-07-2018/DLHE-publication-201617

15 Set at 25 years when the student loan scheme was introduced in 2004.

16 https://assets.publishing.service.gov.uk/government/uploads/system/uploads/attachment_data/file/805127/Review_of_post_18_education_and_funding.pdf, page 171.

17 https://assets.publishing.service.gov.uk/government/uploads/system/uploads/attachment_data/file/805127/Review_of_post_18_education_and_funding.pdf, pages 172–3.

18 https://www.gov.uk/government/speeches/pm-speech-at-augar-review-launch-30-may-2019

19 https://assets.publishing.service.gov.uk/government/uploads/system/uploads/attachment_data/file/805127/Review_of_post_18_education_and_funding.pdf, Chapter 7.

20 https://www.officeforstudents.org.uk/advice-and-guidance/promoting-equal-opportunities/access-and-participation-plans/

21 https://assets.publishing.service.gov.uk/government/uploads/system/uploads/attachment_data/file/805127/Review_of_post_18_education_and_funding.pdf, Chapters 2 and 4.

22 https://www.ucl.ac.uk/ioe/news/2018/feb/every-18-year-old-should-be-offered-ps10000-spend-courses-their-choice-paper-says; https://www.llakes.ac.uk/sites/default/files/63.%20Schuller%20Tuckett%20%26%20Wilson.pdf

23 https://www.hepi.ac.uk/wp-content/uploads/2018/11/Policy-Note-10-Paper-November-2018-Fairer-funding-the-case-for-a-graduate-levy.pdf

24 https://www.timeshighereducation.com/opinion/business-and-universities-should-pay-more-higher-education

Chapter 9 University governance, leadership and the state

1 Jo Ritzen: *A Chance for European Universities*: https://www.amazon.com/Chance-European-Universities-Avoiding-University/dp/90896422

2 https://www.maths.ed.ac.uk/~v1ranick/baked/micro.pdf

3 https://www.amazon.co.uk/Universities-Rankings-Dynamics-Global-Education-ebook/dp/B01HT1F9WG/ref=sr_1_1?keywords=Universities%2C+Rankings+and+the+Dynamics+of+Global+Higher+

Education+Perspectives+from+Asia%2C+Europe+and+North+Americ a&qid=1558795136&s=digital-text&sr=1-1-catcorr

4 In which Charles was actively involved, both at Cambridge and nationally.

5 After a 1965 essay by Herbert Marcuse: https://www.marcuse.org/herbert/pubs/60spubs/65repressivetolerance.htm

6 '*Never doubt that a small group of thoughtful, committed citizens can change the world; indeed, it's the only thing that ever has*', Nancy C Lutkehaus, *Margaret Mead: The Making of an American Icon* (Princeton, NJ: Princeton University Press, 2008), page 261.

7 Lord Acton, the historian and moralist, expressed this opinion in a letter in 1887.

8 https://www.advance-he.ac.uk

9 https://www.timeshighereducation.com/news/female-leadership-moves-backwards-worlds-top-universities

10 https://www.hesa.ac.uk/news/24-01-2019/sb253-higher-education-staff-statistics

11 Advance HE: https://www.ecu.ac.uk/publications/equality-higher-education-statistical-report-2018/

12 https://www.bbc.co.uk/news/business-47723950

13 https://www.timeshighereducation.com/news/universities-scoring-highest-gender-equality

14 https://www.brook.org.uk/data/Brook_DigIN_summary_report2.pdf

15 https://1752group.files.wordpress.com/2018/09/silencing-students_the-1752-group.pdf

16 https://www.humanrights.gov.au/our-work/sex-discrimination/publications/change-course-national-report-sexual-assault-and-sexual

17 https://www.nap.edu/catalog/24994/sexual-harassment-of-women-climate-culture-and-consequences-in-academic

18 https://www.theguardian.com/education/2018/sep/07/uk-university-professors-black-minority-ethnic

19 https://www.bbc.co.uk/news/education-46473269

20 Notably Andrew Adonis and Jo Johnson.

21 https://www.teqsa.gov.au

Chapter 10 Ten questions about the future of universities

1 http://claytonchristensen.com/key-concepts/

2 http://s-f-walker.org.uk/pubsebooks/2cultures/Rede-lecture-2-cultures.pdf

3 https://www.amazon.co.uk/Robot-Proof-Higher-Education-Artificial-Intelligence/dp/0262037289

4 That is, without having to meet particular grade requirements.

Index